FINDING SOLUTIONS TO HUNGER

FINDING SOLUTIONS TO HUNGER

KIDS CAN MAKE A DIFFERENCE

A Sourcebook

For Middle and Upper School Teachers

by

Stephanie Kempf

WORLD HUNGER YEAR
New York
1997, 2001, 2005

JANE AND LARRY LEVINE
New York
2009

Library of Congress Catalogue Card Number: 97 - 90926
Kempf, Stephanie (date)
Finding Solutions to Hunger
Kids Can Make A Difference

1. Hunger - Study and Teaching 2. Poverty - Study and Teaching 3. Community Service - Youth
I. Kempf, Stephanie II. Title
1997   97-90926
ISBN: 0-9660038-0-2

Copyright©1997, 2001, 2005, 2009 by Stephanie Kempf
All rights reserved.

Cover design and illustration by:
Lisa Rivard
lisa@rivardart.com

www.kidscanmakeadifference.org

PRINTED IN THE UNITED STATES OF AMERICA

TABLE OF CONTENTS

	PAGES
Acknowledgments	vi
HUNGER FACTS	viii
IMAGINE: A Letter to Students From the Director of WHY (World Hunger Year)	ix
WHY (World Hunger Year)	x
The Kids Can Make A Difference® Program	x
INTRODUCTION	1
NOTES TO TEACHERS	3
UNIT I: WHAT IS HUNGER?	7
Lesson 1: Food Keeps Us Alive! - A Nutrition Workshop	9
Lesson 2: Eating The Way The World Eats	17
Lesson 3: How Big Is The Hunger Problem?	23
Lesson 4: Hunger Destroys	27
Lesson 5: Two Kinds of Hunger: Famine & Chronic Hunger	33
Lesson 6: The Power of One	53
UNIT II: WHY ARE PEOPLE HUNGRY?	59
Lesson 7: If There Is Enough Food, Why Are People Hungry?	61
Lesson 8: Is Overpopulation A Root Cause of Hunger?	67
Lesson 9: One Planet, Two Worlds	73
Lesson 10: The Legacy of Colonialism	79
Lesson 11: Development - Who Benefits?	95
Lesson 12: Is U.S. Foreign Aid Working To End Hunger?	109
Lesson 13: The Importance of Female Education	115
Lesson 14: Hunger Hurts Us All	127
Lesson 15: Hunger, USA: Children, The Elderly, The Working Poor, Racial & Ethnic Minorities, Single Mothers	131
Lesson 16: Working & Eating	147
Lesson 17: The Homeless	159
Lesson 18: The Media	183
Lesson 19: The Grapes of Wrath	195
Lesson 20: ANCIENT FUTURES: Learning From Ladakh	203
UNIT III: WHAT CAN WE DO TO HELP END HUNGER?	213
Lesson 21: Find Out What People Think	215
Lesson 22: Shine A Light On Hunger	217
Lesson 23: Combine Our Talents	221
Lesson 24: Write Letters	223
Lesson 25: Give Testimony	227
RESOURCE GUIDE	229

ACKNOWLEDGMENTS

Many hands, hearts and minds have nurtured the evolution of this guide. The seed was planted in 1994 by Jane and Larry Levine, two enthusiastic board members of WHY (World Hunger Year). I was teaching literature classes in a public high school in New York City when Jane and Larry began telling me about the hunger-awareness workshops they were presenting to sixth-graders around the northeast. I was struck by Larry's descriptions of young people who were surprised to hear that hunger actually exists in the U.S. Teachers, Jane and Larry explained, were expressing frustration over the lack of time and resources available for teaching extended courses on the causes of poverty. I attended some of the Levines' workshops and saw that they were indeed filling a crucial need within the students, teachers, schools and communities. Before long, informed students began taking bold and imaginative steps to alert their peers and communities to the forces behind hunger. Students were teaching workshops, creating hunger videos, making public service announcements on radio and holding fund-raisers to support food pantries and shelters. Jane and Larry's program had a new dimension: *KIDS CAN MAKE A DIFFERENCE®* was born.

Jane and Larry educated me about the silent hunger crisis enveloping all of us and suggested I visit WHY and think about helping create a teacher's guide that would extend the themes of their workshops as well as provide teachers with information and resources related to hunger and poverty. From that conversation on, nothing seemed more urgent. I am deeply grateful to Jane and Larry for their belief in me and their gentle but persistent prodding. I must also express my appreciation to those young people --- their idealism and moral energy continue to be an endless source of inspiration and motivation.

Bill Ayres and the staff at WHY welcomed me warmly and allowed me to roam freely through their extensive research library. They were always eager to answer my questions, recommend books and videos and introduce me to local hunger activists. My thanks to all of them at WHY: Sue Leventhal, Jonathan Greengrass, Vivian Wong, Noreen Springstead, Yolanda Brooks, Amalia Guerra, Erin Callahan, Mary Painter, Lucy Anderson, C. Carlson and Peggy Hupcy. Bill, Peter Mann, Jennifer Urff and Robin Garr deepened my understanding of the root causes of hunger. Our roundtable discussions of model programs working successfully to end hunger infused me with hope and underscored the fact that **ending hunger is possible**.

As lesson plans began to sprout, Jane and Larry helped guide their development, then distributed copies of an early draft to teachers who tested the lesson plans in their classrooms and provided valuable feedback. Thanks to Ronnie Bowen, Carolyn Carey, Jennifer Castle, Jane Donohue, Nancy Fortier, Marilyn Fraser, Lisa Howlett, Jane Darby and Kelly Keene. Thanks also to teachers and community organizers Harry Moore, Kate Rose, Karen Swann and Rita Kirchgassner-Grathwohl, who teach and work in hungry communities.

Their rebellious spirits and commitment to ending hunger reinforced my belief in the transforming power of education.

I am very grateful to Joan Dye Gussow for reviewing the manuscript so carefully at a crucial point in its development and offering critical insight and encouragement.

I am especially indebted to Bill Bigelow. His pedagogical writing on issues of social justice reshaped my understanding of how to teach. His comments on an early draft and his gentle provocation pushed key lessons to deeper levels.

Jane, Larry and I are very grateful for the interest and generous support from UNITED WAY OF NEW YORK CITY and from all the friends of KIDS CAN MAKE A DIFFERENCE®. Special acknowledgments to our fellow advisory board members Alan C. Handell, for his valuable and on-going assistance with printing, and Julianne Rana, for her research regarding statistics and resources. Without her cheerful and patient commitment to the project, the current revisions would not have been possible.

Many warm thanks to my parents for their unwavering support and excitement about the project and for distributing early drafts to schools and community leaders.

Finally, to James Toback, my love and appreciation, for introducing me to the power of words, and providing the intellectual nourishment and material and emotional support that kept me moving forward.

HUNGER FACTS

U.N. studies show that the world already produces more than enough food to feed everyone on the planet and has the capacity to produce even more, and yet...

World hunger organizations estimate that 1 BILLION people around the world are chronically hungry. (United Nations, Department of Public Information, 2009)

25,000 children die **every day** of hunger or disease resulting from hunger.[1]

Every six seconds a child dies because of hunger and related causes. (Food and Agriculture Organization of the United Nations (FAO), 2004)

65 percent of the world's hungry live in seven countries: India, China, the Democratic Republic of Congo, Bangladesh, Indonesia, Pakistan and Ethiopia. (FAO, 2008)

36.2 million Americans, including 12.4 million children, are food insecure and at risk of hunger. (United States Department of Agriculture, 2007)

13 million children in the U.S. go to bed hungry. (Bread for the World, 2004)

In the U.S. hunger and race are related. 22.4% of Black and 17.8% of Latino households experience food insecurity over the course of the year, as compared to 8.1% of White households. (Children's HealthWatch, formerly known as the Children's Sentinel Nutrition Assessment Program, 2007)

The U.S. Administration on Aging estimates that 1 out of 4 seniors in the U.S. has an inadequate diet.

Around the world the most vulnerable to hunger are: children, pregnant and nursing women, single mothers, the elderly, the homeless, the unemployed, ethnic and racial minorities, and the working poor.

---

[1] This number varies depending on major events that affect people's access to food, such as natural disasters, war, forced migration, environmental degradation, etc. as well as successful hunger-relief programs.

FINDING ANSWERS FOR HUNGER AND POVERTY

Founder
Harry Chapin
1942-1981

President
Charles J. Sanders

Dear Friends,

We are living in exciting times! It is a time of unabashed hope coupled with social and economic challenges we as a nation -- indeed, a global society -- have not had to address for generations.

Imagination is at the root of all progress and so much of our future remains to be imagined. Who better to envision that future but those who will be living it – our youth! With this book in your hands and your teachers and peers as companions, we invite you to **imagine a world free from the injustice of hunger**...

Imagine a coalition of youth around the country joining our new President in his pledge to end hunger by the year 2015 for the 12.6 million children in the United States that are unsure when they will next eat.

Imagine school lunchrooms serving nutritious and tasty hot meals every day to ALL STUDENTS prepared from fresh ingredients many of which come from local farms.

Imagine a Summer Feeding Program that actually feeds millions of hungry children during the summer when they are not receiving school meals.

Imagine vacant lots and roof tops turned into food-producing gardens in every neighborhood in the country.

Imagine soup kitchens and homeless shelters working hand-in-hand with community non-profits and social service agencies to feed and house people today while helping them prepare for a better future tomorrow.

Imagine our country landscaped in small, diversified family farms helping to revive rural townships and local economies.

Imagine a world where access to healthy, fresh food at all times for all people is considered a basic human right and is guaranteed as such by governments and citizens alike.

Imagine youth from every country building a global movement to end hunger and poverty for the more than 900 million people around the world who suffer from hunger on a daily basis and the thousands of children who die from hunger-related causes every day.

Imagine kids making a difference! I can.

**Executive Director
and Co-Founder**
Bill Ayres

Established 1975

This curriculum will both stimulate the imaginations of students and teachers but also lead to activities that can reduce hunger. Imagine the possibilities!

Peace,

Bill Ayres

P.S. Be sure and visit our website at www.whyhunger.org, sign up to receive action alerts and newsletters, check out the Food Security Learning Center, and join us on Facebook!

WHY (World Hunger Year)

WHY (World Hunger Year) is a leading advocate for innovative community-based solutions to hunger and poverty.

WHY's programs and initiatives include:
- Strengthening grassroots organizations across the country with resources and networking opportunities through the **Grassroots Action Network**
- Linking WHY's domestic work to broader global movements for food sovereignty and basic rights through the **Global Movements Program**
- Building just, sustainable food systems through the **Food Security Learning Center**
- Helping children and youth to understand the root causes of poverty through **Kids Can Make a Difference**
- Connecting Artists with grassroots organizations to raise funds and awareness in communities across the country through the **Artist Against Hunger and Poverty Program**
- Fundraising for WHY's programs and informing the general public about hunger and poverty issues through WHY's annual **Hungerthon**

Through these programs and initiatives, WHY promotes the basic right to food in the US and around the world, and advances model programs that create self-reliance, economic justice, and equitable access to nutritious and affordable food.

Kids Can Make A Difference® (KIDS)

KIDS Can Make A Difference is an innovative educational program for middle- and high-school students. Through a newsletter, website and classroom curriculum, KIDS helps students understand the root causes of hunger and poverty and how they, regardless of their family's economic status, can become part of the solution.

KIDS has three major components:
- **Teachers' Guide: Finding Solutions To Hunger**: Kids has provided over 5,000 classrooms, after school programs, and families with tools to help young people to understand the causes of poverty and become informed and effective citizens, realizing their own capacity to change the world. Students learn about the pain of hunger; the importance of food; the inequality of its distribution; and the links between poverty, hunger, joblessness, and homelessness. They are then given the skills to take what they have learned into their communities.
- **KIDS Website:** The KIDS website has been rated one of the top 20 websites for educators by Educational World. The site provides news, a hunger quiz, hunger facts, suggested books, back issues of the newsletter, the table of contents, sample lessons, program notes from the teacher guide; and
- **Newsletter:** The three yearly issues highlight current hunger issues, showcase student initiatives, and feature teachers' experiences teaching the KIDS program and students' experiences making a difference in their community and world.

INTRODUCTION

by Joan Dye Gussow

If I were a teacher struggling to help students remain human in a sea of cynicism and self-absorption, I would grab onto this slim volume as if it were a life raft and use it to bring my class to shore. In *Finding Solutions to Hunger: Kids Can Make a Difference*, Stephanie Kempf overtly sets out to engage young people in the task of helping save their less fortunate peers from hunger and starvation. However, her provocative lessons may prove even more effective in transforming the lives of the young people who participate in them. Utilizing the activities in this book to understand and take action on the causes of hunger may well turn the average child into an informed and effective citizen with a healthy sense of her own capacity to change the world.

How does one begin to help children understand that the world lets 25,000 of their peers die every day from hunger? And if they begin to grasp that fact, how can they be helped to avoid falling into despair about the planet on which they are expected to live as adults? Stephanie Kempf believes understanding and empowerment can save them, and in this manual, she sets out to prove that. The real story behind the catastrophe called global hunger --- the economic and social forces that result in some one billion people going to bed hungry on a planet that produces more than enough food --- is a mystery to most adults. When hunger hits the TV news, or the front pages of newspapers, most Americans accept simple (and usually wrong) explanations of its cause --- and turn away.

This manual is based on the belief that it can be otherwise, that our children can be helped to understand the real causes of hunger and can learn to act to change them. Lesson by lesson she leads students through exercises that teach such things as the pain of hunger, the importance of food, the inequitability of its distribution, the curious lack of relationship between hunger and population density, and the links between poverty, hunger, joblessness, and homelessness here and elsewhere. Through the "Curse of Sugar," students learn the story of colonialism and come to understand how much of the "development" poor countries experience today continues that story.

Throughout the lessons, students are asked to read and write, to calculate and analyze, to role play, and to figure out for themselves what needs to be done. In one lesson "villagers," "World Bank ministers," "government officials," "environmentalists," "loggers," and "trees and creatures of the forest" are asked to join in a debate about whether a proposed development project would really benefit the people and their countryside. In another lesson, students --- playing roles as shopkeepers, activists, government officials, a charitable organization, and homeless individuals --- confront each other at a town meeting called to discuss how to keep the homeless from turning the railroad station into a shelter.

I found myself thinking how much I would enjoy introducing these lessons to a secondary school classroom full of MTV'd seventh graders; the activities are so engaging and they inspire such compassion and hope about subjects usually thought of as too difficult and depressing to teach. Scattered throughout the book, especially after sections presenting difficult problems, are boxes headed "Make a Difference". Here the author lays out action ideas for young people who have just learned something new about hunger --- how they can learn more, how they can team up with other concerned people, how they can reach out into the larger community to help end hunger. The lessons in the last section of the book are devoted specifically to giving students the skills to take into their immediate communities what they have learned from this curriculum, conducting surveys, writing letters, giving testimony, organizing programs to introduce their classmates and fellow citizens to "local heroes" --- people already helping the hungry and homeless in their communities.

This is an inspiring volume. Reading it should encourage anyone to believe that something **can** be done about the problems that face all communities. Reading it, one can even hope that if classrooms all over America would use *Finding Solutions to Hunger*, the nations of the planet would finally live up to their leaders' pledge that no child should ever again go to bed hungry.

Joan Dye Gussow is Professor Emeritus of Nutrition and Education at Teachers College, Columbia University and a long-time nutrition and anti-hunger activist.

NOTES TO TEACHERS

***Please have students check www.kidscanmakeadifference.org for the most up-to-date statistics.**

(1) FOCUS ON ROOT CAUSES OF HUNGER

The activities in this program were collected from various sources: teachers, students, activists, hunger organizations and curricula, etc. They have all been designed to guide you and your students toward a clear understanding of the root causes of hunger. Many lessons also offer examples of the creative and effective actions people around the world are taking to end hunger in their communities.

Projects and discussions emphasize --- not charity --- but a thorough investigation into **why** people are hungry in the first place, what they need to begin feeding themselves, and what we can do to remove the obstacles that prevent people from taking control of their own lives. A few lessons offer students ideas on how to organize fund-raisers or earn money for hunger relief services. These are essential lessons; however, before planning a fund-raiser, hold a crucial discussion with your students on both the importance and the limitations of charitable giving. We don't want to send the message to young people that money or charity will solve the hunger problem. Even if all the world's wealth were somehow magically re-distributed tomorrow, powerful social and political forces would just as quickly and dramatically upset the balance again. We cannot buy social justice which is what hungry people need to become self-reliant; however, food, medicine and shelter cost money. Emergency services save lives, they are the first step in helping people begin to help themselves. Be sure students understand that in addition to raising money, we must continue to work together to understand and eliminate the forces that undermine self-reliance.

Uncovering root causes is an empowering and hopeful experience. Once young people understand that ending hunger is possible, that it is not caused by a shortage of food, but by a shortage of democracy, feelings of guilt, passivity and cynicism are replaced by an exuberant, confident and clear-sighted desire to provoke change.

(2) CREATE A POSITIVE TONE

The most common reaction expressed by students when they become aware of the effects and extent of chronic hunger is guilt. Teachers involved in the hunger program have found effective ways to help students understand their feelings and move beyond them in ways that are constructive and empowering. They suggest setting aside plenty of time after your first hunger lesson to allow students to share their feelings freely. Let them know that most people react in a similar way and that it is natural to feel guilty; however, feeling guilty doesn't **change** anything. It is also appropriate to feel anger toward a system that is so unjust. Tell students that during the course of their study they will begin to understand the forces at work causing and perpetuating hunger. They will also begin to see clearly what they can do individually and collectively to help eliminate chronic hunger around them. The idea of "changing the world" is overwhelming, but working to change yourself, then your family, friends and community is doable. Remind students often that **ending hunger is possible**. It has already been proven! Around the world everyday people are working together to change their communities. This is something to celebrate!

Contrary to the way hungry people are portrayed by the media, they are not helpless and dependent. Everyday poor people overcome tremendous odds in their struggle to obtain life's essentials: food, clean water, a safe home, health care, education, a job, fair wages. They courageously resist and endure oppression in the form of greed, racism, class and gender discrimination, industrial exploitation and environmental degradation. During your study of hunger it is important to balance an honest portrayal of the destructive nature of hunger with a positive portrayal of people working together to change their own lives as well as the lives of others.

(3) CONNECT YOUR STUDY OF HUNGER TO STUDENTS' LIVES

This program opens with a nutrition workshop - **FOOD KEEPS US ALIVE!** in which students examine how fundamental food is to their own survival. Once they realize our shared dependence on the life-giving power of food, they can better understand the seriousness of hunger and the significance of later lessons which focus on how hunger destroys bodies, minds, spirits, families and communities. **EATING THE WAY THE WORLD EATS** is a powerful, personal experience of the injustice of the world's food system. Some teachers have used this provocative activity to kickoff their hunger-study, others have helped students stage the banquet at the end of their study of hunger and invited parents, local government officials and the media to participate. Students read from their journals and presented research on hunger in their communities.

Most of what students know about hunger comes from images of famine projected by the media. In **TWO KINDS OF HUNGER** students explore the political reasons behind famine. They also learn that 90% of hunger deaths are the result of another kind of hunger --- one which is more widespread, less talked about and closer to home --- chronic hunger. Students need to be aware that hunger is not always visible. Most of us probably encounter hungry people everyday without realizing it. As teachers we must be aware of and sensitive to hungry children in our schools. Children suffering from chronic hunger are often embarrassed by their situations. In many communities hard-working parents refuse to take advantage of available relief services because they don't want anyone to know that they can't feed their families. We need to remind **all** our students that every one of us will need help from others many times during our lives. When we do, we need to know there are places to go where we can get that help. It is okay to seek and accept help. At the same time, we must remind students that no one should be in need of food, a home, or a job, and that there are urgent and practical things communities can do to make sure everyone has what she needs to become and remain healthy.

The first thing we can do is to alert others to what we are learning about the causes of hunger. Whenever possible, encourage students to engage their families and friends in discussions and projects about hunger. **THE POWER OF ONE** contains inspiring real-life stories of how one person's efforts provoked positive change. Activities in **UNIT III: WHAT CAN WE DO TO HELP END HUNGER?** emphasize the power of the group in launching an effective hunger awareness campaign, connecting with local hunger activists, writing attention-getting letters, and testifying before legislative committees. It is not necessary to complete activities from Units I and II before planning and performing these activities. Integrate them into your study from the start.

(4) EXTEND SIGNIFICANT LESSONS

This guide presents a broad overview of hunger and poverty. Many sections contain valuable teacher background reading; however, poverty is a complex subject. The topics addressed in some lessons have long and deeply rooted histories and deserve a more in-depth study. For example, **THE LEGACY OF COLONIALISM** is essential to understanding how the world's resources and power became so unequal. A case study reveals how Brazil's land, resources, and indigenous people, as well as African slaves, were exploited for the purpose of enriching and empowering Portugal. Students see that the consequences of colonialism continue today. They connect the severe poverty and hunger in Brazil and other developing countries to the power imbalances and widespread environmental destruction set in motion by colonialism. They also explore evidence of the reverberations of colonialism in their own communities, and connect the present day struggles of workers, Native Americans and African Americans to colonialism and slavery. This key lesson could be expanded to include more comprehensive units on colonialism around the world, Native American cultures, slavery, resistance, racism, the civil rights movement, and the labor movement. To assist in designing these expanded units additional curricula, books for young people, and videos are listed in the Resource Guide. Some examples of other topics to extend are: nutrition, ecology, women, the media and homelessness.

If You Only Have Two Weeks To Spend On A Hunger Program ...

Follow the lessons outlined below and, whenever you can, work other activities and literature related to hunger into your regular classroom subjects. Integrate a group project from **UNIT III: WHAT CAN WE DO TO HELP END HUNGER?** into your two-week study.

Lesson 3: How Big Is The Hunger Problem?

Lesson 5: Two Kinds of Hunger: Famine & Chronic Hunger

Lesson 7: If There Is Enough Food, Why Are People Hungry?

Lesson 9: One Planet, Two Worlds

Lesion 10: The Legacy of Colonialism

Lesson 14: Hunger, USA

IDEAS FOR TEACHING A HUNGER PROGRAM

1. Have students keep personal journals in which they record their feelings about what they are discovering, draft letters and plans for class projects, compose stories and poems, and collect ideas for community action. Their journals should also contain a list of local organizations with addresses and contacts for student volunteers. Encourage students to title and decorate these journals and use them as a permanent resource guide for continued community service.

2. Invite speakers from your area to address issues related to poverty and hunger.

3. Plan a special class hunger project with your students. If possible, involve the entire school. Some students have founded a **Make A Difference** club, organized annual hunger assemblies in other schools, hunger marches and food drives, and forged permanent relationships with local soup kitchens, food pantries, and shelters.

4. Involve students in planning and teaching hunger workshops to students in other classes, schools, the public library or town hall.

5. Ask students to collect current news items related to hunger and poverty. Prepare a special bulletin board where, after discussing these, students can post them for the rest of the school to see. Add poems, essays, drawings and notices for volunteers to the display.

6. Engage other teachers in your school in integrating hunger-related issues into their classes. For example, the biology teacher might teach a full nutrition course, the science teacher an ecology course, the history teacher a course on colonialism, the Industrial Revolution or labor movement, etc.

7. Join an organization working to end hunger in your community and share your experiences and knowledge with your students.

UNIT I:

WHAT IS HUNGER?

...Hunger is a curious thing: At first it is with you all the time, waking and sleeping and in your dreams, and your belly cries out insistently, and there is a gnawing and a pain as if your vitals were being devoured, and you must stop it at any cost...then the pain is no longer sharp but dull, and this too is with you always, so that you think of food many times a day and each time a terrible sickness assails you...then that too is gone, all pain, all desire, only a great emptiness is left, like the sky, like a well in drought.

from *Nectar in a Sieve*
by Kamala Markandaya

LESSON 1: FOOD KEEPS US ALIVE!

This lesson helps students see food as fundamental to human survival. Before they can fully appreciate the injustice of hunger and its truly devastating effects on the human body, students need to reflect on how important food is in their own lives --- how much food they need daily in order to function properly, and what food actually does for their bodies.

For students who have never had to think of food in terms of survival, this is a particularly crucial lesson. Our culture is bulging with food and reminders of food-abundance --- stocked refrigerators, freezers and pantries, supermarkets, fast food, miles and miles of corn and wheat fields, and a bombardment of food ads and packaging. We assume that because there is so much food around that everyone has access to that food. This is not true. Unlike other basic human needs --- air and water --- food is not free. Increasingly, around the world, around our communities, fewer and fewer people have the money to buy the food they need to remain healthy and strong.

To help students begin to view food as the essential ingredient of life, they will keep food diaries that will show them how much food they eat every day as well as the **kinds** of foods they are eating. Later these diaries will be compared with the food diaries of teenagers from around the world. Students will explore the basic elements of food's life-giving power.

If possible, engage the science teacher's participation.

DAY 1: KEEPING FOOD DIARIES

MATERIALS: students' journals
copies of food charts for each student

PROCEDURE:

1. Ask students to reflect on the basic necessities all human beings must have in order to stay alive. List these on the board. Circle food.

    Why do we need food?
    Where does food come from?
    How much food do we need to become and remain healthy?
    What happens when we don't get enough food?

2. Explain to students that over the next few days they will be keeping food diaries. A page of this diary will show them the amount of food they consume over the course of one day.

    They must write down **everything** they eat including snacks, candies and soft drinks. They should not change their eating habits for this exercise. Their diaries should reflect a typical day's worth of food. (Students will not be sharing this information with others.)

3. Have students divide a page of their journals as follows. Each day's worth of food must be listed on a separate page with the day and date at the top. At the end of each day students will add up the total number of calories and grams of protein consumed.

MONDAY, OCTOBER 1

FOOD	PORTION	CALORIES	PROTEIN
Whole wheat bread	2 slices	120	6
Peanut butter	2 TBS.	190	8
Jelly	1 TBS.	35	0

4. Distribute the food charts. Allow students a few minutes to study them. What do they notice about how foods are listed on the charts? (NOTE: Legumes belong to the family of plants that bear their seeds in pods such as peas and beans.) Why are foods divided this way? Draw attention to how foods on the chart are measured: 1 cup, 1 tbs., etc.

5. Explain that a calorie is the measure of how much energy a food contains. Have students find foods on the chart that are high in energy and low in energy. Students will be listing the calories in their food diaries. (More on calories later.)

6. Explain that protein is the nutrient in food that the body uses to build and repair itself. Protein is measured in grams. Have students find some high and low protein foods on the charts. (More on protein later.)

7. Students can list the foods they have already eaten today in their diaries along with the numbers of calories and grams of protein contained in those foods. Discuss how certain combinations of foods (sandwiches, salads, etc.) must be broken down so that each component can be listed separately. If some foods students consume are not listed on the chart, encourage them to check the food's wrapper and package for calorie and protein calculations. If your library does not have a nutrition guide book with extensive charts, help students compare the food item with similar foods in their category and estimate the calories and protein grams as best you can.

DAY 2:
WHY DO WE NEED FOOD?

MATERIALS: A variety of foods to present to students: Whole-wheat bread, crackers or cereals, pasta, nuts, beans, fruits and vegetables, cheese, yogurt, milk, etc.

If possible bring a piece of fresh fruit for each student to enjoy during the third section of this lesson-WHOLE FOODS KEEP US HEALTHY.

PROCEDURE:

What is so important about food that no human being can live without it? What does food do for our bodies?

1. **FOOD GIVES US ENERGY**

    Have students clap their hands. How is it they are able to do this? The energy in the food they eat. Brainstorm reasons why our bodies need energy. Don't forget **internal** energy needed to keep cells repaired and organs and muscles operating - heart beating, blood flowing, etc.

    The energy in food is measured in **calories**. Each body needs a certain number of calories everyday to function. The amount of calories you need depends on your size, age, how active you are and the climate in which you live. Growing children, pregnant and nursing women, and people engaged in sustained strenuous physical activity need more calories than others. Ask students to consider why this is true.

    Ask students to add up the total number of calories and grams of protein they consume in one day's worth of food from their food diaries. Draw their attention to the bottom of the food charts - DAILY RECOMMENDED CALORIE AND PROTEIN REQUIREMENTS. How do their totals compare with the recommended requirements? Remind them that each person's needs will vary: these figures are estimates.

    A healthy body gets its energy from healthy sources. Present some high-energy foods such as bread, crackers, nuts, pasta, cereal, fruits and vegetables...

    Carbohydrates are the most important source of food energy. They are the least expensive and the most plentiful (especially in the plant kingdom) which is why the majority of the world's population relies on carbohydrate foods to supply their daily energy needs.

Have students place an E next to high-energy foods in their food diaries.

If a body gets too many calories and does not burn them off by being physically active, the body will store the extra calories as fat.

WHAT HAPPENS IF A BODY GETS TOO FEW CALORIES FROM FOOD?

2. **FOOD GIVES US BODY-BUILDING MATERIAL**

Have students examine their own hands. What are they made of? How do they heal themselves when injured?

All living things are made of **protein**. It is part of the structure of each of the millions of body cells that together make up bones, blood, muscles, teeth, skin, hair, etc. We get this body-building protein from the foods we eat.

Present some examples of high-protein foods. Protein is found in animal sources such as meat, chicken, milk, cheese, and eggs as well as in grains, beans, nuts and seeds.

Have students compare the total daily number of grams of protein from one day's worth of food in their diaries with the recommended daily requirements.

Have students place a P next to high-protein foods in their diaries. Are they getting most of their protein from animal or plant sources? Worldwide, people get most of their protein from plant sources. Most people in industrial societies such as the U.S. get most of their protein from animal sources.

WHAT HAPPENS IF A BODY DOES NOT GET ENOUGH PROTEIN?

3. **WHOLE FOODS KEEP OUR BODIES HEALTHY**

Distribute the fresh fruit to students.

WHOLE FOODS (fruits, vegetables, beans, nuts, seeds, grain) contain essential vitamins, minerals and fiber that help regulate body processes and functions. They protect our bodies from disease. Too little vitamin A, for instance, can cause blindness; iron deficiency causes anemia.

Have students circle WHOLE FOODS in their diaries. Are they getting five servings a day of fruits and vegetables (total)? Help students distinguish between WHOLE FOODS and processed foods. Processed foods include potato chips, cookies, white flour products, soft drinks and many "fruit" drinks, luncheon meats, cheese spreads, frozen dinners, etc. The more a food is changed from its whole, natural state the more nutrients are destroyed. Processing destroys essential nutrients.

Many ingredients that could be harmful to the body are added during processing: salt, sugar, fat, chemicals, artificial flavors and colors. Processing also uses up many valuable resources. Twice as much energy is used to process our food than is used to produce all our nation's crops! Processed foods require lots of wasteful packaging, and factories that process food are often responsible for polluting our water and air. Our bodies and planet pay a high price for processed foods.

WHOLE FOODS come to us directly from the earth. Nothing has been taken out. Nothing has been added. They require no wasteful packaging. Whole foods pass along to human beings all the rich nutrients they receive from the soil, air, water and sunlight. They give us energy, bodybuilding material and protection from disease.

*WHAT HAPPENS IF A BODY DOES NOT GET **ENOUGH** VITAMINS AND MINERALS FROM FOOD?*

4. Close this class by asking students to look at the pages of their diaries and reflect on how much food they consume in one day. What would happen if for the rest of their lives they could get only half, or a quarter of that much food? How might that feel? How might their bodies change?

FOOD CHART
NUMBERS OF CALORIES AND GRAMS OF PROTEIN IN COMMON FOODS

Food	Calories	Protein (grams)
Grains		
Bread, 1 slice		
white	70	2
whole-wheat	65	3
French, enriched flour	85	2
rye	60	2
Bagel		
Breakfast Cereals, 1 cup		
bran flakes	105	4
bran & raisins	145	4
corn flakes, plain	95	2
corn flakes, frosted	155	2
oatmeal	130	5
rice, puffed, plain	60	1
rice, puffed, frosted	115	1
Cakes, from mix, 1 slice (1/16 of the cake)		
angelfood	135	3
coffeecake	230	5
devil's food	235	3
gingerbread	175	2
white w/white frosting	260	3
yellow w/chocolate frosting	245	3
Cookies		
brownies, 1	90	5
chocolate chip, 4	200	2
fig bars, 4	200	2
oatmeal & raisin, 4	235	3
oreo, 4	200	2
shortbread, 4 small	155	2
Crackers, saltines, 4		
Doughnuts		
cake, plain, 1	100	1
glazed	205	3
English muffin, plain	140	5
Muffins (commercial)		
blueberry	140	3
bran	140	3
cornmeal	145	3
Macaroni with cheese, 1 cup		
canned w/corn oil	230	9
home recipe w/margarine	430	17
Noodles, egg, enriched flour		
1 cup	200	7
Pancakes, enriched flour		
4" diameter, 1	60	2
Pies, 9" diameter, 1 slice (1/7 of pie)		
apple	345	3
banana cream	285	6
cherry	350	4
lemon meringue	305	4
peach	345	3
pumpkin	275	5
Pizza, cheese, 12" diameter		
1 slice 1/8 of pie	145	6
Popcorn, 1 cup		
air popped, plain	30	1
popped in veg oil/salt	55	1
Pretzels		
thin sticks, 10	10	<1
Dutch twists, 1	65	2
thin twists, 10	240	6
Rice, 1 cup		
brown, cooked	217	5
white		
instant	162	3
long-grain	264	6
Rolls, enriched flour		
hot/dog bun	120	3
hamburger bun	120	3
hard	155	5
Spaghetti		
enriched, 1 cup	155	5
LEGUMES, SEEDS, NUTS		
Beans, dried, 1 cup		
red kidney	230	15
black beans	227	15
Peanuts, roasted in oil & salted, 1 cup	840	35
Peanut butter 1 TBS	95	4
Peas, 1 cup	230	16
Sunflower seeds, 1 cup	810	35
FRUITS		
Apples, 1 medium	80	trace
Apple juice, 1 cup		
sweetened	230	trace
unsweetened	100	trace
Apricots, canned		
1 cup in syrup	220	2
Bananas, 1 medium	100	1
Cranberry juice		
cocktail 1 cup	165	trace
Grapefruit, 1 med.	50	1
Grapefruit juice		
1 cup sweetened	135	1
1 cup unsweetened	100	1
Lemonade from concentrate 1 cup	105	trace
Oranges, 1 medium	65	1

Food	Calories	Protein (grams)
Orange juice from concentrate, 1 cup	120	2
Peaches		
1 medium, raw	40	1
canned, 1 cup	200	1
dried, 1 cup	420	5
Pears		
1 medium, raw	100	1
canned, 1 cup	195	1
Pineapple		
raw, 1 cup	80	1
canned, 1 slice	45	trace
Plums, 1 medium	30	trace
Raisins 1 1/2 tbs	40	trace
Watermelon wedge 4x8	110	2
VEGETABLES		(grams)
Beans, green canned, 1 cup	30	2
Bean sprouts, mung		
1 cup raw	35	2
Beets, cooked, 1 cup	55	2
Broccoli, cooked, 1 stalk	45	6
Carrots		
raw, 1 medium	21	1
cooked, 1 cup	50	1
Corn		
ear, 5" long	70	2
canned, creamed, 1 cup	210	5
canned, whole, 1 cup	140	4
Lettuce, raw 1/4 head	20	1
Mushrooms, raw, 1 cup	20	2
Peppers		
sweet green, raw, 1/2 cup	20	1
sweet red, raw, 1/2 cup	14	<1
hot green chili, raw	18	1
Potatoes		
baked w/skin 1 medium	220	5
baked w/out skin 1 med	245	3
French fried 10 fries	158	2
hash browns, 1 cup	345	3
mashed, fresh, 1 cup	135	4
mashed, dehydrated, 1 cup	150	4
Potato chips, 1p chips	115	1
Spinach, cooked, 1 cup	50	2
Tomatoes		
raw, 1 medium	25	1
canned solids, 1 cup	50	2
Tomato catsup 1 tbs	15	trace
Tomato juice, canned 1 cup	45	2
MILK PRODUCTS		
Cheese		
cottage cheese, 1 cup	235	28
cheddar, 1 oz	115	7
American, 1 oz	105	6
Cream, sour, 1 cup	495	7
Cream whipped, (pressurized) 1 cup	155	2
Cream, whipped (heavy), 1 cup	410	2
Milk, 1 cup		
whole	150	8
lowfat (2%)	120	8
nonfat (1%)	90	8
Chocolate milk, 1 cup	210	8
Eggnog	340	10
Ice cream, 1 cup	270	5
Ice milk (hard)	185	5
Ice milk (softserve)	225	8
Yogurt 8 oz		
plain	145	12
fruit-flavored	230	10
EGGS		
egg 1 fried in butter	85	5
hard-boiled	80	6
poached	80	6
scrambled, w/ milk	96	6
SUGARS & SWEETS		
Sugar, white, 1 tbs	45	0
Syrup, Pancake, maple	244	0
Fudge, plain, 1 oz	115	1
Jellies, 1 tbs	49	<1
FATS & OILS		
butter 1 tbs	100	<1
Margarine		
regular, hard 1 tbs	100	<1
regular, soft 1 tbs	100	1
Oils		
corn, 1 tbs	125	0
olive, 1 tbs	125	0
vegetable, 1 tbs	125	0
Mayonnaise, 1 tbs	100	<1
MEAT PRODUCTS		(grams)
Bacon, 2 pcs	85	4
Beef		
ground, lean 3 oz	235	20
roast, 2 slices, 4x2x1/x	37	17
sirloin 2 1/2x2 1/2x3/4		
lean & fat		
lean alone	185	22

Food	Calories	Protein (grams)
Chicken		
breast, fried	185	22
breast, roasted, no skin	142	27
drumstick, fried	120	13
drumstick, roasted	76	13
Turkey, roasted		
dark meat 3 oz	159	24
light meat 3 oz	133	25
Ham, boiled 1 oz	65	5
Pork chop		
lean & fat 2.7 oz	305	19
lean alone 2 oz	150	17
Sausages		
bologna 1 oz	85	3
hot dog 1	170	7
pork link 1	60	2
Salami, dry, 1/3 oz	45	2
FISH PRODUCTS		
Fish sticks, breaded pollo (2 sticks)	155	9
Flounder/sole 3 oz		
baked w/ lemon juice	99	21
baked w/ butter/marger	120	16
Salmon 3 oz		
canned, pink	118	17
broiled or baked	183	23
smoked	99	16
Scallops, breaded, cooked, 6	200	17
Shrimp		
fried, 4 large	218	19
broiled, 18 large	99	21
Tuna 3 oz		
canned in oil, drained	163	25
canned in water, drained	111	25
SOME FAST FOODS		
(from McDonald's Corp, Oak Brook Illinois)		
Big Mac	560	25
Quarter Pounder	410	23
Quarter Pounder w/cheese	520	29
Fillet-o-fish sandwich	440	14
Hamburger	260	12
Cheeseburger	310	15
French fries, small	220	20
McNuggets	270	20
Sauces		
barbeque	70	1
hot mustard	70	1
sweet/sour	60	1
Milkshakes		
chocolate	320	12
strawberry	320	11
Vanilla	290	11
Hot fudge sundae	240	7
Apple pie	260	2
Egg McMuffin	290	8.2
Sausage McMuffin	370	17
BEVERAGES		
Cola, 12 oz	151	0
Ginger ale, 12 oz	124	0
Grape soda, 12 oz	161	0
Lemon-lime soda, 12 oz	149	0
Orange soda, 12 oz	177	0
Root beer, 12 oz	152	<1
Gatorade 1 cup	39	0
Grape drink, canned, 1 cup	112	0
Lemonade, froze, 1 cup	100	<1

DAILY RECOMMENDED CALORIE AND PROTEIN REQUIREMENTS

AGE	CALORIES	PROTEIN
MALES		
7-10	2,000	28
11-14	2,500	45
15-18	3,000	59
FEMALES		
7-10	2,000	28
11-14	2,200	46
15-18	2,200	44

Source: Recommended Dietary Allowances from the National Academy of Sciences, 1989

ADDITIONAL ACTIVITIES:

1. Take students to the source of our food - the land. Visit a local farm or invite a farmer to come to speak to your class. To find farmers visit a local green market or contact your local Farm Bureau. Brainstorm questions for the farmer in advance. What crops are produced? How is the food grown and harvested? Where does it go when it leaves the farm? Together track a favorite food from the farm to your mouth.

2. Have students create a list of everyday foods and research their origins. Create a world food map by taping pictures of foods or food labels onto the country or state that produces that food. More and more people worldwide are becoming dependent on food that must be shipped to them from another area --- food that could be produced locally. When produce is transported long distances it is usually picked before it is ripe so that it doesn't spoil during shipping. Lots of energy is used in refrigerating, packaging and transporting food long distances. Hold a discussion on the consequences of becoming dependent on foods that other people far away grow for us.

3. The majority of the world's population gets it energy and protein from plant sources. Have students research some of the world's food staples.

RICE -	*The food staple of over half the world's people*
WHEAT -	*The most widely grown plant in the world*
ROOTS -	*Yams, potatoes, taro and cassava*
MILLET	
SORGHUM	
MAIZE -	*At one time the food staple of North America, maize sustained entire populations of Native Americans. The word means "Our Mother, Our Life, She Who Sustains Us."*

   Students can consult their food diaries to find out the staple (centerpiece) of most of **their** meals. Countries that rely on animal products as a food staple have the highest rates of heart disease, obesity and cancer.

4. Plan and prepare a healthy feast. If possible wash, cut and cook foods in the classroom or cafeteria. Students could also bring in a favorite dish. Encourage them to find recipes from different countries in order to give the feast an international flavor.

LESSON 2: EATING THE WAY THE WORLD EATS*

This introductory activity allows students to experience firsthand how unfairly food is distributed in our world. Three different meals are prepared in advance - each representing one of three groups: those who have more than their fair share of food, those who have just enough, and those who never get enough food to stay healthy. By sheer "luck of the draw" students end up in one of these groups. After the meal they discuss and write about their experience.

NOTE: Some schools have held this activity close to Thanksgiving and have asked each student to bring a non-perishable food item as a ticket to the event. Later the food is delivered to a local pantry.

MATERIALS: Three different kinds of meals with corresponding colored meal tickets. (See #7 under PROCEDURE for specially marked tickets.)

The figures below are based on a class of 30. Adjust the numbers to suit your class size.

BLUE GROUP (15%)
4 blue meal tickets.
4 fancy meals: Choose foods students love such as hamburgers, pizzas, ice-cream, etc. There should be more than enough food for this group. Leftovers should be sitting out in full view.

These are the overconsumers. They sit together at a large table that is covered with an elegant tablecloth. Use flowers, china plates, silverware and dinner napkins. Teachers serve these students.

YELLOW GROUP (60%)
18 yellow meal tickets.
18 servings of plain rice and vegetables
(or rice and beans).

These students represent the people of the world who get just enough to eat. However, there are inequalities within this group. Some get more than others. These students sit together at their desks and eat off paper plates. They serve themselves from large bowls and use plastic forks. Each

---

* This activity is based on a model provided by Oxfam. Percentages are from the director of Food First, Oakland, CA.

row of students is assigned a specific bowl of food. The amounts inside the bowls should be unequal.

RED GROUP (25%)
8 red meal tickets.
8 small servings of plain rice and one large pitcher of "dirty" water. (Place one drop of green food coloring and two drops of red in the water to give it a muddy appearance.)

These students represent the more than 1 billion people who are chronically hungry. They never get enough food. This group sits on the floor and serves themselves from one large bowl and pitcher. Some students in this group may get no food at all.

PREPARATION: Prepare the meals in advance. Place colored tickets together in one basket for students to choose from. Prepare seating arrangements in your classroom. Do not lay food out until each group is seated.

PROCEDURE:

1. As students enter the classroom ask them to choose a meal ticket from the basket. When everyone has a ticket, announce that they are going to have a lunch that shows how people around the world eat. Their ticket determines which group they will sit with.

2. Invite students with BLUE tickets to sit at the large table. Pull out their chairs and hand each one a napkin. Fill their glasses. Serve their first course while the other students watch.

3. Invite students with YELLOW tickets to serve themselves from the large bowls assigned to their row - then to return to their desks to eat.

4. Invite students with RED tickets to sit in a circle on the floor. Place the large bowl of rice and pitcher of water in the center of the circle. Tell them they must share this food.

5. As students eat tell them that their random choice gave them little control over how much food they receive in the same way people in the real world have little control over which economic situation they are born into.

Share some hunger facts with students: Worldwide over 1 billion people are chronically hungry. This means they never get enough food to become and remain healthy. It is estimated that everyday in the U.S. nearly 36 million people - nearly half of them children - go hungry.

Tell them today they are eating the way the world eats. Let's take a look at the world we've created inside this classroom.

TO THE BLUE GROUP: Those of you lucky enough to end up in this group represent the 15% of the world's people who get more than enough food. You live mostly in countries like the U.S., Australia, France, Switzerland and most other countries in Western Europe, although some of you can also be found in developing regions such as Brazil, Haiti and India. You use more than your fair share of the world's resources. Your children are healthy and attend good schools. This will help them get high-paying jobs later on. You get the best medical care when you are sick. Because of your high-fat, high-sugar diets, however, the leading causes of death in your group are heart disease, cancer and diabetes. (Serve this group their desserts.)

TO THE YELLOW GROUP: Those of you who ended up in the yellow group represent the 60% of the world's population who get just enough to eat. You can be found in more countries than the blue group, including the U.S., Eastern Europe, Thailand, the Philippines and Iran. Most of the time your families get enough food. Sometimes, however, you may not have enough money to pay expensive medical bills, rent and heating bills in the winter. During those times you cannot spend as much as usual on food for your family.

Your children are six times more likely to die of diseases related to hunger than those in the blue group. You could be Lucia, a school teacher in Prague who takes in sewing to earn extra money to support her parents and her children. You could also be MaryAnn, a mother of three in Chicago, who works two jobs cleaning homes and offices in order to feed her children. Some of you struggle to keep from falling into the red group.

TO THE RED GROUP: Those students who ended up in the red group represent the more than 1 billion people around the world who **never get enough food to eat.** You are hungry everyday of your life. Most of you come from the global south - Ethiopia, Mozambique, Haiti, Bangladesh, or Cambodia. Some of you can also be found in wealthier countries such as the U.S., Canada and England. Most of you live on $2 a day. You do not have access to clean water and often drink water that is contaminated. You cannot afford medical care of any kind. You live in makeshift homes or out in the open. For many, especially your children, this means early death.

Some of you work on large plantations that grow sugarcane, coffee or bananas that are shipped out of your country. You would prefer to grow food to feed your families. You could be Doire, a farmer in Haiti, who rents a small plot of land. In the dry season when nothing will grow he makes charcoal to sell or trade for a few day's worth of food. You could be David who is homeless in New York City and earns a few dollars a day opening doors for customers at a local bank. Many of you cannot find employment - without jobs you have no money to buy food or rent a home. You often go a full day with nothing to eat.

6. Allow students plenty of time to express how it feels to be in their group. Does the lunch seem fair? How would it feel to eat this way everyday of your life? (Avoid creating a rich country/poor country discussion by asking students if there aren't hungry and well-fed people in every country.)

7. To emphasize the fact that some people move between groups depending on their economic situations mark some tickets with a symbol or names. Tell students you have some news. Some of them drew special tickets.

If you drew a BLUE TICKET with the name John Drew on it please stand. You work in a company that manufactures television sets. The company has shut down and moved to a country where there are no unions and where they can pay very low wages. You have not been able to find another job. You had no savings and no one who can take you in until you get on your feet. You must go to a shelter for the homeless to get food, clothes and medical care. Please take a place in the RED GROUP.

The price of coffee on the world market has just fallen from $1.20/lb. to 60¢. This news will affect the lives of some of you in this room. If you drew a BLUE TICKET with the name Bob Baker on it please stand. You are the manager of a large coffee company in the U.S. The drop in the price of coffee means your company doesn't have to pay as much as it has been paying for coffee. You can still charge your U.S. customers the same price they've been paying for your coffee. Your company is going to make a huge profit this year and you will receive a healthy bonus. Congratulations! Today you will receive two dinners. I hope you're hungry!

If you drew a RED TICKET with the name of Anna Hernandez please stand. You pick coffee on a plantation in El Salvador. When the price of coffee dropped your employer no longer had enough money to pay all his employees and was forced to cut back on his workforce. You have been laid off. Today you will receive only water.

If you drew a YELLOW TICKET with the name Jose Martin on it please stand. You grow fruit in your garden and sell it at a local market each day. Many of your neighbors and customers were laid off from the local coffee plantation - the town's largest employer. As a result, people are buying less from you. You do not have enough money to buy corn for your family. Please take your place in the RED GROUP.

8. Tell students that the world produces more than enough food for everyone to live a healthy, active life and has the capacity to produce

even more. In spite of this many people go hungry. WHY? Ask students to brainstorm reasons why hungry people don't have access to food. Encourage students to persist in asking WHY? in order to get to the **root causes** of hunger. For instance, people are hungry because they are poor. WHY are they poor? Because they don't earn enough money. WHY don't they earn enough money? Because they can't find a job or aren't paid a fair wage. WHY can't they find a job? Only by asking WHY? do we uncover the real causes beneath hunger.

MORE QUESTIONS:

1. If there is enough food for everyone, why are so many people so hungry?
2. Why do some people have too much while others have too little?
3. Why is this allowed to happen?
4. Were you aware that these inequalities existed?
5. Are there hungry people where you live?

9. As a homework assignment ask students to write their reactions to the activity in their journals. Encourage them to list any questions, ideas, etc., they have as well.

10. Together read and discuss sections of **FAST FOOD NATION** by Eric Schlosser (Houghton Mifflin), an exposé of how burgers, fries and sodas came to represent American culture. The author explains the unappetizing methods used to produce fast food as well as the negative social and dietary consequences we pay. He connects fast food, car culture, suburban sprawl, industrial agriculture and illegal immigration.

11. Have students look at the book **HUNGRY PLANET** (See Resource Section). They can calculate how much their own families spend on groceries in one week and compare the kinds of foods their families eat and the cost to those of families from 24 different countries in the book.

MAKE A DIFFERENCE!

Encourage students to organize and stage a Hunger Banquet for parents and local business leaders. Invite local government officials and the media to participate. Students can show hunger videos, read from their journals, and discuss the root causes of hunger in your community and some practical things people in your area can do to end it.

LESSON 3: HOW BIG IS THE HUNGER PROBLEM?

In this introductory lesson students learn how widespread the hunger problem is and discover that one of the reasons it continues is the lack of attention it receives in the media. **25,000 children die every day from hunger or diseases resulting from hunger.** (This figure fluctuates depending on world events such as wars, famines, natural disasters, political unrest, economics, etc.) Some comparison exercises help students grasp the enormity of this statistic. The day's newspaper is examined for any mention of these unnecessary deaths and a discussion focuses on **why** so many people are unaware of the scope and causes of hunger.

NOTE: Included here is a list of videos. If possible choose one to use with this lesson, since seeing the effects of hunger is a powerful part of helping young people understand that behind every abstract statistic is a real human child and that the victims of hunger are not responsible for their situation. Solving the hunger problem requires all our concentrated efforts.

HUNGER IN A WORLD OF PLENTY
Oxfam
(800) 77-OXFAM
www.oxfamamerica.org

FAMINE & CHRONIC PERSISTENT HUNGER: A LIFE AND DEATH DISTINCTION
The Hunger Project
(212) 251-9100
www.thp.org

From UNICEF:
MISSING OUT
FISTFUL OF RISE
FOR A FEW PENNIES MORE
www.unicef.org/videoaudio

PROCEDURE:

1. Ask students how they think the world would react if 25,000 children died today in some sort of disaster.

2. (If using a video play it now and tell students that **everyday** 25,000 children die of hunger. Allow them time to respond. How did the images make them feel? Did anything about the video surprise them?) If not using a video ask students what their reactions are to this enormous problem.

3. List any questions students have about hunger in a permanent space on the board titled: **QUESTIONS ABOUT HUNGER.** Over the course of this hunger study they can research and answer their own questions.

4. If 25,000 children die every day from causes related to hunger, how many children perish every minute? Hold one minute of silence to reflect on this fact. How many classes the size of yours equal 25,000 children? How many schools?

5. Ask students to speculate on whether most people are aware that so many children perish everyday from hunger.

6. Page through the day's newspaper looking for the headline and article that let the world know that **25,000 CHILDREN DIED OF HUNGER TODAY!** (and yesterday, and tomorrow, and the next day...)

    Why isn't this front page news?

    What sells newspapers, magazines and TV news?

    Were students aware that the hunger problem was as serious and widespread?

    How does a lack of awareness perpetuate hunger?

    Do the people students know **care** about ending hunger and poverty?

    Are there hungry people in your community? Are the **causes** of their hunger explored in the local news?

    If there is enough food in your community, why are people hungry?

ADDITIONAL ACTIVITY:

Nearly 1 BILLION people around the world do not get enough food to become and remain healthy. HOW MUCH IS 1 BILLION?[*]

A. Compare 1 BILLION to the population of your state.

---

[*] Sources: Math problem B above is from *Kids Ending Hunger* by Tracy and Sage Howard. Problem C is from *How Much is a Million?* by David M. Schwartz.

B. If you started counting to 1 BILLION, counting a number every two seconds, how old would you be when you finished? (ANSWER: *62 plus the student's present age.*)

C. If 1 BILLION children climbed onto one another's shoulders to form a tower, how many times would that tower reach to the moon and back to earth? (Figure an average of four feet for the height of the children because they are standing on shoulders, not heads. There are 5,280 feet in a mile. The moon is approximately 239,000 miles from Earth.)
(ANSWER: *The tower would reach to the moon, back to Earth, and to the moon again.*)

MAKE A DIFFERENCE!

The first step in helping end hunger is talking about hunger. Begin teaching your family and friends what you know about hunger. As you learn more, develop and teach hunger workshops to students in other classes and other schools. Educate your community by writing letters to newspaper editors and local government officials.

See Lesson 24 for letter writing tips.

LESSON 4: HUNGER DESTROYS

In this lesson students compare two plants --- one healthy, the other withering --- to prompt a discussion of how hunger breaks down the body and mind. They learn how the Infant Mortality Rate (IMR) exposes the severity of hunger in a particular country. By comparing the IMRs of several countries, including the U.S., students question why certain areas of the world experience a devastatingly higher degree of hunger.

BACKGROUND READING

It is important for students to distinguish between the hunger they feel when they skip a meal and the kind of hunger that kills. Occasional hunger pains are usually satisfied by eating a large meal, but people suffering from chronic hunger **never get enough** food to keep their bodies and minds functioning properly. Children, pregnant and nursing women, and the elderly are especially vulnerable to this kind of hunger, and they are most often the very people with the least access to food and the power to change their situations.

Children's bodies are still developing. Without sufficient nutrients from food to provide energy, bodybuilding material and resistance to infection, their bodies become weak and eventually break down. They cannot perform many physical tasks and have difficulty concentrating and staying awake. This is not the kind of hunger that can be satisfied by eating a large meal. Often by the time a severely malnourished child is brought to the attention of a doctor, the damage is irreversible. Severe hunger results in stunted growth, blindness and organ failure. Without essential vitamins and minerals from foods, chronically undernourished bodies cannot fight off illnesses such as TB, measles, flu, or even the common cold. Every year 500,000 children go blind from a lack of vitamin A. 20% of the children in developing countries suffer goiter, an enlargement of the thyroid due to a severe iodine deficiency.

Pregnant women who are chronically hungry give birth to babies with dangerously low birthweights. The mothers' bodies cannot provide the nutrients their babies desperately need. Many of these undernourished infants do not survive their first year of life.

Elderly people are often on special diets for health problems related to age. Many are housebound and must rely on very limited incomes. Teams of physicians have traveled across the U.S. interviewing elderly people about their diets and inspecting their kitchen cupboards. Their study revealed that may of the elderly go without food for days at a time and that their bodies lack the necessary nutrients provided by fresh fruit and vegetables. Beans, potatoes and white bread were the most common foods found (and in small amounts) in many of their homes. These elderly people were living out their last years in fear and dread with the constant pain and worry of hunger.

Hunger destroys. It destroys an individual's ability to function --- to grow, think and work. It destroys her dignity, sense of self, security, future, and ultimately, her life.

Hunger destroys cultures and societies. It breaks down families, creates hostilities between people, deprives communities of valuable intellectual and physical contributions, drains the economy and threatens the peace and security of our entire world. The existence of hunger in a world of such abundant resources and helping hands mocks our moral values. We can no longer turn away from hunger --- it is destroying us all.

MATERIALS: **Two plants:** 1 healthy and shiny
                                   1 withering

              Optional: One copy of a food diary from around the world for each small group

                                     Songs: *Hunger & Thirst* by Tom Chapin
                                                WHY? by Tracy Chapman

PROCEDURE:

1. Ask students how it feels when they skip a meal. How does their hunger affect them physically and mentally? What if that hunger was never satisfied?

2. Present the two plants. Encourage students to compare them and relate their discussion to the consequences of severe hunger on human bodies. How would it feel to get too few calories? What would a body look like with too little protein?

3. Together map the breakdown step-by-step of a chronically hungry person over a long period of time. Write students' ideas on the board. Remind them to consider the internal physical effects as well as the psychological and emotional ones. Encourage them to use language that keeps this exercise personal - "I would feel tired." "My stomach would hurt." Your map can take many forms. One might look like this:

At first I could still function.
  People might not even know I am hungry all the time.
    My stomach would growl.
      I would feel impatient and grouchy.
        All I would think about is FOOD.
          I would start to lose weight.
            Friends would be bigger and more active then me.
              I would feel embarrassed because I can't keep up.
              I would run out of energy easily.
              I would be tired all the time.
              My grades would suffer.
                I would have difficulty concentrating and staying awake in class.
               It would be hard doing simple things such as walking up a
              flight of stairs, carrying books, opening heavy doors.
             I would feel very frightened.
                My body would be using protein for energy instead of to
              repair damaged tissues, muscles and organs.
              My eyesight would deteriorate.
                I would feel ashamed at my appearance
              and at having to beg for food.
               I would have to stop going to school.
              I would feel powerless.
              There is no future for me.
               If I caught a cold or the flu
                I might not be able to fight it.
                 People would say I died of
                an illness but I would
                really have
                 died
                 of
                  malnutrition.

4. Would a healthy meal save a person in this condition? What is necessary immediately? Over the long-term? What words can students find to describe how it must feel to be this hungry? How must it feel to see a loved one in this condition? What effect does this kind of hunger have on the rest of the community? Do the consequences of hunger also affect people who aren't hungry? How?

5. If your students have kept food diaries have them compare them with the diaries of teenagers from around the world on the following page. Work in small groups and have each group present its findings to the class.

6. **CLASS MATH PROBLEMS:**
Too little vitamin A results in blindness. (Vitamin A is found in fruits and vegetables, but many hungry children, especially in developing countries, rarely get fresh fruits and vegetables.) Blindness can be prevented by taking a megadose of the vitamin --- only two vitamin pills per year are necessary. The cost of each pill is 2¢. 4¢ per year can save

one child's eyesight! Nearly 150 million children around the world need vitamin A desperately.

- A. How much would it cost to supply all of those children with 2 vitamin pills for one year?

- B. How many children's eyes could the class save if each student gave up one soft drink a week for one year?

HOW HUNGER IS MEASURED: THE CHILD MORTALITY RATE

7. Scientists have found a way to measure the severity of hunger in an area by keeping count of how many children die before their fifth birthday. Children who die so young are almost always suffering from malnutrition. Hungry, weak children are more likely to die than well-fed, strong ones. This tells us that hunger is one of the major causes of child deaths.

   The system used to measure hunger is called **THE CHILD MORTALITY RATE**. A country's Child Mortality Rate represents the number of children under five years of age who die out of every 1,000 children born in that country. If 25 out of 1,000 children in a country die before the age of five, we say that country has a Child Mortality Rate of 25. A Child Mortality Rate of 25 or above signals a widespread hunger problem --- too many children cannot get the nutrients they need to stay alive.

8. Have students graph the following Child Mortality Rates. Locate these countries on a world map.

Country	Rate	Country	Rate
Somalia	142	Cambodia	91
Bolivia	57	Mozambique	168
China	22	Guatemala	39
Afghanistan	257	Japan	4
Iraq	44	Israel	5
Sweden	3	USA	8

9. Which countries are having widespread hunger problems? Does a low Child Mortality Rate mean there is **no** hunger in a country? Are students surprised to learn that the U.S. does not have the lowest Child Mortality Rate?

---

[*] Source: *State of the World's Children*, 2009, UNICEF

Explain that the Child Mortality Rate is an average. Among well-fed people in the U S. who can afford enough food, the rate is very low. Among the poor in the U.S. the rate is much higher. The Child Mortality Rate in Washington, D.C., for instance, is 13 --- equal to or higher than the average Child Mortality Rates of some of the poorer countries in our hemisphere such as Cuba (7). What are some reasons for this?

10. Close this class with "Hunger & Thirst" or "WHY?"

MAKE A DIFFERENCE!

Invite students to organize a *Vitamin A+ Kids* penny drive in your school. They can create posters to advertise this important event and they can visit other classes to explain how hunger causes blindness, how many children suffer from it, and how we can stop it. A large jar can be placed in each classroom to hold the coins. When the drive is over have students count the pennies and calculate how many children's eyes will be saved.

Send money to:
The International Eye Foundation
Vitamin A+ Kids Campaign
10801 Connecticut Avenue
Kensington, MD 20895
(240) 290-0263

IMPORTANT: Before beginning this drive hold a discussion with students on the limitations as well as the importance of charitable giving. While it is absolutely crucial to save children's eyesight by collecting money that will purchase necessary vitamin pills, we also need to continue investigating **why** so many children lack access to foods that would prevent them from going blind in the first place. After the drive, consider having students express their feelings in writing about what they have done as well as to reflect on what else needs to be done.

FOOD DIARIES FROM AROUND THE WORLD

DIET OF A TEENAGER FROM INDIA

BREAKFAST	Hot tea
EARLY LUNCH	Khichri --- rice with dahl, salt turmeric and fat Khadi --- soup made from buttermilk
TEA BREAK	Tea, Puffed rice, Banana
DINNER	Bajra roti --- fat cake made from cereal or millet flour Dehydrated vegetable Lentils with spices

APPROXIMATE ANALYSIS: 1,600 Calories
                                     30 Grams of Protein

DIET OF A TEENAGER FROM UGANDA

BREAKFAST	Plantain
SNACK	Plantain, Mango
DINNER	Plantain, Ground peanuts, Sun-dried termites

APPROXIMATE ANALYSIS: 1,200 Calories
                                     20 Grams of Protein

DIET OF A TEENAGER FROM MALAYSIA

BREAKFAST	Eggs, Bread, Butter & Jam, Hot beverage, Milk
MORNING SNACK	Savoury Pie, Biscuit
LUNCH	Rice, Meat, Vegetables
AFTERNOON SNACK	Fruit
DINNER	Rice, Fish or Meat, Vegetables, Soup
EVENING SNACK	Fruit or Noodles

APPROXIMATE ANALYSIS: 2,100 Calories
                                     75 Grams of Protein

DIET OF A TEENAGER FROM CHICAGO

BREAKFAST	1 cup of Milk 2 slices of white bread
LUNCH	1 small bowl of canned chicken noodle soup 1 bag of potato chips 1 soda
DINNER	1 hot dog with white bread 1 soda 1 cookie

APPROXIMATE ANALYSIS: 1,000 Calories
                                     27 Grams of Protein

Source: The World Food Day Packet distributed by the National Committee for World Food Day. (See Resource Guide to order.)

LESSON 5: TWO KINDS OF HUNGER FAMINE AND CHRONIC HUNGER

In Part 1 of this lesson *Maria's Dream*, a short story, takes students inside the world of a twelve year-old refugee as she struggles to recover physically and emotionally from the civil war and drought that forced her family to flee their homeland. In spite of her circumstances, Maria is determined to return to her land and begin rebuilding her family's health and future. Students discuss and write about what is necessary to prepare for and survive a natural disaster such as drought. They measure, prepare and sample food rations and a dehydration cure given to famine victims.

In Part 2 students read and discuss *Really Mister He's Nine*, a true story in which doctors investigating the extent of hunger in the United States discover that nine year-old Lee's growth has been stunted from a life of insufficient nutrients. Students explore the root causes of Lee's hunger and solve math problems that expose the relatively inexpensive costs of preventing serious illnesses caused by chronic hunger.

PART 1: FAMINE

The world has always been slow to notice hunger. We usually pay attention only after thousands of people, mostly children and elderly, have perished from starvation and disease. Famine, the most widely recognized kind of hunger, is responsible for only 10% of the estimated 20 million hunger deaths every year. The other 90% of deaths not portrayed by the media are the result of chronic hunger --- the long-term consumption of too few nutrients.

FAMINE IS AN EMERGENCY. IT MEANS PEOPLE ARE NEAR DEATH.

Famine is a widespread lack of access to food caused when political forces and/or environmental forces disrupt the availability of food in a community that does not have the institutional capacity to compensate for the crisis. Sometimes this food shortage affects a specific ethnic, religious or economic group of people. Food is usually available in other parts of the country, but only to those who can pay for it.

Political Causes of Famine

Famine may result from food embargoes, civil unrest or war. War is the major cause of famine today. It destroys food and water systems, roads, homes and hospitals. It complicates emergency food delivery. Sometimes delivery is purposely blocked and the lack of food is used as a weapon of war.

War forces people to flee their homes and land in search of food and safety. The **refugees** must leave quickly, taking with them only what they can carry and travel long distances usually on foot. **Relief agencies** need to act swiftly to set up make-shift towns called **refugee camps** at a safe distance, usually in a neighboring country. Aid workers must find ways of overcoming tremendous obstacles such as a lack of roads, military blockades, violence and expensive planes that can carry limited amounts of supplies. When so many exhausted, hungry and sick people are forced to gather suddenly in one small area, there is rarely enough food, medicine, clean water and shelter for everyone. Food is **rationed** and consists of items that are easily transportable such as flour, rice, cornmeal, beans and water. Seldom do famine victims get meat, fruits or vegetables.

Initially there is no sewage system in place and limited water sources become contaminated, spreading diseases such as typhoid and polio. People, especially children, suffer severe dehydration caused by diarrhea. Refugees cannot survive long on rations. Relief agencies work together to provide food deliveries from around the world, drill wells, build shelters and begin dispensing tools and seeds for planting.

The unexpected convergence of thousands of needy people into a country already struggling with hunger has devastating effects, economical and environmental, on that country as well. In 1994 1.5 million people escaped Rwanda's civil war and streamed into nearby Zaire and Tanzania at a rate of 500 refugees per minute. Sometimes famine is complicated by a combination of war and natural disaster such as when civil war and drought in Somalia drove millions from their homes.

Environmental Causes of Famine

Earthquakes, floods, hurricanes and drought result in famine when countries lack the resources that would enable them to better prepare for and withstand nature's violence.

Severe soil erosion also leads to regional food shortages. In their desperation to satisfy a chronic hunger, people in poor countries cannot always concern themselves with the long-term consequences of their actions on their environment. In Africa, for example, soil is poor and weak from overuse. Crop yields are meager even in the best of seasons, leaving no food available for storage in case of emergencies. The land needs fertilizer or a rest between plantings to regain its life-giving nutrients, but many African farmers have large, hungry families and cannot afford fertilizer or the time the land needs to renew itself. With each season they are forced to plant in empty soil. This leads to soil erosion.

Rainfall in many parts of Africa is seasonal. Certain regions are prone to drought during which crops wither and livestock die if there is no water storage or irrigation system in place. The thin topsoil is blown away and sand and rock remain.

When there are too few plant roots to bind the soil, sudden heavy rains can cause violent flooding. Crops and soil both are washed away. Hungry people's hard labor is wiped out and they are left without the basic resources to grow or obtain food. To create new farmland farmers cut down forests, but eventually this land is degraded as well by overcultivation, wind and water erosion.

It is not an accident that the most devastating natural disasters have occurred in the poorest nations. People in these countries lack the materials and technology to prepare for, withstand and recover from the violent acts of nature. These resources include fertilizer for improving soil fertility, trees to bind the soil, dams to control flooding, irrigation systems, roads, storage facilities, sturdier homes, medical care and communications systems. The U.S. experiences natural disasters, but we do not suffer famines. Five years of drought in California resulted in no loss of life. Five years of drought in Ethiopia resulted in a famine that killed over 1 million people.

PROCEDURE:

1. Ask students to share news reports they have seen or read involving famine. Do they know what caused these famines?

2. Explain that they will be reading a story of famine based on true experiences. In *Maria's Dream* a family flees Mozambique for a refugee camp in Malawi. Locate these countries on the class map.

3. Read the story aloud or have students read it for homework. They might write, then discuss personal reactions to the story. Discussion questions, writing exercises and activities follow the story.

   IMPORTANT: Encourage students in their discussions and writing to go beyond the traditional ways of helping famine victims --- giving food and medicine and supplies (although these are crucial) --- to a deeper exploration of the **root** causes of famine such as: lack of access to resources to help prepare for drought, lack of negotiating power and credit, and unequal relationships between and within countries (such as between farmers and landlords, armed rebels and peasants, well-fed people and malnourished people). Urge students to focus on how eliminating these inequalities will help people become self-reliant.

   Before planning the fund-raiser activities in the ***MAKE A DIFFERENCE!*** section of this lesson encourage a discussion of **how** providing farm animals or planting trees goes beyond mere charity toward helping people become self-reliant. Be sure students understand the long-term consequences of such gifts.

MARIA'S DREAM

It was still dark when Maria awoke in the mud-pole hut in the refugee camp. She had been dreaming again of going home and, rolling over on her grass mat, she tried crawling back inside the lovely dream, but her work called to her. She stretched her long, thin arms. A life of too little food and too much work had left Maria small for her age, but her will remained unbreakable. She had taken over her father's chores while he was away at the border investigating rumors that it was safe for refugees to return to their homes in Mozambique. It had been nearly a year since the terrible war and drought had forced thousands of them to flee their homes for the safety of this makeshift camp.

Maria pulled herself off the ground and rolled up her mat. Today she would make the long walk to the refugee center for her family's food rations. The sides of the hut were open and Maria saw her mother preparing the last of the dried maize.

"Hurry up, girl," she told her. "You must be back to help with the garden before the sun is too intense." She handed Maria a small clay bowl, refusing her daughter's insistence that they share it.

"You will need the energy for the journey," her mother said.

Maria finished the cold gruel, then, placing the empty food sack around her narrow shoulders, she set out on the dark, dusty road. From the top of a hill she surveyed the gloomy camp. Hundreds of simple mud-pole huts had been constructed hastily to protect the refugees from the blistering sun. Here and there the desolation of the place was broken by the orange glow of a camp fire. This is not home, Maria reminded herself and walked on in silence.

Back in Mozambique before the drought, there had always been warm goat's milk for breakfast. She smiled now, remembering the smallest goat and how soft the white fur had been against her cheek. Maria thought back on the day the small animal had arrived, carried in the spindly arms of a hungry traveler seeking work. Maria's father had traded maize, beans and fruit from the baobab tree for the goat, knowing that one day it would provide milk for his children. Maria had watched the man's bony fingers tear greedily at the fruit as he told how he had rescued the kid after it had fallen into the Limpopo River down south.

"She's a good luck charm!" he had said, whistling his praise. "I saved her life and now she's saving mine!" From then on, Maria had called the goat Popo. She had tied a tiny bell around the goat's neck and had only to follow the tinkling sound to find the curious creature teasing the neighbor's scrawny cow or munching someone else's grain.

Those had been good days! Ever since she could walk Maria had helped her parents work the land - turning over the dark soil, planting seeds, pulling up stubborn weeds, watering the green shoots, then raking in the harvest. The magical seeds had always fascinated Maria. So tiny! Yet they carried inside them the mysterious secret for LIFE! Flowers, maize, pumpkins, even the large baobab tree began in the dark, miniature world of a seed.

Maria yearned desperately for her homeland. She imagined an invisible thread - one end wrapped around her heart - the other tied to the baobab tree that once shaded her yard. The further away she had gone the tighter the knot had grown. The land was in Maria's blood and she felt it. Hadn't it fed her, quenched her thirst, taught her about creation? Hadn't she slept every night of her life with her ear to its heartbeat?

She had been strong then, too, racing her brother in the fields. Sometimes Joao would shove her into the shallow brook and she would pretend to drown, kicking, splashing and waving her arms wildly. He would simply laugh and push her under again.

Maria had gone to the village school for one year and had learned Portuguese more quickly than her brother. It was later decided that she should stay home to help care for her baby brother, Fabio, tend the goats and help till the land. It was essential that Joao remain in school because an education would be necessary to find a good job which would bring more money and food for the family. Sometimes Maria would wrap Fabio onto her back with a long, brightly colored cloth as she collected wild apples or firewood. In the evenings she would help prepare the family's meal over a small stone fire in the yard. Her mouth watered now, and she sat down on the road, closed her eyes and recalled the warm taste of pumpkin leaves, maize and tomatoes.

Maria looked around her at the brittle bodies of the other refugees on the road. Jutting bones, faces permanently marked with hunger and worry --- they saddened her deeply. She examined her own weakened arms and legs. No longer could she run, nor did she **want** to. The desire for play had long been drained from her. Now, she worked full days, after which there was only the desire for food and sleep. If Joao could see her now, she thought, and the heavy loads she carried, he would be proud. How often had he repeated their grandmother's advice to "Become like the grass, girl, so you bend in the wind, not break."

It had been a sad day before the drought when armed rebels had stormed Maria's village, rounding up all the young men to fight their war. Joao, twelve, had been among those taken. He was just a boy, sweet and strong, and Maria wondered now if he was alive and if he thought of her and missed their homeland as much as she did.

A few years before the drought the land had begun to weaken and could produce only a few crops. Maria and her mother would gather up most of the maize and the plumpest vegetables and take them to the market to sell. The money received was set aside for the rent on the land. On the way home they would collect throwaways on the roadside, even spoiled food for the family's meal. The way her father explained it the land was punishing them for all the blood that had been spilled on it since the war had begun up north over six years earlier. Other farmers said the land was tired and needed fertilizer or a rest between plantings, but there was no money or time for either. Somehow the villagers had always pulled through --- until the sky decided to punish them for making the land work so hard. At least, this was her father's explanation for the drought. When the crops were half-grown the sky refused to rain. Every night the neighbors gathered in Maria's yard and prayed, and every morning they searched the heavens for signs of mercy. It seemed to Maria that the skies howled their bright blue laughter at her desperate people. How do you fight the sky? she had asked herself.

To supplement the rent money, her father dug up the baobab tree before it withered and sold it in the marketplace. Day by day it seemed the world grew thirstier. The angry sun choked the crops; their leaves crumpled and their feeble roots released their hold on the earth. Maria gathered them up --- some were boiled for the family's dinner, the rest were fed to the goats.

The brook dried up first, then the river six miles away. Lizards, fish and flamingoes lay gasping in the green mud. The air was so dry it hurt to breathe. Birds fell out of the sky. Several of the elderly perished from the heat. The school was closed down. The endless "fever" cracked open the earth and sucked out all the sweetness from the soil, the people's bodies and spirits. Now, sweetness was found only in distant dreams.

For awhile Maria had secretly shared half her daily meal with Fabio. He had been sick all the time then, crying and twisting in his sleep, and finally sitting limply against the wall of the hut. Maria had noticed when she sang to him that the light had disappeared from his eyes and they no longer followed her when she walked. Like many of the babies in the village, Fabio had lost his eyesight. Nothing could be done. The village doctor and his family, along with many other villagers, had fled at the first signs of drought. Maria kissed her brother's blank eyes.

Her own condition worsened. Her long, dark, braided hair grew thin and lifeless, her skin cracked like the earth's and her flesh melted away. The pink dress that she still wore today hung loosely on her frail body.

Maria's mother had measured out the remaining maize --- enough left for six more days. Even if the rains had come then --- it would have been too late. She shook out a small portion for the family meal and buried the rest in the yard where it would be safe from thieves. That week the family ate all the maize, then they ate the seeds that had been set aside for planting. This meant there would be no harvest again the following season. Popo was traded in the market for a bag of flour. His bones had poked up like horns. Maria cried secretly and hugged him one last time. She whispered her thanks for saving her family. She untied the little bell and placed it around her own neck. In the village square, her father had told her, he'd seen, unbelievably, well-fed people who had bought up most of the food and livestock at the start of the drought and were selling it now to hungry villagers at very high prices. The few families who remained, like Maria's, had traded everything of value they had owned for food. They had nothing left.

The sounds of war grew closer. Maria heard that food trucks sent from other countries had been forced to turn back. Some were attacked by rebels and food was stolen. Late one night a man in uniform came to collect the long over-due rent on the land. Maria's father had not known if the man was a government soldier or one of the rebels. She had heard her father offer the man the small sum from the sale of the baobab tree and her mother's white tablecloth, a gift on their wedding day.

"It is far short," said the man. "You cannot live on the land without full payment. That is the contract." Maria heard her father plead with the man to wait until after the drought broke, he could make up the rest of the rent with a good harvest. With the fighting so near where would his family go?

"You have no seeds," the man replied. "You are weak and have no sons to help you. How will you plant?"

In the full moonlight Maria could see that the man had been eating well. She covered her mouth tightly with her palm to keep from shouting her rage at him. "He must come from the sky," she thought. The cruel sky. How else to explain one so uncaring?

At the refugee center Maria waited in a long line. The crowd was told by a relief worker that rations would be cut today. Soldiers at the border had demanded several bags of food for themselves before allowing the trucks entry to the camp. Who can blame them? Maria thought. Their small country has been invaded by thousands of starving people. We have cut down most of their trees; we are drinking from their rivers and living off their land. How long before it all runs out? They too, must feed their families. She looked at the disappointed faces in line and marveled at what they had all survived.

Maria had never understood the rivalry between the government forces and the rebels. All she knew was that their violence had destroyed her village. Rebels had poisoned the village water source, crushed the market and clinic and set fire to several homes. That awful night when the sky had exploded in red flames and black smoke Maria's father had gathered his family together. Maria was to take only what she was wearing and her sleeping mat. Her mother's hands had trembled as they reached quickly for a blanket in which she wrapped the remaining grain from the sale of Popo, the family's birth certificates so they could identify themselves to the authorities at the border and a family photograph taken by a traveler in exchange for their hospitality.

The villagers could not use the main roads for escape out of fear of land mines or robbery. At night they hid in bushes avoiding strangers --- one could never tell who was carrying a weapon. When Popo's food ran out, they survived on a stew of boiled roots. The food was not appropriate for little Fabio who developed a bright rash. Maria could not believe so many people had once lived in her country. The road at the border was filled with them. Is there no one left in Mozambique? she had wondered. Small children with swollen bellies, tearful and lost, wandered through the crowds. It is a long way, Maria had thought, but it is especially long when you are three and your mother is dead. She and her mother held onto as many small hands as they could and tried to convince others on the road to do the same. Most were too weak, had too many children of their own and no more food or water to share.

Maria's legs grew stiff. She watched bodies collapse in the dust to die, far from home. When she stumbled and fell, her mother reached for her, pulled her on gently, and whispered, "Don't give up, your spirit is strong as the granite hills that surround our village." Maria had forced her feet forward.

Finally, at the edge of the camp she had fallen into her father's arms. Bodies were strewn for as far as she could see, some groaning, some simply staring into space. Their bright red, pink and orange clothes had more life in them than the human eyes and limbs. Relief workers rushed to help the new arrivals, offering food, water and medicine. Maria and Fabio were given a special mixture to relieve their dehydrated bodies.

For weeks Maria and her people could only sit and wait for food. The rations were meager and on some days the trucks never came. There were fights over the smallest morsel of food then. "Fome! Fome!" (hunger) the people cried out. The trees, the rocks and the sky echoed their pleas.

The smell of sickness and human waste thickened the air. Some refugees, mad with thirst, drank from the cholera-infested stream that ran through the camp. Within days they had perished. Maria recalled now the saints she had observed among the crowd of starving bodies. An old man who could barely stand, had taken a few sips of his porridge, then had passed it on to others. Another, a young woman, had picked up an older woman who lay curled in the dirt. The young woman had placed her gently in her wheelbarrow, dampened her parched lips with her remaining drops of water, then wheeled her, stumbling, to the long line at the medical tent.

"Someday," Maria told herself. "I too shall have their strength of body and spirit. I will find a way to make my people well again."

Maria arrived back at the family's hut surprised to find her father there and although exhausted, his eyes flickered with excitement and his hands moved quickly as he told how families were indeed returning to rebuild their villages in Mozambique! A treaty had been signed with the rebels although gunfire continued in some areas. The drought had lifted.

"When our family is strong enough to make the journey, we too, shall return." he announced eagerly and placed his arms around Maria's mother.

"What about the damage from the war?" Maria asked, breathless. "Will we get our land back? No seeds have been planted. How will we eat?"

Caring people from other countries were sending food, seeds, tools, and materials for rebuilding, her father explained. He was hopeful that the soldiers would return their land. Pulling Maria close, he told of how schoolchildren faraway had sent two healthy goats to provide milk for families in one of the villages. "When the first baby goat is weaned, it is to be given to another family and so on until the entire village has shared in the good fortune."

Maria twirled around the poles of the hut, the little bell jingling and her head full of yellow maize, fat pumpkins, red tomatoes, papayas, soft, white baby goats and warm milk! Home! She longed for the hard work to begin.

"Oh, there will be more droughts," her father warned. "It is foolish to believe our land will not punish us for leaving it. We must work day and night to rebuild homes, roads, schools and clinics. The relief workers have explained that planting trees will give our land back its life-giving power. Their roots will keep dry soil from blowing away. Drilling wells and building storage huts will help the villagers stock up on food and water for emergencies. Until we and our land are strong again, we must rely on the generosity of those caring people faraway."

"And the rebels?" Maria asked. Her father lowered his eyes.

"Words must replace weapons. How will we ever convince them?" Maria wondered about the caring people. "How is it **they** can help **us**? she asked. "Aren't they burdened with worries of their own?"

Her father only said the people who sent help had more, **much** more, than they needed. They wished to share it with the people of Mozambique and help them regain their vitality. "The question is, **will** they?" he said, stroking her mother's gray head.

That night Maria felt her land call to her. She knew someday it, like her, could be healthy again. She thought of the people she'd never met who wanted to help and imagined the string that tied her to her land reaching across the seas and continents to the hearts of those caring people. Then, she dozed off to sleep, rubbing the small charm around her neck and dreaming of playful, white goats on the green savannah.

Before dawn, Maria awoke on the damp ground of the mudpole hut to begin the day's work.[*]

---

[*] Sources for this story include a personal interview with Miss Cassa at the Mozambique Embassy, Washington D.C.; *The State of the World's Refugees*, The United Nations, 1993; *A Complicated War: The Harrowing of Mozambique*, by William Finnegan, University of California Press, 1992; and *Nectar in a Sieve* by Kamala Markandaya, J. Day Co., 1954.

DISCUSSION QUESTIONS

1. List each factor you feel contributed in some way to the famine.

2. Was there food in Maria's country during the famine? Why couldn't hungry families get it?

3. What resources would Maria's family have needed in order to prepare for and withstand the drought? How could they have obtained these?

4. What did the land mean to Maria and her family? What was needed to improve its growing power? Why didn't the farmers have access to these resources?

5. Why was it necessary to set up a refugee camp in another country? What were the **immediate needs** of the refugees?

6. What are the **long-term needs** of refugees? Make a list of these.

7. How did Maria and her people survive so many losses? What do you think will happen to her and her family?

8. War is the major cause of flight and famine today. The images we see on television of starvation are most often the results of violence which forces people to flee their land. Make a list of the many ways war leads to famine.

9. How can we help families such as Maria's begin to regain their strength and become self-reliant?

WRITING EXERCISES

1. Choose one scene from the story and imagine your way into Maria's mind and body. Write an interior monologue from Maria's point of view.

2. Write an ending to this story. Do Maria and her family ever return home?

3. Many people believe that overpopulation and too little food cause famine. Write a letter to another class explaining why this is not true. Tell them what does cause famine.

4. Write an essay explaining why five years of drought in California resulted in no deaths, while five years of drought in Ethiopia killed a million people in 1989. Explain what is needed to prepare for drought, why people such as Maria don't have them and people in the U.S. do.

5. Write a poem about Maria. Use words or phrases from the story.

ADDITIONAL ACTIVITIES:

1. A daily ration in a refugee camp consists of:
   400 grams of rice, wheat or dried maize
   60 grams of beans, peas or lentils
   25 grams of oil
   50 grams of corn-soya milk or other fortified blended foods
   15 grams of sugar
   15 grams of salt

   This ration is given to each refugee everyday he or she remains in the camp. It must last the entire day.

   MATH: If there are 454 grams in 1 lb. and 28 grams in an ounce, how much food (in lbs. and ounces) was Maria given each day? (Using the rations listed above.)

2. Show students what the refugee rations above look like and invite them to taste them. What would it be like to eat this amount and type of food every day?

3. Make ORT - ORAL REHYDRATION THERAPY.
   Prolonged diarrhea is the biggest killer of children under five years of age. It causes children's bodies to lose precious bodily fluids. ORT is an easily prepared and inexpensive mixture that saves the lives of 2.5 million children each year. Programs have been set up in many countries to help teach mothers how to prevent diarrhea by using ORT.

   TO MAKE ORT SIMPLY MIX: 2 tsp. sugar
   1/2 tsp. salt
   1 cup of water

   MATH: This life-saving mixture costs 10¢ per packet. How many packets of ORT could the class purchase if each student saved the price of a movie ticket?

4. Research Maria's country of Mozambique to find out more about its people and customs. Why do people in Maria's African village speak Portuguese and bear Portuguese names?

5. Find news items about famine or hunger. Do they explain the true causes of famine or offer any solutions? Tape a television report on famine and critique it with your class. Discuss ways in which the media could educate people about famine and how the world could prevent it.

6. Read *Zlata's Diary* by Zlata Filipovic, Viking Penguin Press, N.Y. 1994. This is the personal diary kept by a thirteen year-old girl during the war in Sarajevo.

7. Watch and discuss the video *The Four Seasons: Winter, Winter, Winter* (1993) about how parents cope during the war in Sarajevo. See Resource Guide to order.

8. Listen to and discuss *Study War No More*, a song by the Weavers.

9. Listen to and discuss *Trouble in the Fields* a song by Maura O'Connell about the impact of famine on human lives.

MAKE A DIFFERENCE!

1. Speak out about the true causes of famine. Be critical of news reports on hunger.

2. Help students organize a fund-raiser in your school or community. Some ideas on how to do this can be found in the Resource Guide. The money raised could go toward the purchase of a heifer or goat that will provide milk for a family such as Maria's. Chickens, sheep, pigs, even honeybees can be purchased and sent to a hungry village to provide a **continual** source of food. For example, $10 buys a share of rabbits, $20 a flock of chicks or share of a llama. For more information contact:

   HEIFER PROJECT INTERNATIONAL
   P.O. Box 8058
   Little Rock, AR 72203
   (800) 422-0474
   www.heifer.org

3. The **JANE GOODALL INSTITUTE** works in villages similar to Maria's to address poverty and support sustainable livelihoods while promoting conservation values.

   Trees are a valuable life-giving resource worldwide. They release oxygen into the air and absorb carbon dioxide, restore nitrogen to depleted soil, shield crops and soil from too much sun, and bind the soil together to prevent erosion by wind or heavy rains. Trees provide lumber, fuel, nutritious fruits and nuts. Their roots and bark are used in making medicines.

   Every hour 500,000 trees are cut down for firewood, shelters or to create fresh farmland. Many of these trees are not replaced. Scientists warn that this rapid destruction seriously upsets the ecological balance of the planet, and turns food producing regions into vast deserts. Families are hit hardest. Without trees valuable topsoil is blown or washed away and the degraded land cannot produce enough food.

   Through the Institute's **ROOTS & SHOOTS** initiative, 45 primary schools and children's centers in 20 Tanzanian villages are taking an active role in developing and implementing projects relating to animals, the environment and their communities. Activities include planting trees and grasses and participating in workshops on children's rights. Roots & Shoots Youth Leaders in the United States are contributing to their efforts through the **REBIRTH THE EARTH: TREES FOR TOMORROW CAMPAIGN**. For more information contact:

   ROOTS & SHOOTS-USA
   The Jane Goodall Institute
   4245 North Fairfax Drive, Suite 600
   Arlington, VA 22203
   (800) 592-JANE
   www.rootsandshoots.org

PART 2:

CHRONIC HUNGER

MATERIALS: *Really Mister, He's Nine*

PROCEDURE:

1. Tell students that only 10% of the hunger deaths each year are the result of famine. The other 90% are the result of chronic hunger. What does "chronic" mean? Have any of the students ever seen a news report about chronic hunger?

2. Read *Really Mister, He's Nine* with students. Allow them time to express their reactions to the story either through writing or discussion.

3. Discussion questions and math activities follow the story. Whenever possible, compare and contrast Lee's hunger with Maria's from the previous story --- the forces behind their hunger, how the hunger affects the children's minds and bodies, media attention to their hunger, their immediate needs, and some ways in which the causes of their hunger could be eliminated.

Really Mister, He's Nine

[The account you are about to read was prepared by doctors traveling across the U.S. investigating hunger. They visited every corner of the country and talked with the local people who were working to end hunger. With the hungry people's permission, the doctors went into their homes, looked inside their kitchens, cupboards and refrigerators, examined their emaciated bodies and talked to them about the amount and kinds of food they eat every day.

Most of the people they met were elderly, children, and women and men who could not find jobs. This is the story of the end of their journey. They have reached the "breadbasket of America" to see if hunger could actually exist in one of the most fertile regions of the world where much of our food is grown. In nearby St. Louis a man who helps collect food for the hungry told the doctors: "People come to the city hospital emergency room and collapse on the floor. Not because they are sick, but because they are hungry. Why should something so important as food be dependent on charity? We don't tell people they can't have air or water, or that they'll have them only twenty days a month. Why do we do it with food?"

In Caruthersville, Missouri the doctors continue their research:]

"The sun was hot as we left the town, and our reprieve was to be the shade afforded by Effie Alsop's front porch. Her wrinkled white face showed the wear of her eighty-six years. She lead us inside, where we began to chat.
"Mrs. Alsop," I asked, "could you tell us what you've been eating?"
"I haven't had nothing yet today."
With some persistence, one of my colleagues learned that she had not eaten for twenty-four hours. We asked again if she was hungry. "I get hungry when I got food in the house. But, when I don't have none I don't seem to get hungry. Isn't that funny, doctor?"
Effie Alsop's husband, also in his eighties, took me into the kitchen. I looked into the cupboard and the refrigerator, finding some dried white beans in a glass jar and several pieces of bread in the refrigerator.
"How often do you eat fruits and vegetables?" I queried. Mr. Alsop simply shook his head, dismissing a question whose answer was obvious.
"Do you and your wife ever go a day without eating?" I followed.
"Yes sir, I'd say at least several days a month."
After speaking with the Alsops, my team split up to make house calls. In a nearby community I visited Mrs. Spain, whose younger black face contrasted sharply with Effie Alsop's wrinkles.

"I've got five children," she said proudly, showing off two well-groomed youngsters. "Yolanda here is two and Natasha is five. The others are in school.

"My husband is out lookin' for work," she reported. "But there's nothin' aroun'. It's a full-time job just lookin' for work aroun' here." Mr. Spain had lost his job several months before. The family lived on $269 a month. There would have been nine to feed, but two of their daughters had died in a fire the previous year.

I asked permission to look into the refrigerator, where I found eight hot dogs, four peppers, a carton of milk, and some eggs.

"Do you ever run out of milk for the children?" I asked.

"All the time," she responded.

Something prompted me to push a little further. "What would you do, if you ran out of food altogether?" Her quick response told me she had already asked herself the same question. "I'd march them to the grocery store, sit them down on the floor and give them food. At least they couldn't arrest me for stealing."

Out on the sidewalk I saw a cute little boy who responded with a smile as I playfully tugged on his ear. Judging from his size, he looked about six years old.

"What's your name?" I asked.

"Lee."

"How old are you?"

"Nine."

Knowing that young children sometimes inflate their age, I laughed and turned to his older sister.

"How old is your brother, really?"

"Really mister, he's nine."

I tried as inconspicuously as possible to signal Naomi Kistin to come over, wanting to rely on her pediatric eye to determine whether Lee could possibly be nine years old.

Naomi took a look at Lee and brought him into his mother's house. I spoke with the mother while Naomi examined Lee in the living room. "The doctor at the clinic said he's anemic," Lee's mother confessed. "I know what he should be eatin', but I can't buy it," she added. "My husband's been trying to find work, but there's nothin' around here for him.

Lee's father, Robert, a man of thirty-five, joined the conversation. "We can't get no help 'cause I live here with my family. They could get help if I left, but we want to keep the family together."

"What do you want?" I asked.

"A job, a steady job. Just the opportunity to prove myself," he said.

As we walked to the car, Naomi said that little Lee seemed to be suffering from growth failure. The actual unemployment rate in the area, we had been told, was around 30 percent of the able-bodied work force, so it seemed unlikely that Robert would find work to bring home more food for his undersized son.[*]

---

[*] Reprinted with the permission of Simon & Schuster from *Living Hungry in America* by J. Larry Brown and H.F. Pizer. Copyright 1987 by J. Larry Brown, Ph.D. and H.F. Pizer, P.A.-C.

DISCUSSION QUESTIONS

1. Is Lee's hunger serious? How does it compare with Maria's hunger? (In both cases stunted growth has resulted from lack of nutrients, and in both cases food is available in the area but the children do not have access to it.)

2. How is it that children living in the "breadbasket of America" are so hungry? Why can't they get the food they need?

3. Why do you think no one knew about Lee's dangerous condition? Which kind of hunger is more likely to be shown on television news reports --- famine or chronic hunger? Why? How might this affect the problem?

4. What do you think will happen to Lee? How could his hunger be eliminated?

5. There are chronically hungry people like Lee in nearly every country on earth. The real cause of chronic hunger is poverty --- the causes of poverty are the same from Mozambique to Missouri. Other than unemployment, what might be some causes of poverty? (Causes include: inadequate wages, high food prices, discrimination, political disenfranchisement, environmental degradation, lack of access to resources such as healthy food, credit, health care and job training programs.)

6. Are there hungry children in your class, school or community? How can your class help them?

ACTIVITIES

1. **MATH:** To measure hunger in a child, doctors compare the height and weight of a hungry child with the height and weight of a well-fed child the same age. Compare the average height of the students in your class with the average height of a child the same age in India.

   The average height of a 12 year-old in India is 135 centimeters. The average height of a 14 year-old is 140 centimeters. There are 2.5 centimeters in one inch. (Work in small groups to find the group's average first.)

2. **MATH:** Immunizations are life-savers for chronically undernourished children who could easily die if they contract a disease. Many children are not immunized because their mothers are not aware of the need for shots or because immunizations are not available to them. $10 immunizes a child against measles, polio, whooping cough, tetanus, TB and diphtheria. If the cost of one U.S. army tank is $1.7 million, how

many children could be immunized if the U.S. government gave up one tank?

3. Watch and discuss *Famine & Chronic Persistent Hunger: A Life and Death Distinction* (1989), an 11-minute video with teacher's manual. See Resource Guide to order.

4. Watch **Hunger In America**, a 58 min. video about hungry families in the U.S. See Resource Guide to order.

MAKE A DIFFERENCE!

1. Have students investigate chronic hunger in your community. What is causing it? Are there enough jobs? Are workers paid adequate wages? Is fresh produce available in all areas? Are food prices too high? Are job-training programs available? Students can interview hungry people, hunger activists, business people, and elected officials, to get their opinions on the forces behind local hunger. Students will also need to research ways your community is helping end hunger. When the interviews, research and analysis are completed, have students write letters to local newspapers, businesses, community leaders and elected officials to inform the community of their discoveries and what needs to be done. (See Lesson 23 for guidelines.)

2. Help feed hungry people in your area by holding a Supermarket Food Drive. Students can get their families and friends involved in this one. Have students contact the manager of a local supermarket to ask if he/she will help feed hungry people. The idea is to get shoppers to purchase one or more food items that will be set aside for delivery to a local food pantry. Have students contact a local food pantry for a list of the kinds of foods needed. Consider holding your drive when food pantry stocks are low. (During holidays stocks are usually high and the hungry are on many people's minds.) Students can create posters advertising this important event and hand out fliers in the market parking lot explaining: (1) how the food drive works, (2) what kinds of foods are needed, and (3) who will be receiving the food. Be sure students get to go along to deliver the food to the pantry. Write a group letter to the supermarket manager thanking him/her and the shoppers and describing the outcome of the drive.

WHERE DOES OUR MONEY GO?

Of course, **giving** money won't end people's hunger --- it can only satisfy it temporarily. We cannot "buy" social justice which is what chronically hungry people need in order to become self-reliant. However, money **can** provide life's essentials for needy people until obstacles to achieving social justice are eliminated. The world certainly has the money to do this --- we simply spend it on other things. UNICEF estimates that $34 billion extra dollars a year could secure basic necessities such as food, clean water, health care and education for all the world's needy children. To help students place this figure in perspective, have them compare it with the amount of money we spend on other things:

$ NEEDED		$ SPENT	
Estimated extra cost of meeting worldwide need for:		Estimates of amounts spent worldwide on:	
	BILLIONS Per Year		**BILLIONS Per Year**
Basic Child Health and Nutrition	$ 13	Golf	$ 40
Primary Education	6	Wine	85
Safe Water and Sanitation	9	Beer	160
		Cigarettes	400
Family Planning	6	Advertising	250
		Military	800
TOTAL	**$ 34**		

(A B-1 Bomber costs $400 million and lasts 4 years. For this same amount lunches could be provided for 250,000 hungry people everyday for ten years.)

Source: The Children's Defense Fund: CDF Reports, 1995.

LESSON 6: THE POWER OF ONE

(Stories of how one person's actions made a difference)

This is an exercise to inspire young people. By sharing stories of how everyday people have helped bring about positive change, students are reminded that every effort, no matter how small, **matters**. They see that the idealism, energy and determination of the young enlighten and motivate others, even those who have become cynical and passive about the world's problems.

MATERIALS: Stories from magazines, newspapers, books or personal experience that reveal how one person made a difference.

Four stories can be found in this lesson. In addition, a list of books on this subject can be found in the resource section at the back of this manual. You can read some of these aloud to students over the course of the program, or have students read different ones and report back to the class regularly on them.

Songs to use for this lesson include:
Man in the Mirror by Michael Jackson
Imagine by John Lennon
Remember the Music by Bruce Springsteen

PROCEDURE:

1. Begin by asking students if any of them has ever tried to change something he/she thought was wrong? Do they know someone who has? Can one person's efforts really make a difference?

2. Read or tell some of the following stories. How do the stories make them feel? What images stayed with them? What do they think of the people in the stories? Do they know anyone like them? Are these people heroes? What if everyone in the world worked at making it a better place?

3. Let students know that **ending hunger is possible**. Emphasize the fact that it is caused by human actions and can be ended by human actions. Everyone's efforts and skills are needed. Despite the complexities of the problem, many courageous people are proving everyday that hunger can be drastically reduced, even eliminated. (Some of those people are working right in the students' neighborhoods.) As we understand more clearly the root causes of poverty and hunger, it becomes apparent that governments, local and international relief agencies and individuals can do a lot to lessen the weight of hunger in our world.

There are three ways people are working to address the problem of hunger:

EMERGENCY FEEDING - This includes famine relief, soup kitchens and food pantries. Hungry people can't wait until the world gets its act together. They need food NOW!

LONG-TERM SOLUTIONS - These include all kinds of ways to help hungry people become self-reliant such as nutrition programs that teach mothers how to stay healthy during pregnancy and how to raise healthy children, agricultural programs that teach people how to care for their environment and how to grow healthy food, drill wells, build irrigation systems, even plant community gardens and train people for jobs that will earn them the money needed to take care of their families.

GETTING POLICY CHANGED OR INSTITUTED - This kind of action means writing letters, organizing media campaigns and lobbying government officials in order to get laws passed that will insure the protection of basic human rights for everyone and that will preserve and protect the environment.

4. Close this class with *Man in the Mirror* or *Imagine*.

ADDITIONAL ACTIVITIES:

1. Have students write about a time when they made a difference in someone's life.

2. Encourage students to interview family members and look through newspapers for local heroes. Present several of these over the course of the study of hunger to inspire students.

3. Invite speakers who are making a difference in your community to talk to the students about their work.

4. Create posters or poems depicting the beautiful, healthy and just world students are hoping to create. What color is this world? What does it look like? What kind of people inhabit it? How does it feel to live there? Title these and display them.

5. Watch the video *Children of Soon Ching Ling* which tracks the history of the children's movement in China and emphasizes the life and work of Soon Ching Ling who fought for children's rights. See Resource Guide - "Videos".

THE STARFISH*

A young boy lived near the sea. Everyday he would walk barefoot on the beach admiring the wondrous creatures and objects that washed up onto the shore. One night there was a terrible storm. The wind raged and howled. From his bed the boy watched streams of water criss-cross his window. He heard the powerful waves crash loudly against the rocks below his house. By morning the wind was calm again. The rain had stopped, but the sea was gray and sullen. It rocked restlessly in its gigantic bed. The boy raced down to the beach and was astonished to see it covered for as far as his eyes could see with starfish.

STARFISH! Golden like the sand! What an extraordinary sight! For a moment it seemed to the boy as if all the stars had been blown out of the heavens by the violence of the storm the night before. Knowing that they would not survive long in the hot, dry sand, the boy began picking them up, one-by-one, and tossing them back into their wet world. An old man watched from his balcony above the beach. He laughed to himself and shook his head at the boy who tiptoed among the star-shapes.

"Hey!" the man shouted. "What do you think you're doing out there?"

"I'm throwing these starfish back into the sea so they won't die here," the boy called back.

The old man stood up and steadied himself against the railing of his balcony.

"Don't be crazy!" he jeered. "There must be **thousands** of them! You'll **never** be able to save those starfish!"

The boy stared back at the old man for a moment. Then, slowly, he reached down, carefully picked up a starfish and sent it sailing out into the deep, rolling sea.

"I saved **that** one, didn't I?" he yelled up to the old man who stood silent, watching. Then the boy bent down and continued picking up starfish. He worked through the morning, paying no mind to the time of day, and keeping his thoughts only on saving the starfish.

After a long while he lifted his head to straighten his aching back. Reaching up, the boy gently rubbed his sunburnt neck and gazed out over the wide stretch of sand before him. There in the hot, afternoon sun, was the old man hurriedly picking up starfish and, one-by-one, tossing them back into the sea.

---

* This story was told to me by Jane Donohue, a teacher in New Hampshire. Jane heard the story at a teacher's meeting. We have been unsuccessful in tracking down the original author.

TRUE STORIES OF HOW ONE PERSON HELPED MAKE THE WORLD A BETTER PLACE

A Young Boy Takes Charge

In 1990 in Philadelphia a boy named Trevor saw a news report on television about a homeless man. It was cold outside and the man had no job, no money, no home and no food. Trevor persuaded his father to help him take the man a warm blanket and some food. He told all his friends at school what life was like for people who are homeless and what the students could do to help them. Trevor's friends began delivering blankets and food as well and convinced their own families and friends to do the same. The newspapers and television stations heard about what Trevor and his friends were doing and told the entire city of Philadelphia how they could also help. Many people responded by sending blankets, food and clothing for the homeless. Today the Trevor Foundation helps feed and care for hundreds of homeless people all over Philadelphia. It all started with one concerned boy and one homeless man.

DELIVERING A MESSAGE TO A WORLD LEADER[*]

This is how Heidi Hattenbach describes her feelings the first time she heard that 25,000 children die every day from hunger. "It hit me so deeply. I cried. It just didn't make sense, so I decided to do something about it."

What Heidi did was to join an organization called YOUTH ENDING HUNGER (YEH) where she met other young people who were speaking out against hunger and finding creative ways to help stop it. At the time there was a terrible war and famine in Ethiopia. The governments of the U.S. and the Soviet Union were sending weapons to the war zone. The people at YEH were encouraging people all over the world to write letters to the presidents of both countries, Bush and Gorbachev, demanding an end to the war and starvation. Heidi and some of her friends visited several schools in her city. Hunger assemblies were organized and Heidi told the students about the war and famine, and urged them to write letters to the presidents saying that it was **not** all right with them that so many people were so hungry, and that they wanted the leaders of the world to take responsibility for the children who were dying.

Because of Heidi and many other young activists the organization collected 65,000 letters from people in Europe, Africa, the U.S. and Canada. Some of the messages in the letters were conveyed in pictures by children too young to even write. YEH organized a delegation to deliver all the letters to Gorbachev in Moscow. One person from each country represented by the letters was chosen. Heidi was among them! Her friends and family raised the money to pay her way.

Mikhail Gorbachev was out of the country the day Heidi and her friends from twelve countries walked into the Kremlin carrying several heavy bags of letters, but Mrs. Gorbachev greeted them with hugs and told them of her own hope of ending hunger. She promised to pass on their message and letters to her husband. The delegation was invited to speak about their mission over Russian television. Their words reached over five million people!

HOW A YOUNG WOMAN INFLUENCED HISTORY*

In 1990 Detra, a 15-year-old high school student in Louisville, Kentucky turned in a report she had just written on Booker T. Washington, the famous African-American educator who founded a college in Alabama. It was February and Detra's school was celebrating Black History Month. So far, this report was the only assignment Detra had been given connected to Black History, and she wondered why none of her other teachers had discussed the contributions of African-Americans in **their** classes. Didn't they know that young people like Detra were interested in knowing about them? And why was Black History celebrated during the **shortest** month of the year?

With her friend Ian, Detra wrote up a petition and took it around school asking students if they would like to hear more about black history. Over 300 people signed Detra's petition. Inspired by this and encouraged by her mother, she then called the Board of Education and asked if she could make a special speech at their next meeting.

Her legs shook as she stood in front of several adults, including the Superintendent of Jefferson County Schools, and asked them three questions: Who was the woman who freed over two hundred slaves in the underground railroad? Who was the man who out-ran a steam-driven machine? Who was the man who chopped down the cherry tree? In a strong, clear voice, Detra told her audience that most students at her school could only answer the third question. Few of them had ever heard of Harriet Tubman and John Henry, two African-Americans whose accomplishments, Detra insisted, were part of **American** history, not just Black History. She gave the Board members the petition to show them that over 300 students - black and white - wanted to know about the people of color who had shaped America.

Not long after Detra's speech, the Board formed a special committee made up of teachers and students (including Detra) to decide what should be taught in a course on Black History. Thanks to Detra's determination, the following school year there was a Black History class in five schools in her county and every single one of them was filled! Detra plans to continue studying history and to become a teacher herself. Her advice to other young activists: "**Never** give up what you really want."

---

*The stories on Heidi and Detra in this lesson were adapted with permission from
  No Kidding Around! America's Young Activists Are Changing Our World & You Can Too by Wendy Schaetzel Lesko, Information USA, Inc. Maryland, 1992. (See Resource Guide to order.)

UNIT II:

WHY ARE PEOPLE HUNGRY?

LESSON 7:
IF THERE IS ENOUGH FOOD, WHY ARE PEOPLE HUNGRY?

Each small group of students examines the food supply as well as the child mortality rate (a measure of hunger) in a particular country to learn that food scarcity is not a cause of hunger. As students discuss some of the forces behind each country's hunger problem, they discover that the forces creating hunger are the same worldwide.

TEACHER BACKGROUND READING

It has long been widely assumed that food scarcity is a major cause of world hunger, but United Nations statistics show that the world produces enough grain to provide **every** person on the planet with at least 2,700 calories everyday. This figure does not even include calories from abundant non-grain sources such as fish, legumes, fruits and vegetables. The **adult** recommended daily calorie requirements fall between 2,000 and 2,700 calories per day.

Enough food is often produced even in countries where people suffer from severe hunger. War and natural disasters can decrease food production in a specific region, but even during famine food is often available to those who can pay for it. In 1992 Niger, in sub-Saharan Africa, had the highest child mortality rate in the world - for every 1,000 children under the age of five 320 died. Yet enough grain was produced in Niger that year to provide every person in the country with 2,230 calories worth of food everyday. In 1991 Somalia, a country Americans often associate with starvation, EXPORTED more than twice as much food as it imported. In Bangladesh, where some of the world's most fertile farmland can be found, enough food was produced to allow each person 2,100 calories worth of grain everyday. 3 out of 5 children under the age of five in Bangladesh suffered stunted growth caused by undernutrition. In most developing countries where enough food is grown, the majority of the populations consume fewer than 1,500 calories per day.

To understand that hunger exists alongside abundance we need only examine the United States' food supply and level of hunger. Millions of tons of grain are produced each year - most of it going to feed livestock. Despite an overflowing food supply, it is estimated that between 30 and 35 million Americans go hungry every month, 13 million of these are children.*

---

* USDA, Economic Research Service, *Household Food Security in the United States, 2001*.

Around the planet, as food production has increased so have the numbers of hungry people. WHY?

1. A small minority controls most of the world's farmland. In developing countries nearly 80% of the arable land is controlled by fewer than 3% of the people who own land. In the U.S. the top 5% of landowners own 86% of the land.[*]

2. The governments of developing countries allocate a very small percentage of their total expenditures to growing **local food staples**. Most of the money, attention and best land are used to produce cash crops (coffee, sugar, tea, cotton, tobacco, etc.) which are exported to people in industrialized countries.

3. Over half the grain grown in the world and half the fish caught are fed to livestock.[†]

4. In many countries the violence of war destroys crops and food supplies. Often food aid is deliberately blocked and starvation becomes a weapon of war.

5. Food costs money. Poverty, on the rise around the world, is a major cause of hunger. Causes of poverty include: unemployment, inadequate wages, unfair distribution of resources, lack of medical care, political disenfranchisement, discrimination and environmental degradation.

6. A lack of awareness and a lack of will are also at the root of the hunger problem. Many people who **could** make a difference in ending the injustice of hunger simply don't.

MATERIALS: One country card for each small group[§]
(Enough copies for each student)
World map

---

[*] Food and Agriculture Organization's report on the World Census of Agriculture, Rome 1970. (Frances Moore Lappé in *Diet For a Small Planet* writes that since then landholdings in most countries have become even more concentrated.)

[†] Lappé, Frances Moore. *Diet For a Small Planet*, Ballantine Books, NY 1991 Edition.

[§] Statistics for the country cards are from *The State of the World's Children*, 2009, UNICEF.

PROCEDURE:

1. Explain to students that most people have assumed that food scarcity is the major cause of hunger. (Students could interview family members first to find out what **they** think causes hunger.) Today students will investigate this assumption to see if it is true. Tell them that the world's food supply is measured by estimating the number of calories per ton of **grain** produced in each country. Remind them that this total does not include other sources of calories and nutrients such as fruits vegetables and legumes.

2. Tell them that the average **adult** needs between 2,000 and 2,700 calories every day to remain healthy. Children need fewer calories. (If your students have kept food diaries, they can add up one day's worth of food to find out how many calories they need each day to remain healthy and active.)

   Review with students "*How Hunger Is Measured - The Child Mortality Rate*" from Lesson 4. Remember, a Rate above 25 means serious hunger.

3. Divide students into small groups and give each group a country card. Students must discuss the facts on their card and answer the following three questions:

   1. Is enough food produced in your country to supply everyone with enough calories?
   2. Are there hungry people in your country?
   3. Why can't people get food?

   Encourage students to discuss how the facts on their card prevent people from getting food. For instance, **how** does civil war create hunger? **How** do cash crops keep people within the country hungry?

4. After 20 minutes ask each group to make a presentation on its country. They must locate the country on the class map and explain some of the root causes of hunger in their country. List each cause that students discover on the board under a permanent title: **ROOT CAUSES OF HUNGER**. Are many of these causes the same worldwide? As your study proceeds, add to this list.

ADDITIONAL ACTIVITY:[*]

1. Have students create their own country cards based on their own research and current news reports.

2. Watch *Harvest of Hunger*, a video which demonstrates that food scarcity is not a cause of hunger, by Oxfam. See resource guide - videos.

---

[*] This lesson was inspired by a lesson in Sonja Williams' high school curriculum called *Exploding the Hunger Myths*. From Food First, 1987.

Group #1
RWANDA
Child Mortality Rate – 181

You and your family must work the land in order to survive. Instead of using the **best** land in the country to grow food, the government uses it, as well as most of its money and farm equipment, to grow acres and acres of coffee which is shipped to industrial countries such as the U.S.

Families such as yours, who must grow your own food, are pushed onto rocky or weak land. Your family cannot afford fertilizers and irrigation systems that would improve the land, so the soil cannot produce enough food for you.

In a typical year enough grain is grown in Rwanda to provide every person with 2,000 calories worth every day, but most Rwandans cannot get their share of that food. Food costs money. There aren't many jobs here except for those in the coffee fields which is back-breaking work for very little pay. There is little chance of being trained for a better job since the average person here receives only one year of schooling during his or her lifetime.

Like most families in Rwanda, you would rather have sons than daughters. Strong sons can help farm the land. Because boys are valued over girls, girls receive less food, less health care and less education than boys. Half the children in your country suffer stunted growth because they do not get enough food.

Is there enough food?

Are there hungry people in Rwanda?

Why can't hungry people get food?

Group #2
SOUTH AFRICA
Child Mortality Rate – 59

You live in the most highly developed country on the African continent. Enough grain is grown in South Africa to provide every person with at least 3,000 calories a day. That's a lot of grain! Many people, including you and your family, cannot afford to buy that food. Your skin is black and your country has had a long history of apartheid. You earn only 1/5 what white workers earn and this is not enough to live a healthy life. When you become sick it is nearly impossible to find a doctor who will care for you. Half the black children in your country suffer stunted growth because they cannot get enough food.

Many of your friends are having difficulty finding jobs. There just aren't enough to go around. Seasonal work can be found in the fields of large, wealthy landowners who grow tobacco, cotton, sugarcane or grapes (for wine). These cash crops are shipped to other countries. This work is hard and the pay is not enough to support a family. You would like to see more of the land that is used to grow cash crops used instead to grow food for hungry people.

It is unlikely that your friends or you will find work. There are few jobs available and there is little chance of being trained for a better job. The average South African receives only 3 1/2 years of schooling over a lifetime.

Is there enough food?

Are there hungry people in South Africa?

Why can't hungry people get food?

Group #3

RUSSIA
Child Mortality Rate – 15

Farmers in your country grew enough grain in 1992 to provide every person with 3,000 calories worth each day. Unfortunately, you and your family couldn't get much of that food.

Your country has experienced much political violence over the past few years. This has made it difficult to get food to the markets in your town. The little food that **does** get to the market is very expensive.

You have been unable to find a job so you cannot afford expensive food. The food you eat is cheaper and of poor quality. The environment and the food supply in your area have been contaminated by the overuse of chemical fertilizers, pesticides and toxic waste.

Even your friends who **are** working are not earning enough money to pay their rent, heating and buy enough food for their families.

One out of every four people in Russia lives in poverty and suffers chronic hunger.

Is there enough food?

Are there hungry people in Russia?

Why can't hungry people get food?

Group #4

THE UNITED STATES
Child Mortality Rate – 8

There are miles and miles of farmland in your country. Enough grain is produced to provide every person with 3,300 calories worth every day. All across the nation "super" markets are stocked with food. There are restaurants in every city and town. Advertisements for all kinds of foods are found everywhere: television commercials, billboards, magazines and radio.

Unfortunately, many people like you and your family cannot get much of this food. Over half the grain grown in the U.S. is **exported** to other countries and fed to livestock. Fresh fruits and vegetables are not available in **your** area. You must eat cheaper foods that are low in nutrients.

Food costs money. You, like more and more people, cannot find a job. You must rely on special government food programs and soup kitchens for food until a job is available. If a job can be found, you hope it will pay enough money to cover your rent, heating and medical bills **and** buy enough food. Many of your working friends are earning inadequate wages and must buy less food each week.

While it is true that many people in your country suffer from diseases related to **over**-eating (obesity, heart disease, diabetes), between 20 and 30 million in the U.S. go hungry at some time during each month. 13 million of those hungry people are children.

Is there enough food?

Are people hungry in the U.S.?

Why can't hungry people get food?

Group #5

HAITI
Child Mortality Rate – 76

You and your family must grow your own food. This can be difficult because much of the best land, fertilizer, seeds and tools needed are given to the small group of people who can pay for them.

In a typical year in Haiti, enough grain is produced to provide every person with 2,100 calories worth everyday. People like you, with little money, cannot afford to buy that food. More food could be grown but the best land is used for growing coffee that is shipped to industrial countries such as the U.S.

In recent years, the government of your country has been accused of violating human rights. This has led to fighting within your country. Other countries have refused to trade with Haiti or send aid until your government stops violating its people's rights. Your people depend on these other countries for farm supplies for growing food. When these countries stopped trading with your government, you had no access to the things you need to grow food. As a result, less food is produced here. What little food there is can be very expensive and is found only in areas where people with enough money can buy it.

You have not been able to find a job that pays enough to cover your rent, medical care **and** buy enough food. There are few job training programs in Haiti. The typical Haitian receives 1 1/2 years of schooling. Nearly half the children under five in Haiti suffer stunted growth from insufficient food.

Is there enough food?

Are people hungry in Haiti?

Why can't hungry people get food?

Group #6

INDIA
Child Mortality Rate – 72

Enough grain is grown in your country in a typical year to insure every single person 2,400 calories everyday; however, nearly 210 million people are too poor to buy their share of that food. In spite of all those hungry people, your country **EXPORTS** (!) three times as much food as it imports. Much of your country's best land, resources and money are used to grow "cash crops" such as rice, tea, cotton and tobacco which are shipped to industrial countries such as the U.S.

When so much food is sent OUT of your country, the food that stays in the country becomes expensive. Many people cannot find jobs and so do not have the money to buy food. Those who **do** work in the "cash crop" fields or factories are paid wages that are so paltry they cannot pay their rent, medical care **and** buy enough food for their families.

Most families prefer sons over daughters. Strong sons can help work the land or perform other jobs that might bring money for food. Because boys are valued over girls, girls receive less of the family's food, less health care and less education than boys.

Over half the children under five in India are underweight for their ages.

Is there enough food?

Are there hungry people in India?

Why can't hungry people get food?

LESSON 8:
IS HUNGER CAUSED BY OVERPOPULATION?

Many myths surround the subject of world hunger. Myths block a clear understanding of the **real** causes of hunger. In this lesson students analyze a popular hunger myth which blames overpopulation for widespread hunger. Students compare the population density and child mortality rates (a measure of hunger) in different countries to discover that some densely populated countries experience very low levels of hunger, while other countries with low population density experience severe hunger problems. Students explore other forces behind hunger in these countries and discuss the role myths play in perpetuating hunger.

TEACHER BACKGROUND READING

The world's population **is** increasing and this increase certainly compounds all the crises with which the world is trying to cope --- hunger, environmental degradation and poverty, etc. Slowing population growth will, no doubt, ease those pressures, but before we blame overpopulation for the growing hunger problem, let's consider: (1) why needy people in developing countries **want** so many children? (2) how potential farmland is used around the world, and (3) who consumes most of the world's resources?

(1) WHY DO NEEDY PEOPLE IN DEVELOPING COUNTRIES **WANT** MANY CHILDREN:

The majority of people in developing countries spend their lives working the land --- their survival depends on it. **The more helping hands a family has, the more food it can produce for consumption or for sale.** Many urban families also depend on the labor of children who earn small wages as street vendors, domestic and factory workers.

In impoverished regions where child mortality rates are high, parents lose many of their children to disease and hunger before the children are five years old. This prompts parents to have **more** children with the hope that a few will survive to care for the parents when they are old and unable to work.

The two reasons above indicate that economic insecurity causes parents to have more children. In societies where women have little or no access to education or paid job opportunities, producing children is a woman's primary source of social identity and self-esteem. Fertility is a status symbol.

These facts suggest that **hunger and poverty cause overpopulation** - not the other way around! Recent studies carried out by the UN in forty countries indicate that educating girls is a crucial strategy for reducing population growth and ending poverty and hunger. Women who have access to education and jobs outside the home have fewer and healthier children. The reasons: school delays marriage and children; educated women are more apt to plan for their babies according to how well they will be able to care for them --- these women have options in life other than child rearing, and their earnings make them more valuable outside the home. Families who are assured of access to basic necessities have fewer children.

(2) NOT ENOUGH LAND FOR ALL OF US? THINK AGAIN!

Before we blame too many people for taking up too much potential farmland, we must consider how the world's farmable land is currently being used. In both the developing and industrial worlds, arable land that could be used to grow food staples is lost every year to industrial development and cash-crop agriculture. How is the land used where you live?

(3) NOT ENOUGH RESOURCES FOR ALL OF US? DON'T BLAME OVERPOPULATION, BLAME OVERCONSUMPTION.

At current rates world population is projected to rise 48% (to 8.3 billion) by the year 2025 --- mostly in developing countries. While we should focus on empowering women as a means of lowering fertility rates, it is important to remember that even though developing countries have most of the world's people, people in industrial countries use up most of the world's resources. For instance, every new inhabitant of the U.S. makes a sixty-fold greater contribution to global warming than does an additional Mexican. Lowering consumption of the world's limited resources by industrial countries and distributing resources more equitably are crucial elements in eliminating poverty and hunger, **and** reducing population growth.

PROCEDURE:

1. Tell students that many people believe that overpopulation is a root cause of hunger. What do they think?

2. If this were really true it would mean that crowded countries are the hungriest countries of all. Right? Let's examine two countries and see. Place the following **hectares** on the board:

THE NETHERLANDS
(Population Density = 16)

AFGHANISTAN
(Population Density = 3)

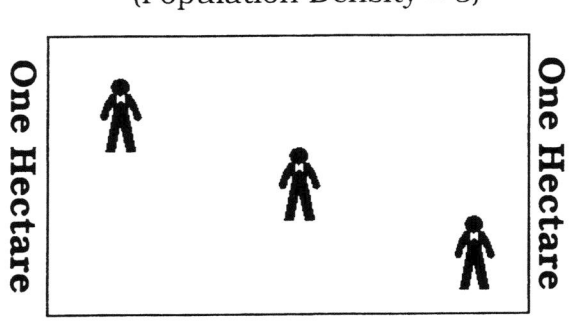

3. Students need to know:

A **hectare** is 2.5 acres of farmable land.

POPULATION DENSITY is the number of people for every hectare of farmland in a particular country. If a country has a population density of 2 it means there are only 2 people for every hectare. A population density of 7 or above is considered high.

4. Which country above is most crowded?
Which country is more likely to be having a severe hunger problem? Why?

5. Place the following information under the appropriate hectare:

THE NETHERLANDS
Enough grain grown to provide every person with 114% of the daily calories required.
*Child Mortality Rate – 5.

AFGHANISTAN
Enough grain grown to provide every person with only 72% of the calories needed to function healthily.

*Child Mortality Rate – 257.

6. Is overpopulation causing hunger in the Netherlands?
   Is overpopulation causing hunger in Afghanistan?

   If time allows, have students research Afghanistan to find out what might be behind its severe hunger problem. (By 1994 Afghanistan had experienced 14 years of uninterrupted violence that displaced more than a million people. Armed groups still controlled access to food in major cities. The fighting left farms abandoned and irrigation systems destroyed. Because of the food shortages, food prices sky-rocketed.)

   Students should also research the Netherlands, a colonizing power. Have groups of students compare the two countries' histories and determine what factors contribute to hunger in Afghanistan, and which factors help prevent hunger in The Netherlands.

7. Remind students that in certain crowded areas of our cities everyone has access to food and is healthy and well-fed. (In other crowded areas of our cities there is a high degree of hunger.) In certain rural areas of our country where population density is very low, people are hungry. What do students think - does overpopulation cause hunger?

8. Tell students that studies show that hunger and poverty cause people to have more children. Can they explain this? (Explore with them the three reasons explained in the Teacher Background Reading of this lesson.)

9. Have students consider if land is being taken up by too many people in their communities. What takes up most of the land? Is the land used fairly and wisely to provide for everyone? Who benefits from the way land in your area is used?

10. Tell students that most of the world's people live in developing countries in Africa, Asia and Latin America. Most of the world's resources are consumed by industrial countries. Have students brainstorm how overconsumption, not overpopulation, might affect the hunger problem. (Unequal distribution of resources is explored in depth in the following lesson.)

---

* Remind students that a Child Mortality Rate above 25 means serious hunger. **To review the Child Mortality Rate, see Lesson 4: "*How Hunger is Measured – The Child Mortality Rates*".**

ADDITIONAL ACTIVITIES:

1. Tell students that one reason the hunger problem continues is that there are a number of myths (such as the overpopulation one) clouding the truth. What is a myth? On the surface a myth appears to be true, but once we investigate it, a myth falls apart. Can students think of any other hunger myths? Have them write about the role myths play in perpetuating hunger and why it is important to dispel them. (Another example of a myth is: Boys are better athletes than girls.)

2. Provide small groups of students with the following information and ask them to prepare a presentation to teach other classes about overpopulation and hunger.

JAPAN	ETHIOPIA
Population Density - 23	Population Density - 2
Child Mortality Rate – 4 [*]	Child Mortality Rate – 119 [*]
% of required calorie supply per person - 125%	% of required calorie supply per person - 73%

3. Take a class walk around your school's neighborhood. Make a list of the different ways in which land is used. Is it used mainly for industrial development or for growing food?

4. Have students create posters dispelling the overpopulation myth, the "not enough food" myth, and others. Exhibit these or present to other classes.

5. Some of the statistics used in this lesson are from the Population Reference Bureau which puts out a World Population Data Sheet that contains statistics on population density, land area, fertility rates, life expectancy, infant mortality rates, etc., for each of the world's countries. This is an excellent tool for math, social studies and geography projects in your classroom. To order contact:

> THE POPULATION REFERENCE BUREAU
> 1875 Connecticut Avenue NW
> Suite 520
> Washington, D.C. 20009

---

[*] Source: *State of the World's Children*, 2009, UNICEF

LESSON 9: ONE PLANET, TWO WORLDS*

Students learn why countries are grouped into "DEVELOPING" NATIONS and "INDUSTRIAL" NATIONS. The classroom is turned into a miniature version of the world to demonstrate the fact that while most of the world's people live in "developing" nations, most of the world's wealth is delivered to industrial nations. Students examine how this unequal distribution of the world's wealth causes hunger and poverty. (Present this activity in a classroom with lots of space or in the gym or lunchroom.)

IMPORTANT: The words "developing" and "industrial" have become universal descriptions of two different types of countries; however, the word "developing" often carries a negative connotation. It implies that a country has not yet "developed" according to our western industrial standard --- that its people have not yet reached the "standard of living" enjoyed by many people in industrial nations and are therefore, "backward". Should a country's level of industrialization be the standard by which it is judged or grouped? Once students have completed the activity in this lesson which explains why countries are categorized this way, bring this discussion of labels into the classroom. Do students think these descriptions (and all they imply) are fair? (We have used the words "developing" and "industrial" in this guide because we believe students should be aware of how these words are being used today in the media - other descriptions such as **rich world - poor world**, or **first world - third world** seem to carry even more negative and misleading connotations.) What do students think? What other words do they prefer to describe different countries?

MATERIALS:
- 100 small food items or other objects to represent "wealth". If using food, try a combination of favorite foods such as cookies, crackers and pretzels and nuts.
- 5 clear bags
- 5 small signs: **ASIA, AFRICA, U.S. & CANADA, EUROPE & RUSSIA, LATIN AMERICA & CARIBBEAN**
- 2 larger signs: **DEVELOPING NATIONS, INDUSTRIALIZED NATIONS**

PROCEDURE:
1. Designate five areas of the classroom - one for **ASIA**, one for **AFRICA**, one for the **U.S. & CANADA**, one for **EUROPE & RUSSIA**, and one for **LATIN AMERICA & THE CARIBBEAN**. Use the table below to assign the appropriate number of students to sit in each area. Give each group their sign to hold.

(These figures are based on a class of 30. The percentage next to the number of students represents the portion of the world's population that can be found

---

* This activity is from *Children Hungering for Justice* produced by the Office on Global Education in cooperation with the Center for Teaching International Relations, University Denver.

in that area. Use these figures to tailor this activity to the number of students in your class. Let students do the calculating.)

	NUMBER OF STUDENTS	NUMBER OF FOOD ITEMS
ASIA	17 (58%)	18
AFRICA	4 (11%)	3
U.S./CANADA	1 (5%)	29
LATIN AMERICA/ Caribbean	3 (8%)	5
EUROPE/RUSSIA	5 (17%)	45

(Figures based on world population and GNP. Data is from World Military and Social Expenditures 1989; 13th edition, by Ruth Lever Sivard. Washington, D.C.: World Priorities.)

2. Count out loud the appropriate number of food items for each group and place them in a clear bag. Announce the total for each group. Give each bag to the corresponding group.

3. Explain to students that you have distributed the food according to the distribution pattern of wealth in the world. The number of students in each group represents the relative population of each region. The number of food items represents the wealth of that region.

4. Tell them that the world is divided into two groups - INDUSTRIALIZED NATIONS and DEVELOPING NATIONS according to the way wealth is distributed.

5. INDUSTRIALIZED NATIONS are ones where most people's basic needs are met (food, shelter, clean water, and medical care). These are the countries with the industrialized economies. They have developed elaborate infrastructures --- roads, bridges, dams, communication systems, and social institutions such as schools and hospitals. Slightly less than 1/4 of the world's people live in industrialized nations. Ask students to guess which countries belong in this category. They are the U.S. & Canada, Europe, Russia, Japan, Australia and New Zealand. Have student representing **the U.S. & Canada** and **Europe & Russia** join together. Give them the INDUSTRIALIZED NATIONS sign.

Ask these students why the word "industrialized" is used to describe these countries.

6. More than 3/4 of the world's people live in countries where the basic necessities of life are not always easy to get. These people struggle everyday to survive. These are the DEVELOPING NATIONS. They include AFRICA, ASIA, LATIN AMERICA & THE CARIBBEAN. Ask these students to join together. Give them the DEVELOPING NATIONS sign.

DEVELOPING NATIONS are mainly agrarian societies (most of their people work the land.) Their economies rely on a few export crops (called cash crops) --- coffee, tea, bananas, tobacco, cotton, sugarcane, etc. The workers who produce these crops are paid very low wages, much lower than what workers in industrialized nations are paid. The infrastructures of most developing countries are incomplete. Most people living in developing countries have the least access to food and clean water. They have the poorest health and lowest levels of education. **Ask students why this is so.** Many developing countries are former colonies.

Developing nations also have the most impoverished resource base. **Ask students why natural resources such as forests, clean water, land, etc., become depleted and degraded in regions where people are poor and hungry.**

DISCUSSION QUESTIONS

1. Which group has most of the world's people?
2. Which group has most of the world's wealth?
3. How might this unequal distribution cause poverty and hunger?
4. Why do some countries have so much while others have so little? How would it feel to have such limited access to the basic necessities of life?
5. Are there hungry people within the industrialized nations who do not share in the wealth? How is this possible?
6. How did the distribution of wealth become so unequal?
7. Who decides how the wealth is distributed?
8. Should wealth be distributed equally?
9. How does the unequal distribution of wealth affect the powerful groups within countries?
10. Is wealth distributed equally within your community? How do you know? What problems might be eliminated if the wealth were more evenly distributed?

Ask each group to find a way to distribute its food equally among its members. (Students from the DEVELOPING NATIONS group might ask that some of the wealth from the INDUSTRIALIZED NATIONS be shared with them. Allow the students to work this out.) Have a member of each group explain how they decided to share the wealth equally.

ADDITIONAL ACTIVITY:

1. Play and discuss the song *We Are the Champions of the World* by Queen.

2. Brainstorm ways in which industrial countries use up most of the world's resources --- energy, water, trees, plants, land, minerals, etc. Most people in "developing" nations don't have automobiles, electricity, and the kinds of household appliances used in many homes in industrial countries such as washing machines, dish-washers, microwave ovens, television, VCRs, computers, etc. Natural resources are wasted and the environment is damaged

in developing countries as well, but this is most often the result of severe poverty and large-scale development projects which use raw materials from developing countries to produce products that bring more wealth to industrial nations. The results of this kind of development - cash crops, clothing, rugs, machinery, etc. are delivered to people in industrial nations. In this way the wealth, resources and labor of developing countries are used to enrich industrial countries.

3. Have students find examples of **ONE PLANET, TWO WORLDS** in their own communities. Encourage them to use their examples or some of the examples on the following page to create comic strips, poems and posters to display around school. Keep asking "why?" these two worlds exist.

4. Listen to and discuss the song *Because All Men Are Brothers* by Peter, Paul & Mary.

SOME EXAMPLES OF ONE PLANET, TWO WORLDS:[*]

A. In California 6th graders work on computers in air-conditioned classrooms while kids in Mozambique use sticks and bark to learn to write in open-air classes. One of four South African children does not go to school at all.

B. A designer handbag in Paris costs $1,500 - more than the annual per capita income in more than forty countries.

C. Rival British and American shipping companies vie to build the world's largest and most luxurious cruise liners while hundreds of thousands of homeless live atop massive garbage dumps in Mexico City and Manila.

D. There are 793 billionaires in the world and more than 1 billion people who survive on the equivalent of $1 a day.

E. Industrial countries average one doctor per 400 people, while developing countries average one doctor per 7,000. Some African states have only one doctor for every 36,000.

F. Every **minute** 27 children die for want of essential food and inexpensive vaccines. Every **minute** the world's military machine takes another $1,900,000 from the public treasury.

G. In Indonesia girls who make NIKE shoes are paid wages that start at $1.35 per day. In 1992 the **entire payroll** for the Indonesian factories that made NIKES was less than Michael Jordan's reported $20 million fee for promoting NIKES. It costs $5.60 to produce one pair of NIKES in Indonesia. In the U.S. one pair of NIKES sells for between $45 and $80. (A study by the International Labor Organization found that 88% of girls and young women earning minimum wage in Indonesia were undernourished.)

---

[*] Sources: A,B,C & E - *The Los Angeles Times*, June 14, 1994
D - *Forbes Magazine*, March 11, 2009
F - World Military & Social Expenditures, 1989.
G - *The New York Times*, February 13, 1994.

LESSON 10: THE LEGACY OF COLONIALISM

How did the world's resources and power become so unfairly divided in the first place? How did the industrialized countries end up with so much more than their share? A case study in this lesson takes students back 500 years to a bountiful paradise called Brazil where a strong indigenous people, their rich and colorful culture, and environment thrive. Students discover that this land is invaded by Portuguese colonists who savagely exploit the healthy people, their land and resources, along with imported African slaves, in order to enrich and empower Portugal. Students explore the role colonialism played in laying the groundwork for the future of land ownership, racism, and the severe poverty experienced today in Brazil. *The Curse of Sugar* serves as a mirror through which students can begin to question and research the continuing effects of colonialism and slavery in North America, the rest of South America, Africa and Asia.

MATERIALS: One bag of sugar
One small sugar bowl
The Curse of Sugar

PROCEDURE:

Read the following descriptions of 16th century Brazil taken from the diaries and letters of three early European explorers who were seeing Brazil for the first time:

> "The lush land belongs to all, just like the sun and water. The people live in a golden age and do not surround themselves with ditches, walls, or hedges."
>
> *(Pietro Martire d'Anghiera, 1500)*

> "The people are stronger and better fed than we are. They are well cared for and very clean and in this way they seem to me rather like birds. Their bodies are so plump and so beautiful that they could not be more so."
>
> *(Pero Vaz Caminha in a letter to King Manoel I, 1500)*

> "They exist on a succulent diet of exotic fruits, herbs, game and an infinity of fish: crabs, oysters, lobsters, crayfish and many other things which the sea produces. This is a delightful land with brightly-colored birds, evergreen trees that yield the sweetest aromatic perfumes and an infinite variety of fruit. I fancied myself to be near the terrestrial paradise."
>
> *(Amerigo Vespucci in a letter to Prince de Medici, 1503)*

Read the following description of Brazil adapted from the research of Nancy Scheper-Hughes in 1992:

Today the Northeast region of Brazil is one of the poorest areas in the world. Scenes of hunger, disease and child death are commonplace. Two-thirds of all rural children suffer stunted growth from inadequate food. Hunger has made the people lean, nervous and desperate. The Brazillian press refers to the region as "The Valley of Death". The country's rivers are "spoiled, brackish, salty, putrid and contaminated by pollutants." Their fish are gone. Children search through piles of garbage for food. Every four minutes two children under one year-old die in Brazil from starvation and disease.

WHAT HAPPENED? How did Brazil change from a "terrestrial paradise" to the "valley of death"? What do students think?

Read or tell students the story of *The Curse of Sugar* during the day (or two days) stopping to discuss or write about the questions at the end of each segment. DO NOT READ THE TITLE as students must try to guess the name of the substance that would play a major role in shaping Brazil's hungry future.

ADDITIONAL ACTIVITIES:

1. After the story have students role play colonists and natives in small groups. They must improvise dialogue between Brazilian natives and Portuguese colonists who want to take over the land and local labor for sugar plantations.

2.* There were no newspapers in Brazil in the early 1500's. What do students imagine might have been in the papers if there had been newspapers when the Portuguese began colonizing Brazil? Students can work in small groups to create an imaginary issue of *The Brazil Herald*. Bring in a copy of your town newspaper to find the different sections students will need to create - front page with headlines and articles, interviews with the King of Portugal, the plantation owners, indigenous people, Africans kidnapped from their homes and brought to work as slaves, (students can play these roles and interview each other); opinion columns, letters to the editors, advertisements, Dear Abby, comic strips, society pages, jobs wanted, etc. Have each group or student work on one or more sections of their choice.

3.* Much of what we know about the early European exploration and colonization of Brazil comes from the diaries and letters of explorers and travelers who made the journey from Europe to Brazil. Have students imagine that they are aboard a 16th century Portuguese ship which leaves Lisbon filled with guns, colonists, beads and cloth. Their ship

---

* Activities #2, #3 and #8 have been reprinted with permission from *Colonialism in the Americas: A Critical Look*. This is a compact and powerful teaching guide by Susan Gage, produced by Victoria International Development Education Association (VIDEA) in 1991. (See Resource Guide under COLONIALISM, SLAVERY, RACISM & RESISTANCE to order.)

stops first in Africa where the captain trades the ship's cargo for African slaves. Then, with its hold crammed full of shackled slaves, it sails for eight weeks to Brazil. There the crew unloads the slaves and reloads with sugar and brazilwood, then heads back to Lisbon with its bounty. Students write a brief diary or a letter to a family back in Portugal describing their feelings and experiences during the journey. (Trace the journey on the world map.)

4. Olaudah Equiana was born in Benin, Nigeria in 1745. He was kidnapped at the age of eleven and sold to slave traders who sent him on a slave ship to Barbados in the West Indies. Years later, he wrote about his time on that ship:

> I was soon put down under the decks and was greeted by such a stench as I had never experienced in my life. I became so sick and low that I was not able to eat, nor had I the least desire to taste anything. The crew watched us closely. The crowding which meant that each had scarcely room to turn himself, almost suffocated us. There was sickness among the slaves of which many died. The situation was aggravated by the rubbing of the chains and the filth of the lavatory buckets. The shrieks of the women and the groans of the dying rendered the whole a scene of horror. I became so sick that, as I was young, my chains were removed and I was allowed to stay on deck. One day, two of my countrymen who were chained together, preferring death to such a life of misery, jumped into the sea.
>
> From Equiano's autobiography, *The Very Interesting Narrative of the Life of Olaudah Equiano* published in 1789.

According to Equiano's own account, after reaching America he was sold to a Captain Pascal who renamed him Gustavos Vassa and sent him to England where he became the servant to two women who taught him to read the Bible. Vassa was sold and resold. He was bought by a Philadelphia merchant and "allowed" to earn money to pay for his freedom. Once free, Equiano returned to England where he worked to end slavery.

The Portuguese felt that their race and culture were superior to those of the Africans and the native Brazilians. This is **racism**. Discuss evidence of racism in the colonization of Brazil. Of North America. Discuss evidence of racism in your community today. Is it connected to the colonization of North America by Europeans? Does racism play a role in the high rates of poverty among people of color in the United States today?

5. By the time the African slave trade ended in 1870, Africa had lost millions of her people. Estimates range from 5 million to 40 million. Research, discuss and write about the effects slavery had on **Africa**. (See

Resource Guide for information on *COLONIALISM IN AFRICA: A Critical Look.*)

6. What was happening in our own country while Brazil's indigenous people, culture and resources were being pillaged? How did the people of North America live before the arrival of Columbus? What did colonialism do to them, their culture, food supply and environment? Who benefited? Who was hurt? What were the effects of slavery in North America? How different would North America be today if it had not been colonized by the Europeans? What are some of the continuing effects of colonialism and slavery on North America today?

A thorough and honest critique of colonial history is crucial if young people are to understand the social, economic, political and environmental injustices with which we struggle today. For an extended study refer to the Resource Guide for curricula, books and videos.

7. Invite Native American speakers into your classroom to discuss their cultures, the problems with which they struggle today, and any resistance movements against government or corporate oppression. How can students support them in their struggle? (It is crucial to help students see that the people hurt by colonialism and oppression are not helpless, but are instead continuing their struggle for freedom in courageous ways.)

8. Colonialism wiped out and suppressed entire civilizations around the world. Urge students to research different Native American cultures which thrived for centuries before the arrival of Columbus. Consider investigating the groups of indigenous peoples who lived in **your** area. Students can use the following list of tribes and questions as a guide for shaping presentations.

SOUTH & CENTRAL AMERICA: the Zapotecs, the Mayans, the Aztecs, the Incas, the Hiuchol.

NORTH AMERICA: the Yaqui, the Hopi, the Navajo, the Pueblos, the Apache, the Cherokee, the Iroquois, the Algonquins, the Sioux, the Cree, the Kwakiutl, the Nootka, the Haida, the Dene, and the Inuit.

1. How did they get their food, clothing, shelter?
2. How did they organize themselves? Who made the decisions and how?
3. What was their justice system like?
4. What was their attitude toward the land?
5. What were some of their customs, games, stories?

6. How did they communicate? Did they have a written language?

7. How did their lives change once the white people came?

8. What can we learn from them today?

9. Students can create poems, paintings and stories depicting how different their community might be today if North America hadn't been colonized by the Europeans.

10. Discuss Chief Seattle's message on the following pages. Have students choose a line from the message and write about it. Or they can imagine they are listening to Chief Seattle speak to them and they must write a response to Chief Seattle explaining how land in your area is being treated.

11. Discuss the poem *The Earth is a Satellite of the Moon* on the following pages. Students can write another verse for the poem or use the poem to inspire a poem of their own.

12. Have students investigate their local supermarkets for cash crops such as sugar, coffee, cocoa, etc. which are produced in great quantities in many developing countries as well as in certain regions of the U.S. The people who produce these crops are overworked, underpaid and very often chronically hungry. Students can find out where the cash crops in their markets come from by reading labels or interviewing the store manager. Use a world map to track sources by attaching a label with the name or picture of each cash crop on its country of origin. Are most of these countries in the Northern Hemisphere or the Southern Hemisphere? Are the countries former colonies? How are workers treated? Is most of their land used to produce these crops? Is hunger a serious problem? (Remember, the child mortality rate is a measure of how widespread hunger is in a particular country.) Some cash crops, their countries of origin, and the countries' child mortality rates are listed on the following page.

    A child mortality rate of 25 or above signifies serious hunger. After your project review how cash crops cause hunger by exploiting land and human labor and damaging the environment.

13. A natural segue from a study of colonialism is a unit on global sweatshops created by U.S. and transnational corporations which exploit adult and child labor as well as natural resources in third world countries. For some fascinating ideas on how other teachers have taught this subject, as well as a list of resources, fact sheets and student poetry on sweatshops send for Volume 11, No. 4 of *Rethinking Schools*. (See Resource Guide for information.) In this issue, for example, history teacher Bill Bigelow asks students to write descriptions of a soccer ball placed in front of them. After they have described what they see, Bertold

Brect's poem "A Worker Reads History", is read aloud. Students rewrite their descriptions -- this time "seeing" the humanity inside this everyday consumer product. Bill's account of his experience teaching about sweatshops includes a game he developed called "The Transnational Capital Auction: A Game of Survival", as well as student writing, current news articles and videos, an assignment which engaged students in finding ten personal belongings not produced in the U.S. and tracking the origins of the goods on a world map, and final projects that take what students have learned outside the classroom to make a difference. (See Resource Guide under **WORK** for more resources to order for your study of global sweatshops.)

SOME CASH CROPS AND COUNTRIES OF ORIGIN

BANANAS - Brazil, Ecuador, Guatemala, Honduras, Somalia

BEEF - Argentina, Brazil, Uruguay

CASHEWS - Guinea-Bissau

COCOA - Benin, Brazil, Congo, Ecuador, Ivory Coast, Ghana

COCONUTS - Guinea-Bissau, Philippines

COFFEE - Angola, Benin, Brazil, Central African Republic, Congo, Costa Rica, Ecuador, El Salvador, Haiti, Honduras, Mexico, Nicaragua, Rwanda, Dominican Republic

COTTON - Benin, Central African Republic, India, Ivory Coast, South Africa

GRAPES - Chile, South Africa (for wine)

JUTE - Bangladesh

PINEAPPLES - Philippines

RICE - Belize, India, Thailand, China, Dominican Republic

RUBBER - Thailand, Brazil

SHRIMP - Ecuador, Mexico

SOYBEANS - Brazil, China

SUGARCANE - Belize, Brazil, China, Guatemala, Cuba, Honduras, India

TEA - India

TIMBER - Belize, Central African Republic, Ivory Coast, Laos

TOBACCO - Brazil, Guinea-Bissau, Honduras, India, Ivory Coast Dominican Republic, Cuba

CHILD MORTALITY RATES[*]
FOR ABOVE COUNTRIES

Country	Rate	Country	Rate
Angola	158	Guinea-Bissau	198
Argentina	16	Haiti	76
Bangladesh	61	Honduras	24
Benin	123	India	72
Brazil	22	Ivory Coast	127
Central African Republic	172	Laos	70
Chile	9	Mexico	35
Congo	125	Nicaragua	35
Costa Rica	11	Philippines	28
Cuba	7	Rwanda	181
Dominican Republic	38	Somalia	142
Ecuador	22	South Africa	59
El Salvador	24	Thailand	7
Ghana	115	Uruguay	14
Guatemala	39		

---

[*] For an explanation of the Child Mortality Rate see Lesson #4 - "How Hunger is Measured". Source: *State of the World's Children*, 2009, UNICEF

THE CURSE OF SUGAR*

When the Portuguese explorer Pero Cabral sailed along the dazzling coast of Brazil for the first time in 1500 - believing he was in India - the native people greeted him and his hungry crew warmly and generously. Brightly colored feather-headdresses were bestowed upon the exhausted sailors, along with strings of tiny pearls and a feast of mais, beans, pumpkins, manioc and game.

Once the Portuguese had a closer look at this "paradise", they saw that the land was covered with dense forests of the coveted brazilwood trees and exotic animals and birds. They persuaded the friendly natives to chop down several of the trees and to load the wood onto their ships. In exchange for their bruising work, the natives were given some beads and a few pieces of cloth. Jean de Lery wrote that after seeing so many brazilwoods felled, an old man asked him, "why do you people come from so far away to seek wood to warm you? Don't you have wood in your country?" Jean de Lery explained that this particular kind of tree did not grow in Portugal and that they wanted the wood for the red dye it produced which was in great demand among textile merchants in Europe. This response must have puzzled the old man whose own culture held the Earth's gifts in the highest esteem and believed trees should be loved and protected, not killed, hoarded or sold. From across the ocean, the King of Portugal laid claim to this wonderful land called Brazil (never mind that it had been inhabited by indigenous people for centuries). The king ordered hundreds of miles of the best land along the coast of Brazil be divided up quickly and granted to wealthy Portuguese businessmen who sailed immediately to begin clearing their new properties. These colonists soon discovered that the tropical climate and fertile soil of Brazil was perfect for growing something else which was in great demand - and which could not be grown back in Europe - something that would change the landscape of Brazil forever.

Can students guess what this "something" was?
HINT: The substance was called "white gold" by the colonists.

(Empty some of the sugar into the sugar bowl and set the bowl alone on a table in front of the class. Tell them that until the discovery of America sugar was a luxury as rare and as expensive as gold, tasted only by the very rich. Produced in small quantities in parts of India, miniature sugar loaves were sold or traded to European aristocrats and wealthy merchants who locked the sweet treasures away to be eaten sparingly - never added to food or drinks. Physicians prescribed sugar water for their wealthy patients believing sugar possessed mystical qualities.)

When they realized the business opportunities this healthy land and people could bring them, the King, Queen, merchants and landowners must

---

* Information for "The Curse of Sugar" comes from *Red Gold: Conquest of the Brazilian Indians 1500-1760* by John Hemming, Harvard University Press: Cambridge, 1978; and *Death Without Weeping* by Nancy Scheper-Hughes, University of California Press: London, 1992.

have had more than sugar plums dancing in their heads. Of course, the colonists had no intention of doing the hard work of cultivating sugar themselves. Instead they tried to persuade the hospitable natives to chop down the forests and plant the cane and build the sugar mills. Unfortunately, the colonists plans hit a major snag. Everything about this kind of work was alien to Brazil's native people. In **their** view, no one owned the land, it simply belonged to the Earth, and they could not bring themselves to destroy forests that provided food, cool shelter and beauty. The work the colonists insisted upon was brutish and destructive and required the use of none of the natives' prized skills --- hunting, forest lore, and archery. The natives simply refused to work long, hard hours destroying their forests and land, for a bunch of strangers, and not have time to rest or enjoy tribal life.

This attitude, of course, did not sit well with the greedy and heavily armed colonists who resorted to force, rounding up as many natives as they could find. The natives, armed with bows and arrows, fought back courageously. They waged long battles against the colonists. Some natives fled inland but were hunted down and taken back to work as slaves. Others returned to set fire to the canefields, mills and white settlements. Many natives died from exposure to European diseases such as smallpox, measles and flu --- so many, in fact, that by 1560 the native population of Brazil was cut in half and the colonists faced a serious labor shortage. Where to look for workers? To Europe for more cattle and to Africa for men and women.

Most of the Africans were immune to European diseases, but once they set foot on the sugar plantations of Brazil, the average life span of a slave was only seven years. The work was backbreaking. It involved cutting down acres of forests, tilling the land, planting, weeding, then cutting down the cane stalks and transporting loads of stalks by oxen to the mill some distance away. All this under a broiling sun and the watchful eyes of armed colonists, far from home and family, with very little food or drink and no time to rest. When the cane reached the mill it was crushed (to squeeze out the sweet juice) by large rollers powered by harnessed slaves or oxen. The juice was then boiled in huge bubbling vats, cooled, crystallized, bagged and loaded onto ships where it was carried to the trading posts of Europe. The Portuguese earned huge profits from this sugar. By 1560 many of the sons of plantation owners were the richest men in Brazil. Like the native people, the African slaves also rebelled. Some set fire to the plantations and killed their masters. Without access to food or weapons, many slaves were overcome, severely beaten, and forced to continue to work. A small band of African slaves did manage to escape deep into the Brazilian forest where they started a kingdom of their own called Palmares which grew to one-third the size of Portugal.

Each plantation owner had about 100-200 slaves and because they were so cruelly overworked and underfed, slaves were replaced regularly by fresh new arrivals. Many African slaves died from overwork, exposure to excessive heat in the fields and mills, inadequate and spoiled foods, overcrowded living conditions and a lack of medical attention.

The plantation was built around the master's grand mansion which was elegantly furnished with gold, silver, handcarved furniture and rich textiles from Europe and the Orient. The plantation owner and his family spent their days and evenings entertaining, dancing, resting, and sporting the finest linens and shoes. They feasted on lavish meals prepared by slaves. At a distance from the master's home stood a row of connected one-room huts with dirt floors where the slaves lived. Near these huts stood the noisy mill, and surrounding all of this were the canefields.

SOME IMPORTANT QUESTIONS

How would it feel to have strangers invade your town and grab up all the land and trees for themselves?

How would it feel to be kidnapped from your home and forced to spend all day working for a stranger with no pay or rest and little food in a foreign land?

The holding onto all the best land by a few wealthy men might have some effect later on. Can you think what that effect would be?

Taking Africans to America and forcing them to work as slaves might even have some effects on the descendants of those slaves generations later in America. What would those effects be? How would African-Americans be looked upon and treated by others? How might this make them feel about themselves? About whites?

PLANT EATS COUNTRY

A sugarcane plant lasts seven years in the soil before it uses up the soil's nutrients, leaving it weak and unable to produce anything else. After so many harvests, the plantation owners abandoned their useless fields in search of new land. When the mills ran down they were left to rust and new ones built further down the road.

While some of the Portuguese colonists were raking in lots of money from their sugar plantations, other colonists were overseeing large areas of forest land in Brazil's interior which had also been cleared by slaves to create land for grazing European cattle --- the beef from which would be sold back in Europe. Still other Portuguese colonists hacked their way deep into the heart of Brazil in search of gold and silver. Brazil was not the only country the Portuguese were ransacking. They were also colonizing the west coast of Africa and Southern India, and carrying away shiploads of sought-after spices --- pepper, ginger, cinnamon, cloves as well as animal skins, dyes, medicinal herbs, ivory and timber. In addition, shiploads of sugar, gold, brazilwood, jaguar skins and slaves from Brazil streamed into Portugal's main port of Lisbon. With all these stolen treasures, Lisbon soon became the envy of Europe and one of the world's largest commercial and cultural centers. Some of this pillage went toward the creation of palaces, monuments and lavish mansions throughout Portugal and its colonies --- the rest bought the Portuguese bigger ships and more weapons.

The African slaves (millions of whom had also been taken from Africa to the rest of South America and North America as well as Europe) were freed in 1870. The wealthy plantation owners in Brazil continued to own and control most of the country's land. To entice the slaves into continuing to do the work on the plantations, the owners gave them small plots of land on which to grow their own food --- but these plots proved to be weak and rocky and could not grow much. Many "freed" slaves starved to death. The rest, in order to survive, continued working on the plantations in exchange for a little food.

With the money from the sale of so much sugar, the Portuguese built sugar factories and developed equipment which could produce even more sugar --- and faster! Before long the Industrial Revolution was rocking a world whose sweet tooth was out of control. (Ever since the middle and working classes had gotten a taste of sugar, the world had begun to spin a whole lot faster.) Everywhere people clamored for sugar and every inch of arable land was used for the production of sugar (or coffee, or cocoa which were also in great demand and could not be grown in Europe).

Landholdings in Brazil were combined to form even bigger plantations. Animal-powered rollers had been replaced by shiny black steam engines. Overworked, underpaid and hungry workers loaded 6,000 huge bags of sugar a year onto railroad cars that crisscrossed the scarred landscape belching dirty smoke into the blue Brazilian sky. As the sugar fields grew bigger, the land once covered with forests and used to produce food grew smaller.

MORE QUESTIONS

What might be the consequences of so much sugar production on Brazil's environment later on?

What did Portuguese colonialism do to the culture and native people of Brazil?

What did colonialism do for Portugal? What effect might this have on Portugal's future?

IS BIGGER BETTER?

Today a few giant corporations control most of the sugar plantations of Brazil. With their advanced technology and huge landholdings these corporate plantations supply the world with hundreds of TONS of sugar every year. Each corporate plantation employs around 2,300 workers and is still built around the owner's grand mansion which now boasts a swimming pool, tennis courts and sculpture gardens. A few miles down muddy unpaved roads live the cane and factory workers in long rows of small cement cubicles. Electricity in the cubicles is unpredictable so the workers must share a public washstand and cook outside over open fires. After long, hard days in the sweltering fields and factories (which are enclosed with metal fences) the workers are too exhausted to tend their small community garden or gather firewood for cooking. Caneworkers are expected to cut 200 kilos of cane everyday. Men are paid $10 a week. Women are paid $5 and are not eligible for medical care provided for male workers. Workers who complain are often fired. Wastes from the factories are dumped into nearby rivers.

With much of the country's land used to produce cash crops instead of food, most food must be imported, is in short supply, and very expensive. Workers are paid paltry wages and compete for second or third jobs in order to earn more money to bring home food for their families. They are chronically hungry and malnourished, surviving mainly on beans, spaghetti and cornmeal, rarely getting fresh fruits and vegetables. Two out of three children in rural Brazil suffer stunted growth. Many women must leave their own children unattended while they work as maids and caregivers in the big homes of the wealthy.

THE GREAT EXPERIMENT

In the 1970's the government of Brazil borrowed billions of dollars from industrial nations such as Germany, Japan and the U.S. to modernize Brazil. Superhighways were built, gigantic hydro-electric power plants, airports, factories, hospitals and laboratories and sleek new skyscrapers and shopping malls. These "improvements" were hailed around the world as an "economic miracle". Unfortunately, only the richest 10% of the people in Brazil benefited from these expensive improvements. The workers could not afford cars to drive on the new highways, electricity from the power plants, medical care from the new hospitals, or clothes from the mall. With the money earned from the sale of cash crops, the wealthy landowners and business people bought imported food and clothes, microwave ovens, computers and VCRs, the best medical care and day-care services for their children.

In order to repay its great debt (and the interest on the debt) which by 1992 had reached $112 billion, the government of Brazil increased the production of cash crops (sugar, coffee, soybeans and cattle). The workers had to work even harder. At the same time the government cut back on services to the poor --- nutrition centers, health clinics, child-care programs, and job-training. Millions of hungry peasants fled the countryside in search of work only to find themselves barely surviving on the edge of the sparkling new cities. They live in dangerous shantytowns, drink from polluted groundwater and scavenge through huge piles of garbage for food. Many Brazilian mothers, when asked how many children they have, answer with the number who are alive and the number who are "angels". Listen to a grandmother describe the changes she has witnessed:

> I am seeing things in the world today that I never saw before in all my seventy years. I am seeing women with only two or three living children. In days past they would have eight or ten children, and before this time

we always had good winters with lots of rain and everyone's house was filled with fresh vegetables from their rocados (gardens) to "kill" their hunger. No one went as hungry then as they are suffering today. In these times we are living all you can see in the middle of the world is cane. That is our curse. The small gardens are gone and we have been chased away. Our lands have been eaten up by sugar.

Once a rare luxury, today sugar can be found in nearly every household in the world and is responsible for widespread tooth decay. Filled with empty calories we eat fewer, healthy foods. Sugar has taken many slaves during its long history. Will the curse continue another 500 years?

MORE QUESTIONS

How different are today's corporate plantations from the early slave-driven plantations?

What would you change about the way the corporate plantations are run?

Why didn't everyone benefit from the "economic miracle"? Do you have any suggestions on improvements that would have benefited everyone?

We can't turn back the clock of history. Colonialism continues today. What ideas do you have on how to stop it?

Are you a slave to sugar? Nearly 28 pounds of table sugar are consumed each **week** for every man, woman and child in the U.S. For many Americans sugar makes up 20% of their diets. Why is the world mad for sugar? Together make a list of foods that contain sugar. Does it surprise you to learn that these foods often contain sugar: ketchup, salad dressing, peanut butter, hot dogs, ham, bacon!

THIS WE KNOW

CHIEF SEATTLE

THE PRESIDENT IN WASHINGTON SENDS WORD THAT HE WISHES TO BUY our land. But how can you buy or sell the sky? The land? The idea is strange to us. If we do not own the freshness of the air and the sparkle of the water, how can you buy them?

Every part of this earth is sacred to my people. Every shining pine needle, every sandy shore, every mist in the dark woods, every meadow, every humming insect. All are holy in the memory and experience of my people.

We know the sap which courses through the trees as we know the blood that courses through our veins. We are part of the earth and it is part of us. The perfumed flowers are our sisters. The bear, the deer, the great eagle, these are our brothers. The rocky crests, the juices in the meadow, the body heat of the pony, and man, all belong to the same family.

The shining water that moves in the streams and rivers is not just water, but the blood of our ancestors. If we sell you our land, you must remember that it is sacred. Each ghostly reflection in the clear water of the lakes tells of events and memories in the life of my people. The water's murmur is the voice of my father's father.

The rivers are our brothers. They quench our thirst. They carry our canoes and feed our children. So you must give to the rivers the kindness you would give any brother.

If we sell you our land, remember that the air is precious to us, that the air shares its spirit with all the life it supports. The wind that gave our grandfather his first breath also receives his last sigh. The wind also gives our children the spirit of life. So if we sell you our land, you must keep it apart and sacred, as a place where man can go to taste the wind that is sweetened by the meadow flowers.

Will you teach your children what we have taught our children? That the earth is our mother? What befalls the earth, befalls all the sons of the earth.

This we know: The earth does not belong to man, man belongs to the earth. All things are connected like the blood which unites us all. Man did not weave the web of life, he is merely a strand in it. Whatever he does to the web, he does to himself.

One thing we know: Our god is also your god. The earth is precious to him and to harm the earth is to heap contempt on its creator.

Your destiny is a mystery to us. What will happen when the buffalo* are all slaughtered? The wild horses tamed? What will happen when the secret corners of the forest are heavy with the scent of many men and the view of the ripe hills is blotted by talking wires†? Where will the thicket be? Gone! Where will the eagle be? Gone! And what is it to say good-bye to the swift pony and the hunt? The end of living and the beginning of survival.

When the last Red Man has vanished with his wilderness and his memory is only the shadow of a cloud moving across the prairie, will these shores and forests still be here? Will there be any of the spirit of my people left?

We love this earth as a newborn loves its mother's heartbeat. So, if we sell you our land, love it as we have loved it. Care for it as we have cared for it. Hold in your mind the memory of the land as it is when you receive it. Preserve the land for all children and love it, as God loves us all.

As we are part of the land, you too are part of the land. This earth is precious to us. It is also precious to you. One thing we know: There is only one God. No man, be he Red Man or White Man can be apart. We are brothers after all.

THE EARTH IS A SATELLITE OF THE MOON[*]
By Leonel Rugama

Apollo 2 cost more than Apollo 1
Apollo 1 cost plenty.

Apollo 3 cost more than Apollo 2
Apollo 2 cost more than Apollo 1
Apollo 1 cost plenty

Apollo 4 cost more than Apollo 3
Apollo 3 cost more than Apollo 2
Apollo 2 cost more than Apollo 1
Apollo 1 cost plenty.

Apollo 8 cost a fortune, but no one minded
because the astronauts were Protestant
they read the bible from the moon
astounding and delighting every Christian
and on their return Pope Paul VI
        gave them his blessing.

Apollo 9 cost more than all these put together
including Apollo 1 which cost plenty.

The great-grandparents of the people
        of Acahualinca
           were less hungry than the grandparents.
The great-grandparents died of hunger.
The grandparents of the people of Acahualinca
        were less hungry than the parents.
The grandparents died of hunger.
The parents of the people of Acahualinca were less
        hungry than the children of the people there.
The parents died of hunger.

The people of Acahualinca are less hungry
        than the children of the people there.
The children of the people of Acahualinca,
        because of hunger, are not born
they hunger to be born, only to die of hunger.
Blessed are the poor for they shall inherit the moon.

---

[*] The poet Leonel Rugama was a Nicaraguan who died in 1970 while fighting for the Sandinista National Liberation Front. His poem from *The Earth Is A Satellite of the Moon* is reprinted here with permission from Curbstone Press, Willimantic, CN. (Translations by Sara Miles, Richard Schaaf and Nancy Weisberg)

LESSON 11: DEVELOPMENT - WHO BENEFITS?*

A role play turns the classroom into an "underdeveloped" country --- rich in natural resources but lacking the conveniences and technology of industrial countries. The World Bank has agreed to loan the government of this country money to "develop" its natural resources. In the name of "progress" the country's president announces that the money will be used to turn a "useless" forest into "profitable" eucalyptus plantations which will supply a good part of the world's computer paper. The money earned from the sale of these raw materials will be used to further "develop" the country--- to build roads, bridges, dams, power plants, factories, etc.

A National Debate is called to decide if this really is the best way to "develop". Half the class assumes the roles of World Bank ministers, local government officials and loggers who favor industrial development and the economic benefits it will bring --- jobs, global trade, money, new technology, etc. Countering their argument are students representing local villagers (dependent on the forest for survival), environmentalists, and the trees and creatures of the forest who must address the social and environmental problems such development is sure to bring. Both groups must weigh the pros and cons of this project and answer the question "Who will benefit?" Students are also encouraged to question who benefits from development in their own communities.

MATERIALS: Enough for all students:
Copies of - *The President's Statement on Development*
- *Role Sheets*

TEACHER BACKGROUND INFORMATION

To develop - "to bring out the capabilities or possibilities of; to bring to a more advanced or effective state."

"Development" is often viewed as positive --- it signifies growth. The word "development" is used interchangeably with "progress" and "modernization". Traditionally, development projects around the world have focused on building up a country's economy by constructing internal systems that mainly benefit industry --- huge electric power plants, dams, railroads, highways, factories and communications systems. In many underdeveloped countries this has also included increased export crop production. The people behind these kinds of "improvements" (most often the International Monetary Fund and the World Bank using billions in loans from industrial countries, along with the support of government officials and business leaders within the developing countries) insist that technology, investment

---

* Role sheets for this activity were created using information from eyewitness accounts documented in *Behind the Smile: Voices of Thailand* by Sanitsuda Ekachai, 1991 - reprinted from The Bangkok Post.

The structure of this activity is based on an activity described and created by Bill Bigelow in *Rethinking Our Classrooms:Teaching For Equity and Social Justice* - See Resource Guide.

and increased global trade stimulate economic growth and elevate a country's standard of living. They contend that the benefits of all these improvements will eventually filter down to improve the lives of the poorest.

Voices from the other side, however, --- social scientists, human rights activists, environmentalists, as well as the people directly affected by these expensive, large-scale modernization projects --- argue that this kind of development is actually **producing poverty** and increasing the gap between the rich and poor people in developing countries. They refer to an increasing number of development projects which have resulted in the extermination of millions of the Earth's species, polluted the soil, air and water and uprooted millions of the world's poorest people. Consider:

> From 1947 to 1991 in India, World Bank and government- sponsored development projects such as the large-scale construction of dams and coal mines resulted in the eviction of more than 20 million poor people from their homes and land.[*]

> In Thailand the broad expansion of industrial shrimp farming financed by the World Bank destroyed nearly half that country's mangrove forests between 1985 and 1990, and devastated fish habitats and polluted water supplies necessary for growing rice for hungry people.[†]

> Between 1981 and 1983 the World Bank spent $443.3 million to "develop" the northwest region of Brazil. A highway was constructed and miles of rainforest were razed to create land for grazing beef-cattle and for growing coffee and cocoa for export. The project attracted scores of hopeful settlers who migrated from the populous south-central region in search of land, jobs, wages, food and a better life. Instead they found the area controlled by powerful export companies and large land-owners. The weak forest soil was unable to produce food without large inputs of expensive chemical fertilizers and pesticides. No credit or agricultural services were available to the poor settlers. 250 became infected with malaria. Indigenous tribes were lost to measles, flu and malaria and over 1,000 farmers and activists were killed in conflicts over land.[§]

Around the world local populations whose lives have nearly been destroyed in the name of "progress" are mobilizing to defend the rights of local people and ecological balance. The best organized of these groups have halted massive development projects. THEY ARE NOT AGAINST ECONOMIC DEVELOPMENT -

---

[*] From Clarence Maloney in *Environmental and Project Displacement of Population in India*, University Field Staff International Report #14, 1990-91. Indianapolis, Indiana.

[†] From *Behind the Smile: Voices of Thailand* by Sanitsuda Ekachai, 1991, reprinted from the *Bangkok Post*.

[§] From *Mortgaging the Earth* by Bruce Rich. 1994 PPS 27-28

THEY DESIRE IT, but they insist on maintaining **control** over the resources upon which they depend for survival. They promote small "human-scale" development projects initiated from **within** the community which preserve the local culture, respect **everyone's** rights, and preserve natural resources.

Some examples of this "bottom-up" development include:

1. In Guinea people in villages far from agricultural markets and health clinics created their own system of roads 69 miles long. Teams of construction workers from other countries trained local laborers in road construction and maintenance and loaned them money for the necessary tools and materials. The villagers themselves designed the roads so that every village would benefit from them and so that no one's land or home was harmed. Today 2,000 Guineans have the training to earn incomes and contribute to the development of their own country according to their own needs. Local farmers have roads that connect them to markets and people in other villages.

2. A community in the Amazon forest received a loan from an international agency. The villagers used the money to organize and maintain cooperatives that help people gather and sell products from the forest without damaging the existing trees, plants, animals, soil, water or air. Villagers work together to collect and sell Brazil nuts and resin from the trees. The money earned is shared among the workers. Some of the income goes back into the cooperative to provide new tools, medical care and other business opportunities for workers and their families.

PROCEDURE:

1. Close the door. Tell students the classroom has just been turned into an "underdeveloped" country --- there is no industry here --- no highways, supermarkets, factories, automobiles or even electricity. Instead there are miles of tropical rainforests, palm-fringed beaches, coral reefs, green fertile valleys, mountains rich in minerals, sparkling rivers, exotic flowers, fishes, birds and animals. The people are hard-working. Most till the land, hunt, fish or gather fruits, nuts and insects from the forest in order to survive. Ask the class to suggest a name for this lush country.

    Tell them that lately people inside and outside the country have been talking about different ways to "develop" this region. Some people want to bring this "primitive and backward" country into the modern age. They say people's lives could be made easier by building power plants for electricity, and bringing in machines to do much of the work now done by hand. Not everyone in this country can agree on the best way to "develop".

    Let students know that they will be working in small groups.

Each group will represent a group within this country with strong opinions on the best way to "develop". Once their groups have shaped their opinions, they will participate in a National Debate on Development.

2. Divide students into six equal groups and distribute the role sheets. (All members of one group play environmentalists, all members of another group play loggers, etc.)

3. Ask students to read their role sheets carefully to themselves. In order to help them get into character, suggest that they discuss the questions on their role sheets. After their discussion YOU can interview a member of each group briefly in-front of the class. (If you do this, try to play groups against each other by asking questions such as "How do you **really** feel about those environmentalists, government officials, etc. over there?")

4. Each group should write the name of their group on a placard and place it so that other groups can see who they are.

5. **After** students have had time to assimilate their roles, hand out a copy of ***The President's Statement on Development*** to each student. Have a student introduce you as the "President of _____" (name of country determined by class). Read the statement with much conviction. Allow students to criticize or applaud the proposal but don't respond. You want them to save their energy and criticism for the National Debate.

6. Ask the small groups to discuss the National Debate Questions on the bottom of the President's Statement sheet. They should be ready to present their opinions at a National Debate on Development. After 10 or 15 minutes, remind students that there may be other groups who share their opinions and can serve as allies during the debate. Have each group select two "traveling negotiators" who will visit other groups who share their opinions. Students must remain in character during these discussions. Traveling negotiators may only meet with seated groups, **not** with other traveling negotiators. During this time you can circulate among groups, asking provocative questions and stirring up discussion: "Do you know what those villagers are saying about the World Bank Ministers?" or "What do you think those government officials will do if you try that?"

7. After 15-20 more minutes call the National Debate to order. Groups and allies should sit together. This is a time to express opinions, hear others out and debate the worth of this project. Allow students to run the discussion as much as possible. You can point out contradictions, raise questions, etc.

8. More questions to consider:

    Will villagers be better off or worse off as a result of this project?
    Should development come from inside or outside a community?
    Who should make decisions that affect an entire community or country?
    Who should benefit from local development?
    How should the 50 million dollar loan be used?

Should countries who loan money have a say in how that money is used by the developing country?

9. Give students time to debrief after the debate. Have them talk or write about how it felt to play their character. If this were a real debate, which side would they have taken? Why? Did any other character's opinions appeal to them?

10. Tell students this role-play was based on an actual event which took place in Thailand in the 1980's. Have them speculate on how this development project played out in real life. Who do they think won? Tell them that:

> The project to tear down the forest began at a time when nearly half the forests in Thailand had already been divided up among logging companies. There was no National Debate to hear all voices. The government and The World Bank insisted that the eucalyptus project go ahead despite the objections of environmentalists and villagers. The forest was bulldozed and the stumps burned. Black smoke hung over the villages for weeks resulting in widespread respiratory illnesses among villagers. Hundreds of new eucalyptus trees were planted and a fence was built around them to protect the plantations.
>
> The villagers had always prided themselves as the protectors of the forest. One day, armed with knives and shovels, several villagers -- young and old, men and women -- marched to the plantation, climbed the fence and swept clean several acres of eucalyptus saplings. Two days later they burned down the government Forestry Office which had given the contracts to the logging companies.
>
> Their protest inspired similar actions in other parts of the country. Villagers, environmentalists and human right activists from Thailand as well as other countries organized. They wrote furious letters to their government officials denouncing the development project. They sent lobbyists to the industrial nations to demand these nations stop loaning money to the World Bank for projects that uproot people and destroy their environment.
>
> Thanks to their efforts, the government of Thailand and the logging companies retreated. A 15 year ban was placed on logging. Today the area of forest that was destroyed is growing back. The villagers intend to press on with their commitment to protect the forest. They continue to petition their government officials using environmental and academic studies that show that the forest is essential to the well-being of the community and the country.

ADDITIONAL ACTIVITIES:

1. Watch and discuss *The Burning Season* - a 1994 movie on videocassette in which Raoul Julia plays real life activist Chico Mendes, who was murdered trying to protect his people and the Amazon forest which sustained them.

2. Development projects take place in our communities everyday. Take a field trip around your school's neighborhood and make a list of examples of development --- shopping malls, power plants, fast-food chains, factories, highways, resorts, movie complexes, etc. Debate their worth to the local community: Who benefits? Does the development improve life for **everyone**? Does the impetus come from a need **within** the community or from outside interests? What are the social and environmental consequences? Are natural resources and labor used fairly and wisely?

MAKE A DIFFERENCE!

The School Partnership Program (SPP) at IDEX links students in the U.S. with communities overseas that are working on development projects that promote self-reliance. Each school partnership is unique and is shaped by the creativity of the students and teachers involved. For example: Children in Anilady, India prepared a book using pictures, maps, and stories called **KNOW OUR COMMUNITY** for students at San Francisco High School. At the same time, the students at SF High School raised funds for a library and job information center in Anilady. (IDEX also has a Global Economics curriculum that assists students in understanding the implications of international trade on communities worldwide. Students examine global economic policies such as GATT and NAFTA. For information on school partnerships and the curriculum contact: The IDEX Education Program, 827 Valencia St., Suite 101, San Francisco, CA 94110. (415) 824-8384

HANDOUT

PRESIDENT'S STATEMENT ON DEVELOPMENT

Ladies and gentlemen, the time has come for our small country to catch up with the rest of the modern world. We stand today at the start of the 21st century --- and yet most people in our country continue to live without electricity, running water, automobiles and telephones. This is going to change! I am proud to announce that The World Bank has agreed to loan our country $50 million to help develop our land and resources. This money will come from industrial countries such as the U.S. who are eager to open businesses and trade with our country. This will bring money and modern technology to our country.

We have many valuable resources such as land, trees, water minerals, fish, etc., that could be earning us much needed money --- money with which we can not only pay back the loan, but become independent and build our own highways, power plants, factories, airports and resorts --- all of which will bring us even more money and comfort.

I am proposing today that the $50 million be used to tear down several miles of useless wild forests in the Northeast region and to create several large eucalyptus plantations. This is a great business opportunity because eucalyptus trees are used to make computer paper. This paper is in great and growing demand all around the world. Eucalyptus trees grow very well in our climate and soil. Our country could earn millions from the sale of these trees. This kind of development will also create thousands of jobs for needy people.

The plantations will remain the property of the government. The villagers now living in the Northeast region will be relocated to other areas of the country and a fence will be erected around the profitable area to protect it and to keep trespassers out.

This is an exciting opportunity for our country! If we do not take advantage of this chance to develop, another country will. Today, before we move ahead with the project, different groups within the country will have an opportunity to express their opinions on this development project. The project is scheduled to begin tomorrow morning.

NATIONAL DEBATE QUESTIONS:

Do you favor this development project? Why or why not?

What effect will this project have on poverty and hunger in this country?

How should the $50 million be spent? (If you don't favor this project)

GROUP #1 - ROLE SHEET

WORLD BANK MINISTERS

You do not live in this small, under-developed country. You live in a powerful, industrial nation and you work for The World Bank. This large bank receives lots of money in loans from your country and uses the money to help other countries "develop". Today you are visiting this small country to make sure that the money your bank is loaning them will be used wisely.

You look around you here and see people living without the modern comforts you enjoy in your own country --- electricity, heat, air-conditioning, running water, telephones, cars, TV and computers. You cannot imagine living here for long without these conveniences. You would like the government of this small country to use the money from the World Bank to turn this country into an industrialized country like yours.

You are a banker and you understand the power of money. When you look around you you see many natural resources such as land, water, trees, minerals, fish, animals, as well as human labor, simply sitting there untapped --- instead of earning this country money. For instance, the land could be used to grow products such as coffee, cocoa or tea that other countries would pay money for. Much of the fish off the coast here could be caught, packaged and sold to other countries to bring money to this country. Money that could then be used to build roads, bridges, power plants, hospitals, hotels, schools, even resorts. You know that if some of these wonderful resources could be used to produce something that the rest of the world needs and wants --- and is willing to pay for --- then this small, backward country could earn lots of money to build itself up. Some of that money could be used to pay back the World Bank. The rest could be used to improve life for the people here. For instance tractors could be purchased to till much larger sections of land and at a faster pace than people can by hand.

In the future when highways, airports, convention centers, skyscrapers and resorts are built here, they will attract visitors from all over the world who will spend even more money in this country! You believe that eventually these improvements will lift up even the poorest. Building roads and bridges and factories means more jobs. Jobs mean people can earn money to buy food, clothing, medicine, education, cars, TV's, and take vacations.

Of course, the villagers in these under-developed countries are always afraid of change and new technology. They have never even seen a TV or a computer or an industrial country like yours. They cannot imagine what you want to do for them. They will not like your idea of development at first, but you must convince them that once they see all the wonderful luxuries it will bring, they will thank you. They do not yet understand how to use their abundant resources to earn them money. It is your job to provide the money that will bring in the experts and the machines to help them improve their country.

QUESTIONS TO HELP YOU GET INTO CHARACTER:

1. What industrial nation do you live in?

2. How does your country compare with this underdeveloped country?

3. As a minister for the World Bank, how can you help the people of this country develop their natural resources?

GROUP #2 - ROLE SHEET

LOCAL VILLAGERS

You are a villager who lives in the natural forest in the northwest region of this country. Your ancestors lived in this forest. Your history and culture are rooted here. The forest has always provided you and other villagers with food such as fruit, nuts, plants, roots, mushrooms, eggs and insects as well as herbs and medicines. You depend on the branches of the trees for use as fuel for cooking and heating. You villagers know just how to cut the limbs so that it doesn't hurt the rest of the tree. You know your very survival depends on the well-being of this forest, land, air and water.

Your ancestors never paid for this land. It was always believed that the forest belonged to the Earth --- trees, land water and animals could not be owned by human beings. Every part of the forest is sacred to your people --- every shining leaf, shady mist, humming insect and proud tree. From the beginning the villagers created and followed rules that protect every inch of the forest.

Twenty years ago your government suddenly declared this forest a "national reserve" which means that it no longer belongs to the Earth but to the government. If the government tries to force you villagers off this land you will refuse to leave.

The forest has become more crowded in recent years as people from other parts of the country have been forced to leave their homes and move to your area. They have told you stories of how their own forests were destroyed by the government and logging companies in order to provide land for golf courses and hotels to attract wealthy tourists and business people from far away. The evicted villagers were told to go to **your** forest to find food, build homes and raise their families. You wonder if this was part of the government's plan to make the villagers fight with each other instead of against the government. These poor settlers have had to start all over again. Many have built shacks on the hillside and are among the poorest of the poor.

You are opposed to development projects that force people from their land. If people from other countries want golf courses, resorts and cash-crops, why don't they produce them in their own countries instead of yours? People who know nothing about you, your forest, your culture or your needs are taking over your land and leaving thousands of your people homeless.

Your government would like to use your country's natural resources to earn money to build roads, bridges, power plants and communications systems. You know these "improvements" only benefit local and foreign businesses and wealthier landowners --- not hungry villagers who need food, shelter, clean water and health care. You want the government to know that you villagers are not against development; but you demand that your rights be respected. You want to be included in deciding what kind of development is best for **you and other villagers**. You insist on maintaining control over your ancestral land and forest.

QUESTIONS TO HELP YOU GET INTO CHARACTER:

1. What does this forest mean to you?
2. How do you feel about the development projects in your country?
3. What kind of development would help local villagers?

GROUP #3 - ROLE SHEET

GOVERNMENT OFFICIALS

You are a high-ranking government official in this small country. You and your family are lucky enough to live a comfortable life. It is your job to oversee industrial and agricultural development projects in your country. You believe these projects --- building roads, factories, hotels and airports --- will attract more business people and tourists to your country. You hope that one day your country will become one of the powerful industrial nations like the United States and there will be no poverty here. Life will be so much better then.

You are very good at your job. One of the projects you managed was the construction of a large shrimp factory and highway in what was once a shantytown on the edge of a forest. The people of this poor area were moved to another part of the country and their shantytown and forest were bulldozed clean. A shiny new factory with the latest technology and machinery was built where today tons of shrimp caught off the coast are cleaned, packaged and shipped to markets in Europe. You were proud to have participated in turning a deteriorated area into a money-earning business for your country! This project created jobs and the sale of the shrimp brings much needed money to your poor country --- which can be used to build hospitals, factories, roads and schools. Projects such as this are going to modernize your country and make life better and easier here.

Sometimes you have to deal with these wacky environmentalists and local villagers who know nothing about development. They do not understand that cash-crops and factories are going to make your country powerful and wealthy. They would like to keep the country primitive and unproductive. They think **they** own the forests, land, air and water! Well, these precious resources do not belong to villagers or environmentalists. They are a national reserve under the protection of the national government. Development projects involving the country's resources are legal. You have met with important people from industrial countries --- experts --- who know all about the best way to turn these resources into money. You will try to educate the villagers. When they refuse to recognize the authority of the government, they leave you no alternative but to use the military to force them off government-owned property. They must respect the law. Ignorant villagers cannot be allowed to run the country. Your job would be so much easier if these villagers understood that everyone must work together and sacrifice for the good of the entire country. They will thank you in the future when they see the new kind of country you are trying to create for them.

QUESTIONS TO HELP YOU GET INTO CHARACTER:

1. How do you earn a living?

2. What changes would you like to see take place in your country?

3 How do your feel about villagers who refuse to give up control of local resources such as forest land?

GROUP #4 - ROLE SHEET

ENVIRONMENTALISTS

You are worried and angry. For many years you have studied the environments of other small countries which are just beginning to "develop". You have watched as miles of forests are chopped down to make room for highways, cashcrop plantations and factories. You have felt the clean air become polluted from factories and automobile fumes, and the fertile land become weak and poisoned from chemical fertilizers and pesticides.

You have committed your life to educating people about the importance of trees. Trees bind the soil together. When large areas of forest are cleared away, the land becomes prone to erosion --- there are no roots to hold the soil together and the top-soil is blown away or washed off by heavy rains. In some small countries you have even seen flooding so severe that thousands of people were driven from their land. Trees could have prevented this flooding but they were all cut down to provide land for growing cash-crops.

Trees are also important because they hold moisture in the air and release it slowly. In countries where forests have been cleared away you have noticed that less rain falls today. Large regions of these countries are becoming extremely dry.

More and more you are seeing the governments of these countries tear down their natural forests in order to plant eucalyptus trees that can be used for making computer paper. Now that computers are so popular you suspect more and more eucalyptus trees will be planted. This worries you. Eucalyptus trees grow very quickly--- this is why paper companies like them. Because they grow so quickly, they use up much of the soil's nutrients and water. Their greedy roots rob nearby plants of nutrients and water --- no other plants can survive near a eucalyptus tree. To replenish the soil requires large inputs of expensive chemical fertilizer. The leaves of the eucalyptus tree make many animals sick.

You know that when people destroy natural resources such as forests, land and water, they are destroying themselves. You will continue to advise governments to protect and respect their environments and resources because they keep people, animals, and the world alive and healthy.

QUESTIONS TO HELP YOU GET INTO CHARACTER:

1. Why have you committed your life to protecting the environment?

2. Why are trees so important?

3. **How** should governments protect the world's resources?

GROUP #5 - ROLE SHEET

LOGGERS

You are a logger in this small country. It is your job to cut down or bulldoze trees and transport them to companies who sell the lumber or use it to build homes, furniture or turn it into paper. Sometimes the government hires you to help clear away wild forests so that the land can be used to farm or build on. You think this is a good idea because it provides jobs for people like you and cash-crops grown on the new land can be sold in markets around the world and bring your country more money.

Logging is your only source of income. You depend on it to provide food, clothing and shelter for your family. A few years ago there was a ban on logging --- all these crazy environmentalists were upset about losing too many trees. Can you believe it! You were out of a job, your family was hungry and the environmentalists were worried about the trees! You borrowed money from your relatives to get by while you searched for another job but none could be found. Now the government has begun many development projects that require clearing the forests and using the land to build highways and factories. You are thrilled to be working again. You work hard for your pay. Someday you hope to buy some land for your family and build a house on it.

Of course, you love the forests --- but there are so many of them and they take up valuable land that could be used by businesses to earn money and provide jobs for people. The forests aren't earning any money just standing there! Your country needs to invest in projects that will help make people's lives better. There are so many poor people in your country --- these environmentalists should worry more about **people** than trees!

Another thing --- trees are useful. They give us building materials for homes and they provide fuel. They can always be replanted. Come on! The earth will never run out of trees! You want to tell villagers to use trees wisely --- sell them, plant more and sell more. Use the money to build up your country. You have heard about industrial countries where everyone drives a car, has a TV, even a computer! You would love to have these things too! You would like to see your country "modernize". You are tired of being viewed by the rest of the world as poor and backward.

QUESTIONS TO HELP YOU GET INTO CHARACTER:

1. Do you like working as a logger? Why?

2. How do you feel about the trees you cut down?

3. What kinds of changes would you like to see take place in your country?

GROUP #6 - ROLE SHEET

TREES AND CREATURES OF THE FOREST

The forest has been home to your species forever. You trees have stood side-by-side, proud, majestic and peaceful for centuries. You are lime, mango, jackfruit, taad and tamarind and thousands of others. You provide food for animals and humans, building materials and shade. Your roots nourish and bind the soil of the forest out of which grow the millions of other species of plants used by animals and humans for food and medicine. You share a special kinship with local villagers. When they take your limbs for fuel or fruit or leaves for food they are gentle. You feel their respect. They have always protected you, in turn you care for them.

One of the ways you keep the planet in balance is by cleaning the surrounding air. Lately you have noticed that the air is drier and dirtier. The wind has whispered to you that huge man-made machines and fires are destroying your kind by the thousands. The villagers? Your limbs and leaves shiver at this news. You are afraid.

You creatures of the forest --- sloths, anteaters, blue morpho butterflies, toucans, macaws, jaguars and monkeys share this cool, green home. You all depend on the trees and plants for building your homes and providing food. Each of you performs a life task, no matter how small, that keeps the Earth healthy and in balance and adds to its glorious beauty and richness.

QUESTIONS TO HELP YOU GET INTO CHARACTER:

1. What kind of tree or creature are you?

2. How do you contribute to the health of the surrounding region? Be specific.

3. What is your idea of a peaceful, healthy world?

4. How do you feel about the villagers? loggers? environmentalists?

LESSON 12: IS U.S. FOREIGN AID HELPING END HUNGER?

Students analyze the different packages that make up U.S. Foreign Aid: FOOD AID, DEVELOPMENT AID, ECONOMIC AID, and MILITARY AID. They speculate on which areas of the world need each 'package." By comparing a list of the top ten POOREST countries in 2007 with a list of the top ten U.S. foreign aid RECIPIENTS in 2007, students discover that politics plays more of a role than poverty and hunger in determining who receives aid. They examine two graphs to discover that even though the U.S. gives the MOST money to help poor countries, several smaller countries give a far larger share of their gross domestic product.

PROCEDURE:

1. Ask students for a definition of "foreign aid." What might that aid consist of? Explain that our foreign aid is divided into different "packages:"

   A. **FOOD AND HUMANITARIAN AID** – This includes sacks of wheat and maize for starving refugees and victims of natural and human-made disasters such as earthquakes and famine. It also includes food for the victims of on-going crises.

   B. **DEVELOPMENT AID** – This is aid designed to reduce poverty and to encourage economic growth in low-income countries. It comes in different forms. Sometimes development means loans to help a country start a health program to immunize children against disease or a loan program to help farmers improve their food-growing methods so they can grow more crops. Most often, however, development means building cash-crop farms, power-plants, highways, bridges, mines and factories-- the benefits of which most often go to enrich the large landowners and the donor country instead of the local needy people. Needy people are often exploited by this kind of development which drives them off their land and pollutes and damages their environment. In many cases development aid means using money to create investment opportunities for U.S. businesses or using cheap labor in developing countries to provide cheap goods for U.S. citizens.

   C. **ECONOMIC AID** – Often economic aid is loaned to poor countries only if they promise to use it to buy U.S. products even if they can get those same products somewhere else for less money.

   D. **MILITARY AID** – This is help in the form of guns, tanks, missiles, ammunition, and military advisors. This kind of aid often increases fighting in war zones.

   Using the day's newspaper ask students to brainstorm different countries that may receive the different kinds of aid.

QUESTIONS FOR DISCUSSION:

1. Do wealthy nations have an obligation to provide aid to poor nations? Why or why not?

2. Does it matter what a donor nation's motives are when they provide aid? Why or why not?

3. Most of U.S. Foreign Aid comes in the form of military and development aid. Who benefits most from this type of aid?

4. If you lived in a severely impoverished region which type of aid package would you prefer?

5. What should be the purpose of foreign aid? How would you divide the money?

6. How could U.S. aid be used to help people become self-reliant?

WHO GETS THE MONEY? Ask students to speculate on who receives most of the aid from the U.S. They may be surprised by the charts below. (To review the Child Mortality Rate see Lesson 4.)

TOP RECIPIENTS OF U.S. FOREIGN AID IN 2007:	Child Mortality Rates CMR	TOP TEN NEEDIEST COUNTRIES IN 2007:	Child Mortality Rates CMR
Israel	5	Sierra Leone	262
Egypt	36	Afghanistan	257
Afghanistan	257	Chad	209
Pakistan	90	Equatorial Guinea	206
Columbia	20	Guinea-Bissau	198
Sudan	109	Mali	196
Ethiopia	119	Burkina Faso	191
Jordan	24	Nigeria	189
Kenya	121	Rwanda	181
South Africa	59	Burundi	180

(Sources: UNICEF – the State Of The World's Children, 2009
US AID – FY 2009 International Affairs)

1. Were any of the world's neediest countries among the top ten recipients of U.S. aid in 2007?

2. What reasons can students think of for why the U.S. would send most of its help to countries that are not among the neediest? Have small groups of students research each country to find out why it receives U.S. aid.

The following reasons will help clarify.

U.S. Aid may be given:

- **to strengthen a military ally**
- **to reward a government for behavior we desire**
- **to provide building projects needed by the U.S. to use a developing country's resources**
- **to influence the politics of a country**
- **to help eradicate HIV/AIDS**
- **to stop the production of illegal drugs**

When students have presented their findings have them consider the following: **Is U.S. Foreign Aid helping end hunger?**

WHO GIVES THE MOST MONEY TO HELP DEVELOPING COUNTRIES?

Show students the charts on the following page. The top chart shows that when compared with 21 other donor countries the U.S. donated the most toward development in 2007. The bottom chart shows that when the Gross National Incomes (GNI) of all the donor countries are compared the U.S. comes in last.

Ask students to examine the charts to determine which countries are giving a fair share to poorer countries.

Net Official Development Assistance (ODA) in 2007

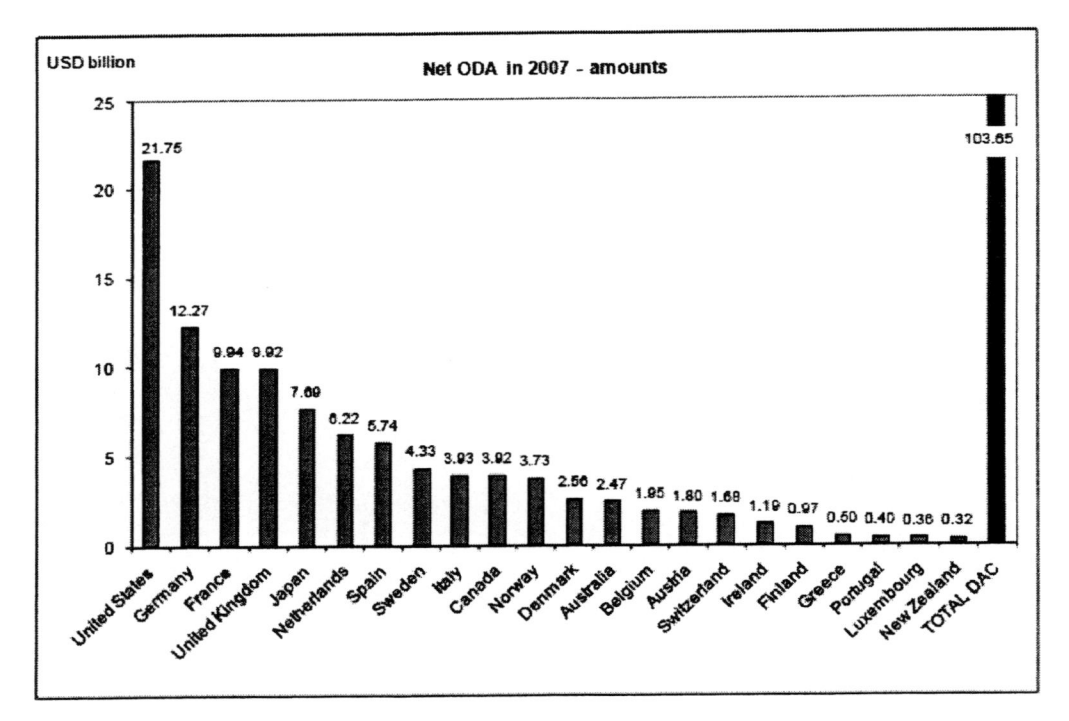

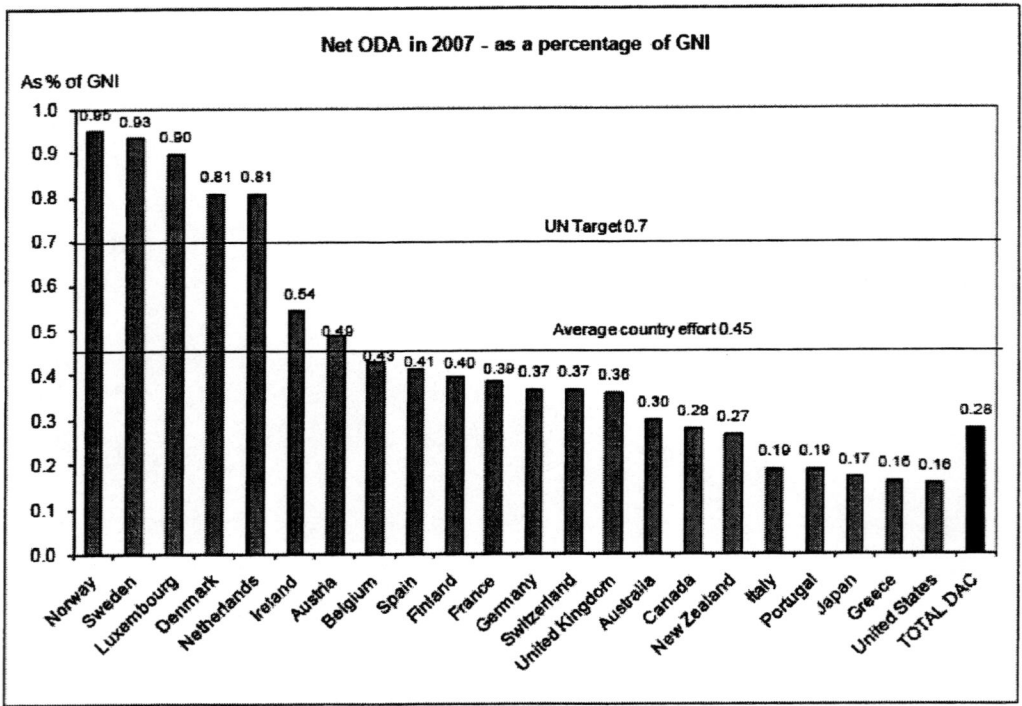

Net ODA in 2007 – amounts (USD billion)

Country	USD billion
United States	21.75
Germany	12.27
France	9.94
United Kingdom	9.92
Japan	7.69
Netherlands	6.22
Spain	5.74
Sweden	4.33
Italy	3.93
Canada	3.92
Norway	3.73
Denmark	2.56
Australia	2.47
Belgium	1.95
Austria	1.80
Switzerland	1.68
Ireland	1.19
Finland	0.97
Greece	0.50
Portugal	0.40
Luxembourg	0.36
New Zealand	0.32
TOTAL DAC	103.65

Net ODA in 2007 – as a percentage of GNI

Country	As % of GNI
Norway	0.95
Sweden	0.93
Luxembourg	0.90
Denmark	0.81
Netherlands	0.81
Ireland	0.54
Austria	0.49
Belgium	0.43
Spain	0.41
Finland	0.40
France	0.39
Germany	0.37
Switzerland	0.37
United Kingdom	0.36
Australia	0.30
Canada	0.28
New Zealand	0.27
Italy	0.19
Portugal	0.19
Japan	0.17
Greece	0.16
United States	0.16
TOTAL DAC	0.28

UN Target 0.7
Average country effort 0.45

(Source: The Organization for Economic Cooperation and Development, 2008.)

ADDITIONAL ACTIVITY

1. Bill Ayres, co-founder of World Hunger Year, uses a version of the following role play to help students understand how "aid" can sometimes hurt hungry people instead of help.

   MATERIALS: One large container of water

   Close the door. Tell students to move their desks to the far end of the room as closely together as possible. Explain that you own most of the land in this village. They have very small plots of land that is dry and weak. They must walk to a polluted river several miles away to get water for their few crops every couple of days. Their families are hungry, there is never enough food.

   A U.S. aid agency has offered to help build a well in your village so clean water is more accessible. Since you own most of the land in the village and are the most powerful person in the village, you have convinced the U.S. agents that the well should be built on your land.

   (Place the container of water on a chair on your property. This is the well.)

   Now that the well is completed and the Americans have left, you tell the rest of the villagers that because the well is on **your** land and because you helped pay for some of the construction of the well, the rest of the villagers must pay you for any water they receive from your well. How will they pay? If they can't pay you, offer to buy their land from them and rent it back to them. Is anyone willing to sell? If they refuse to sell their land, you refuse to give them any water. What can they do? Appoint two students to serve as your "police" to guard the well so that no one takes water without paying.

   Remind students that their families are hungry and thirsty. If students agree to sell their land to you, they must get out of their desks and stand against the wall. You now own their plot of land. Your landholdings are getting bigger. You grow cash-crops such as coffee and sugar on your land and earn lots of money from the sale of these to other countries. Because you have the money you can afford fertilizer which regenerates the weak plots of land the villagers sell to you. (Stop the game when the majority of students have sold their land or have found a way to take control of the well.)

   1. Did this aid make their lives better or more difficult?

   2. What could have been done differently to insure that everyone benefits from the well?

2. In September 2000 world leaders came together at the U.N. in New York to adopt the **UNITED NATIONS MILLENIUM GOALS** committing their nations to a new global partnership to reduce extreme poverty and setting out a series of goals with a deadline of 2015. Have students research these eight goals at **www.un.org/millenniumgoals**. They should also research the progress that has been made toward these goals. (The website also contains a 4 minute video called "Make It Happen.")

3. Create a WALL OF HOPE with images, news stories, ideas that inspire and remind us of the possibilities to be achieved with aid. There are many success stories for students to research. Go to the websites for Oxfam America, CARE, and The Peace Corps.

4. Often the U.S. provides military aid to regions (such as the Middle East and Central America) where it has concerns related to national security. How could feeding and teaching the needy help strengthen national and global security?

5. One of the root causes of poverty lies in the powerful and rich nations having formulated most of the trade and aid policies which have more to do with maintaining dependency on industrialized nations by providing sources of cheap labor and cheaper goods for citizens back home and increasing personal wealth and maintaining power over others. Have students bring in objects found around their homes that were made in other countries. Check labels—these might include clothing, sneakers, baseballs, dolls, etc. Each student should research the history of their item and report to the class. Together discuss how cheap labor exploits people in poorer countries and the effects of this on people in both that country as well as the U.S.

LESSON 13
THE IMPORTANCE OF FEMALE EDUCATION

Students experience firsthand what happens when boys receive preferential treatment over girls. This leads to a class discussion on (1) **why** many societies prefer sons to daughters and (2) the consequences of the discrimination on girls' self-esteem and opportunities as well as boys' attitudes and behavior toward girls. Students hear some personal stories of what it is like to be female in a country with a long tradition of gender-discrimination. They learn that worldwide females receive less nurture, food, education, health care and fewer opportunities to develop job skills, own land and receive financial credit than males. Students analyze current research which shows that educating women has dramatic effects on lowering poverty and hunger - educated girls and women are more likely to have fewer and healthier children and are more likely to immunize their children against disease. Developing knowledge and skills allows women to work outside the home, to pass on what they learn to their children and to become more active in shaping policies that affect their communities.

Teacher Background Reading[*]

A 1993 study conducted by UNICEF found that infant and toddler girls in many countries receive less nutritious food, fewer visits to health centers, lower rates of vaccination and less nurture than boys. Cultural attitudes stressing the value of sons over daughters were primarily responsible. In Asia, Africa and Latin America preference for sons has resulted in physical, emotional and intellectual neglect of girl children. In China it is estimated that the One Child Policy has resulted in the deaths of more than one million first-born girl infants. In many societies the social pressure on women to give birth to a boy child is intense. Failure to do so can result in violence or become grounds for desertion or divorce.

In most societies sons carry on the lineage and the family name, prestige and possessions and perform religious rituals and burial rites. This discrimination against girls is not merely a casual whim but the result of a complicated combination of cultural and social attitudes and economic circumstances. Many parents see little or no value in investing in girls' education, instead they invest time and money to educate their sons who will support them when they are too old to work. Daughters are viewed as household labor who, once married, will become part of the labor force of another household. Discrimination against women in the labor market and in salaries reinforces parents' negative attitudes towards educating girls. Religious traditions also restrict women's activities to domestic tasks.

---

[*] Adapted with permission from *Girls and Women: A UNICEF Development Priority*, United Nations. 1993.

"Nurture discrimination" against females begins with the lack of enthusiasm that greets a girl baby, her mother's early abandonment of breast feeding as she attempts another pregnancy hoping for a son, the infant girl's extra susceptibility to diarrhea and respiratory infection, lack of food and clothing. In the developing countries studied by UNICEF --- Bangladesh, India, Nepal and Pakistan --- girls were consistently discriminated against when it came to parenting and health services. Compared to boys, girls carried an extra household workload and had little access to schooling (sometimes none).

In many African and Asian families it is common for men and boys to eat first at meal times and to consume the best food. This leads to higher rates of malnutrition and disease among girls. By the age of 19 as many as 60% to 70% of girls in Africa and Asia reach marriage lacking the education and training that could provide them with the knowledge and skills to develop healthy bodies and minds, to raise healthy children, to run a household and to perform a job for pay. They also reach marriage with bodies that are inadequately developed for pregnancy and birth. (Every year 585,000 women die from causes related to pregnancy and childbirth --- one quarter of them are teenagers.) Their female children will repeat this same cycle.

Half the world's food supply is cultivated by women --- in Africa, two-thirds. Men are most often in charge of tending livestock which often represent a family's economic reserves. In parts of the developing world where men grow food crops for cash, girls and women are expected to provide **all** their family's food from a plot of land set aside for this purpose. (Women very rarely own the land they cultivate.) Girls and women plant, weed, harvest and winnow. They process the grains, pounding, grinding, sieving, crushing, pulping and drying berries in the sun. Girls and women grow the family's grains, fruits and vegetables. They tend poultry, collect firewood, and must often walk long distances for the family's water. (In addition to these daily chores, they must also feed and care for their many children, cook the family's meals, clean their houses and wash the family's clothes. This lack of discretionary time means they often miss meals, are chronically exhausted, and suffer poor nutrition and disease.) Results of a study made by the Women's Programme of the International Council for Adult Education concluded that the daily activities of women in Africa, Latin America and Asia began on average between four and six in the morning and ended between ten and eleven at night.

In rural areas where women are secluded they trade or sell surplus food from their plots in nearby markets. This money is used to purchase household necessities such as matches, paraffin, cooking oil, salt and medicines. When food becomes scarce in a region, men migrate to other areas - usually cities - to find work in factories, leaving the women behind alone to provide for themselves and their children. In Bangladesh girls begin working as maids for urban employers at the age of six or seven. They work around the clock, usually living in a corner of the kitchen and eating scraps.

In both developing and industrialized countries sickness, hunger, poverty, unemployment, lack of education and lack of access to credit are compounded simply by the fact of being female. In order that women not become trapped in a downward spiral and pass on the same disadvantages to their children (particularly girl children), major changes in policies and attitudes are urgently required.

EDUCATED WOMEN:

- **have fewer children.**
- **understand their own as well as their children's health and nutritional needs.**
- **are more likely to have their children immunized against disease.**
- **develop skills that are valued outside the home.**
- **are more active in shaping government policy in their communities.**

Development programs have been initiated worldwide to encourage governments to change policies that discriminate against women and to make education, health care, credit, job training and jobs available to all women.

PROTECTING WOMEN'S RIGHTS HELPS END HUNGER AND POVERTY.

PROCEDURE:

1. During the day before this lesson show strong favoritism toward the boys in the class (call on them more often, compliment them, give them special privileges, exempt them from certain assignments and responsibilities, etc.) When the girls protest call the class together for a discussion.

    1. How did it feel to be discriminated against for being a girl? Did any of the girls protest?

    2. What might happen if the girls were discriminated against on all levels of society: family, school, workplaces, etc. over the course of their entire lives?

    3. How did the boys feel when they received special treatment? Did any of them speak up in support of the girls? Why or why not?

    4. What would happen to the girl's self-esteem, confidence and opportunities in life if this gender-discrimination continued?

    5. What would happen to the boys' attitudes and behavior toward girls if this treatment continued?

6. Many countries have long histories of discrimination against females. Are females discriminated against in the United States? In what ways? (Students can interview women in their families and communities for their opinions.)

7. Many societies prefer sons to daughters. Why do you think this is the case? Are the reasons fair? Or are they the result of sexist cultural, social or economic practices that can be changed so that men and women are treated fairly? (Use the Teacher Background Information to help students understand the consequences of this discrimination on girls' and women's' lives -- less food, health services, education, nurture, etc.)

2. Read the following accounts of gender-discrimination.
Ask the students to take notes on **why** boys are favored over girls in these stories and what some of the consequences of this discrimination are on the girls.

1. From ***The Price of a Dream*** by David Bornstein, Simon & Schuster, New York, 1996. Pages 137-140:

"(In Bangladesh) news of the birth of a baby girl is often received by a family like news of a debt incurred. For months before his child is born, a father may pray five times a day for a son. A son brings prosperity and security. He is an asset. He can work the land or try his hand as a trader, a shop-keeper, or a carpenter. He can travel to Dhaka to look for work, and if he finds it, send money home. When he matures, he will bring a wife into the household, and if he is a dutiful son, he will care for his parents as they grow old, protecting their land and ensuring for them honorable burials when they die.

A daughter earns nothing. She may care for the children, cook, tend animals, carry jugs of water hundreds of yards each day, and do countless jobs in and around the homestead, but her work is assigned little value. Not only is she underprized for her work, she is viewed as a liability. Sometimes as a catastrophe. Ultimately, she will cost her parents a great deal. The cause is dowry. From the day his daughter is born, a father is obsessed with one event: her marriage. Even the poorest villagers in Bangladesh must provide substantial dowries of furniture, clothing, and gold jewelry. A wealthier villager may offer a TV, a refrigerator, or a motorcycle to lure a promising bachelor. Dowry can cripple a poor family. A poor father may marry his daughter to a man who already has one or more wives...or he may resort to a moneylender. To not marry off a daughter is an unthinkable disgrace.

Sons are typically better nourished--they eat first at meals and receive larger portions than daughters--and they are more likely to be given medicine by their parents or taken to a doctor when ill."

2. From ***Bound Feet & Western Dress*** by Pang-Mei Natasha Chang, Doubleday, New York, 1996. Pages 6-12:

(The author's great aunt tells the story of growing up female in China.)

"Before I tell you my story, I want you to remember this: in China, a woman is nothing. When she is born, she must obey her father. When she is married, she must obey her husband. And when she is widowed, she must obey her son. A woman is nothing, you see...There were twelve children in my family--eight boys and four girls--but my mama always told people she had eight children because only the sons counted. Sons would carry forth the family name, while daughters would marry and take on the duties of their husbands' families.

When a boy was born to the house, the servants saved his umbilical cord in a jar under Mama's bed. When a girl was born, the servants buried her umbilical cord outside the house. A girl left her father's house as soon as she came of age.

You must understand how I had to act in front of Baba (father). It was very formal...I never entered Baba's presence unless asked, and I never left it without his telling me I could. Unless he spoke to me first, I did not speak in his presence...I never addressed my father by "you". I never said to him, for instance, 'Would you like another cup of tea?', I had to say, 'Baba, would Baba like another cup of tea?'. Most of the time, though, I never even asked Baba about refilling his tea cup, I just did it.

It was the custom when I was little for a woman to have tiny, tiny feet. Westerners call them bound feet, but we call them something so much prettier in China: new moon or lotus petals...When I was three, my amah (nanny) instructed me to eat an entire glutinous rice dumpling by myself. She said it would help to soften me, but I did not know what she meant until the next morning. Mama and my amah arrived at my bedside with a basin of warm water and strips of heavy white cotton. They soaked my feet in the water then proceeded to bind them with the thick wet bandages. When the bandages completed their first tight wraps around my feet, I saw red in front of my eyes and could not breathe. It felt as if my feet had shrunk into tiny insects. I began shrieking with pain, I thought I would die. Mama said I would grow used to it, that there was nothing she could do.

For three days I sat before my amah and Mama, enduring the ritual: the removal of bloody bandages, the soaking, the rewrapping and tightening. But on the fourth morning something miraculous happened. Second Brother, who could no longer bear my screams, told Mama to stop hurting me. Second Brother said that foot binding was a custom that was no longer beautiful. Mama asked Second Brother who would marry me if she let my feet alone. Second Brother then said: 'I will take care of her if no one marries her.' Second Brother was only fifteen at the time, but he had been raised to be true to his word, and Mama relented...From that day forth I never had my feet bound again."

*(Up until ninety years ago young girls' feet were bound this way in China to meet unrealistic standards of physical beauty imposed by their culture. Does **our** culture impose unrealistic and harmful standards of beauty on females?)*

QUESTIONS

1. Current research has shown that educating girls and women is one sure way to reduce hunger and poverty. How would an education benefit the girls in the above stories?

2. What **kind** of education would best benefit girls in developing countries? (learning about their rights, health and nutrition, child care, family planning, history and culture, reading and writing, math, cooking, agriculture, fishing, civic education, job skills, etc.)

3. Some of the other benefits of female education can be found in the graphs and charts on the following page. What do these graphs tell us about the importance of female education?

HANDOUT

FEMALE EDUCATION AROUND THE WORLD*

	School Life Expectancy (Ave. Years of Schooling)	CHILD
COUNTRIES	FEMALE RATES*	MORTALITY**
AFGHANISTAN	4.0	257
MOZAMBIQUE	7.0	168
ETHIOPIA	7.0	119
BANGLADESH	8.0	61
INDIA	9.9	72
CHINA	11.0	22
PERU	14.0	20
ISRAEL	16.0	5
FRANCE	17.0	4
USA	16.0	8

* Source: *UNESCO Institute for Statistics, June 2009*
** Source: *State of the World's Children*, UNICEF, 2009.

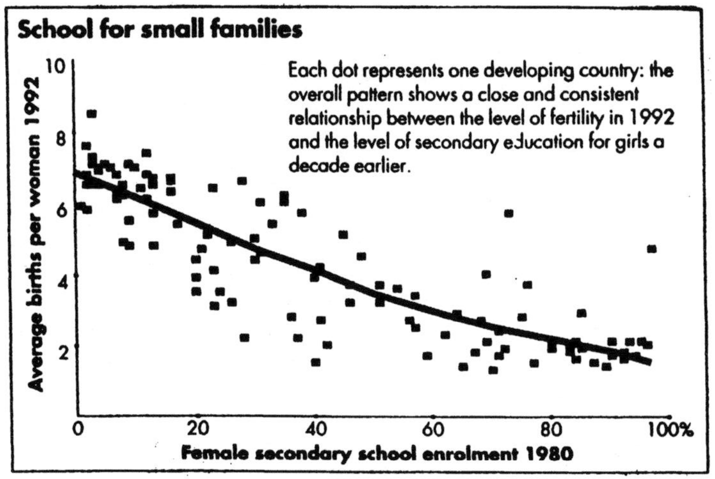

School for small families

Each dot represents one developing country: the overall pattern shows a close and consistent relationship between the level of fertility in 1992 and the level of secondary education for girls a decade earlier.

(Average births per woman 1992 vs. Female secondary school enrolment 1980)

Source: Total fertility rate: United Nations Population Division, *World population prospects: the 1992 revision*, 1993. Education; UNESCO, *Statistical yearbooks*, 1993 and earlier years.

What happens to infant mortality rates as female education increases?

Why do educated girls and women have healthier children?

Why do educated girls and women have fewer babies?

How can educating females help end poverty and hunger?

How can educating females help improve communities?

WOMEN AND POVERTY

Women are more than one-half of the world's population
and
work two-thirds of the world's working hours
yet
they own one-tenth of the world's wealth
and
one-hundredth of the world's land
and
are two-thirds of the world's illiterate people
and
more than three-fourths of the world's starving people are women
and their dependent children

Why is it important that women and men gain literacy skills?
- to read newspapers
- to read labels on food products
- to read medical directions
- to read maps, bus & train schedules, and road signs
- to help children with homework
- to read contracts, insurance forms, etc.
- to read warning labels on poisons and pesticides
- to read letters from family, friends, school -
    and to write a response
- to keep their own accounts
- to read menus
- to read telephone directories
- to get a job requiring reading and writing

Have students work in small groups to create their own lists of reasons why it is important to learn to read and write. Then compare their lists with the list above.

ADDITIONAL ACTIVITIES:

1. In many developing countries girls must stay home from school to work in the family's fields growing crops or caring for smaller children while their brothers attend school. Write a letter to the parents of such a girl convincing them that education is just as important for their daughter. (Letters can be written in journals.)

2. The South Asian Association for Regional Cooperation has called the 1990's *The Decade of the Girl Child.* With UNICEF's assistance South Asian countries are making educational programs a priority for girls. Create posters explaining the importance of The Decade of the Girl Child and why it is necessary to draw attention to the social position of females in many societies. Display these around your school.

3. Have students interview mothers and grandmothers or other women in the community about their educational history and views on the treatment of women in the U.S.

4. Have students share or write about their own experiences with gender discrimination. (You can initiate this discussion by giving an example from your own experience.)

5. Watch and discuss the video *Meena* (1992). This is an animated video by UNICEF depicting the life of a young Indian girl and how she is discouraged from pursuing education. The story explores traditional cultural values that often emphasize the educational advancement of young males and suppress the educational development of young females. (For elementary age students.) 14 minutes. To order refer to Resource Guide.

6. Watch and discuss *The Flame*, a video about how WILD (Women in Livestock Development Program) is helping impoverished women worldwide care for themselves and their families. (See Resource Guide - VIDEOS)

7. Watch and discuss *With These Hands*, a video from Church World Service which focuses on the lack of support for Africa's women farmers. Three women's stories reveal the major role women play in producing much of the world's food, the obstacles they face and what can be done to change their lives and their children's lives. (See VIDEOS).

MAKE A DIFFERENCE!

In many countries governments do not spend enough money on education. Often there is only one school to serve many different villages. Students must walk long distances to reach their classrooms. Because girls are usually not allowed to walk alone, they are kept home to care for younger siblings, work the fields, or perform other domestic tasks.

Today, however, many organizations are designing special programs especially for girls and women near their homes. Some of these organizations include UNICEF, women's labor unions, the YMCA and even the Girl Scouts.

One very successful program in India set up small classrooms in several villages far from the major school. Because they don't have to walk long distances these girls and women spend their mornings learning reading, writing and math, and can still spend several hours performing their usual chores at home. The program also set up child care centers near the classrooms to take care of small children while their sisters and mothers study. The program didn't stop there. The girls and women also learn skills that will help them earn money to support their families and themselves. For instance, some are learning to make soap, do silk-painting, and even secure a loan to start a business of their own. Some of the girls and women who have graduated from this program have gone on to become teachers who actively promote education for females.

These organizations are working hard to make their governments aware of the importance of education for **all**. Some have set up centers where men and women learn about sharing domestic tasks such as child care, food preparation and cleaning. The most successful of these programs have proven that families and communities are healthier when women are allowed access to education, jobs and credit.

LESSON 14: HUNGER HURTS US ALL

This lesson focuses on the social, environmental and moral consequences of hunger on everyone --- including people who are not chronically hungry. First, students create a universal declaration of human rights, then they explore how the violation of those fundamental rights affects the rest of the community and the world.

MATERIALS: Handouts: *We Are The World* (one for each student)

Optional: (but highly recommended)
The Universal Declaration of Human Rights by Ruth Rocha and Octavio Roth, United Nations Publications, The United Nations. (This is an adaptation for children that is clear and short enough to be read aloud and discussed. Every classroom should have one!)

PROCEDURE:

1. In large or small groups have students brainstorm fundamental human rights. (Have them reflect on their **own** basic needs.) Make a list of the rights to which **all** human beings are entitled. Should everyone have access to food? Clean water? A safe home? A good education? A job? An adequate wage? Medical care? Why or why not? (Do children have special rights?)

2. Sitting in a large circle, read *The Universal Declaration of Human Rights*. Add any of these rights to your list.

3. How many people around the world actually have access to some of those basic necessities? Hand out *We Are The World*.

4. Go over the list together. What do students think? (Be sure students understand that the comparisons made in your classroom are based on **real** percentages in the larger world.)

5. To begin your discussion of how the lack of access to basic necessities affects everyone choose a fact from the handout. As you read it aloud, ask the appropriate number of students to sit **outside** the circle. Have students discuss ways in which the rest of the class might be affected. For example, if your class represented the world, 21 students would not know how to read. 21 students must sit outside the circle. How would the entire class be affected if 21 of them could not read? How is our world affected when 70% of us cannot read?

6. **DISCUSSION QUESTIONS:**

    1. Should we care about ending hunger? Why?
    2. Are we responsible for making sure other people's rights are respected and protected? Why or why not?
    3. How can the world insure that everyone's rights are protected?
    4. Do the consequences of hunger affect even people who aren't hungry? (Some ways in which widespread chronic hunger affects the world are: forced migration, violence, environmental destruction, and a breakdown of the supports --- trust, respect, caring, a shared sense of morality, etc. --- that hold societies together.)
    5. Would hunger and poverty exist in a true democracy?

ADDITIONAL ACTIVITY:

1. Have students write in journals on how chronic hunger breaks down families. What are the effects of this breakdown on the rest of the community?

MAKE A DIFFERENCE!

Examine your lifestyle! Making a real commitment to ending hunger includes assessing the way we and our families and community members use limited resources. There are practical, everyday ways in which each of us can conserve precious resources. Brainstorm a list of what these might include. Some ideas are:

1. Be frugal. Prevent waste by taking only what you need (food, water, paper, etc.)

2. Turn off lights and water when not immediately needed.

3. Recycle and repair. Reusable items such as cloth towels, napkins and bags save valuable energy and resources. Take time to repair broken items instead of buying new ones.

4. Use public transportation whenever possible. Bicycle, walk or carpool.

5. Eat **local** whole foods (fruits, vegetables, grains, legumes, etc.) Besides being more nutritious, whole foods save resources. Processing foods (juice drinks, cheese spread, luncheon meats, frozen dinners, potato chips, etc.) uses up **lots** of energy and water. Processing robs foods of their nutrients and pollutes the environment. Packaging them also wastes resources. Whole foods require no or minimal packaging.

6. Eat less meat. To produce 1 pound of meat a steer must be fed 16 pounds of grain! Processing that pound of meat requires 2,500 gallons of water! A high demand for meat (mostly by people in industrialized countries) has resulted in over 1/2 the world's grain being fed to livestock.

7. Be a conscientious shopper. Ask your local merchants where their products come from. Support local farmers by buying produce at greenmarkets. Food produced locally is most often fresher and earthfriendly - no valuable resources are wasted or polluted by packaging, refrigerating and transporting food long distances.

8. Clean up vacant lots. Use the space to plant a community garden.

9. Knowledge is also a precious resource! Spread it around! Teach someone to read or how to preserve resources.

10. Speak out! Hold a family or class meeting and decide how everyone can help conserve resources in your house or school. Teach other classes about the unequal distribution of resources and encourage them to prevent waste and overconsumption.

(Students may not think that by doing these simple things they are making a difference in the vast imbalance in the world, but they will be taken more seriously by others in their commitment to end social inequality; they will be setting an example for others; and they will be living more closely to the kind of healthy and just world they are trying to create.)

HANDOUT
WE ARE THE WORLD*

IF THIS CLASS REPRESENTED THE WORLD:

NUMBER OF STUDENTS IN A CLASS OF 30		% WORLDWIDE
11	Would NOT ALWAYS have enough food to remain healthy and strong	36%
9	Would NOT have access to clean and safe water	29%
8	Would NOT know how to read	26%
4	Would NEVER go to school	14%
30	Would NOT go on to college	99%
11	Would be children under age eighteen (Of those eleven who represent the children of the world, 4 (39%) would suffer from stunted growth)	35%
1	Would own or control almost all the land available for growing food	3%
2	Would be Americans and would hold 33% of the world's income, and would use up 40% of all the energy and minerals in the world	6%

* Statistics are from *The State of the World's Children 1997*, UNICEF, Oxford University Press.

LESSON 15: HUNGER USA

Who is hungry in our communities?

Chronic hunger is not always visible. In this exercise students work in teams to shine a light on five different social groups within our communities who are the most vulnerable to hunger. After discussing the reasons behind each group's hunger, the teams teach the rest of the class about their discoveries.

TEAM #1 studies and teaches about a news report on hungry **children**.

TEAM #2 examines and teaches about a news report on hunger among the **elderly**.

TEAM #3 must balance a household budget for a **poor working family** by cutting back on food expenditures in order to cover a medical emergency.

TEAM #4 explores statistics and graphs related to U.S. population and poverty and discusses why **racial and ethnic minorities** are so vulnerable to hunger.

TEAM #5 imagines its way into the life of a **single mother** with three small children and discusses the special difficulties she faces providing enough food for her family.

(Separate lessons in this guide focus on the **homeless** and the **unemployed**.)

NOTE: This can be a one-day lesson or teachers can make this a research project by turning students into detectives. Before each team teaches its lesson, have the students investigate programs in your area which are helping end hunger among a specific social group. Encourage students to advise each other on where to look and who to interview to find out the answers.

MATERIALS: Handouts: **Hunger, USA** Team Sheets
(A different set for each team and enough copies for every student on the team. One group studies children, another the elderly...)

PROCEDURE :

1. Have students brainstorm who is chronically hungry in your community. List answers on the board.

2. Divide students into five teams. Tell them that today they will each investigate a specific social group particularly susceptible to hunger --- then their team will teach the rest of the class what they have learned together.

3. Distribute the handouts. Tell students they are to read their information sheets quietly, then discuss the questions. Each team also discusses a program that is helping end hunger for the group they are representing.

4. After students have had time to discuss their sheets, ask them to decide how they will teach this information to the rest of the class.

5. To close this class, brainstorm ways in which young people can make their community more aware of who is hungry and why.

ADDITIONAL ACTIVITIES:

1. Encourage students to give their presentations to other classes. Before they do it they can research local programs helping to end hunger for each group and supply other classes with phone numbers and addresses of places where they can volunteer --- nursing homes, food pantries, soup kitchens, shelters, day-care centers, etc..

2. To help students explore in greater depth why African-Americans, Latinos and Native Americans are more susceptible to hunger than whites, use materials listed in the Resource Guide to create a unit on **Racism** and **Discrimination**.

   The following activity is from *Open Minds to Equality* by Nancy Schniedewind and Ellen Davidson. Copyright 1983 by Allyn and Bacon. Reprinted by permission. (See Resource Guide)

   This activity gives students a chance to "walk in another person's shoes", and to see that group problem-solving is often more effective than isolated, independent problem solving.

PROCEDURE:

Ask each student to write on a slip of scrap paper a brief answer to the following question: What is one way racism / sexism has affected you personally and how did you handle it? Students should **not** write their names on the paper. Have them fold it in quarters.

Divide students into groups of six. Students within a group put their slips of paper in a container and mix them up. Students draw a slip. No one should get her own slip.

Each student must read her slip quietly and spend a minute thinking about the problem and possible solutions. Each group chooses a first speaker. That person reads aloud to the small group the problem on her slip. She must **own** the problem, reading it as though it is her own, then spend a minute talking about how she is going to deal with her problem. After one minute call "TIME". The group has two minutes to discuss the problem and give their ideas before moving on to the person seated on the first-speaker's right. Continue in this manner until all problems have been discussed.

1. What was it like to hear your problem read by someone else as though it were that person's problem?

2. What was it like to have to talk about a problem as if it were your own, when it wasn't?

3. Did you get any good ideas on your own problem? On other problems?

4. What ideas came up during the two minutes of group discussion that the speaker hadn't thought of? Why do new ideas come up this way?

5. What are some advantages of having your problem be anonymous? Disadvantages?

3. Students can write about, role-play or discuss the following situations:

You are a child who looks forward to eating breakfast at your school each morning because there is so little food in your house. Both your parents work hard, but they aren't paid enough to meet all the monthly payments and buy enough healthy food. You have just learned that some people in your community want the schools to stop serving breakfast so that children like you will eat breakfast at home with your family.

Your family discovers that the elderly couple living next door to you often goes without food because they do not have enough money.

Your best friend never accompanies you and the rest of your friends to movies or the local pizza parlor because his family does not have the money.

4. Watch and discuss the following videos listed in the Resource Guide: *The Face of Hunger in America* and *Hunger in America.*

5. Listen to and discuss one of the following songs related to hunger in the U.S.:

The Banks of Marble
by The Weavers

Brother Can You Spare a Dime
  by Peter, Paul & Mary

In the Ghetto
  by Elvis Presley

6. Read and discuss *The Grapes of Wrath* by John Steinbeck. Listen to and discuss Bruce Springsteen's song the *The Ghost of Tom Joad*.

TEAM #1

HUNGER, USA - CHILDREN

(The following report was adapted from an article in the *Los Angeles Times* on November 20, 1994 called "The Hunger Wars.")

The symptoms have swept through Edgewood Middle School in southern California. By 10 o'clock many mornings there is a long line outside the nurse's door. Some children clutch their stomachs. Others grasp their heads. In this mostly middle-class community, these children share a common ailment. They are hungry.

One boy came into the Assistant Principal's office last year and confessed to stealing food from a 7-Eleven store. "Every night I go to bed hungry," the thirteen year-old told her, bowing his head. "There isn't enough food." The American Dietetic Association estimates that **one in four children comes to class undernourished**.

America's hunger is not the starvation of Somalia or Rwanda that galvanizes the world's attention: bloated bellies, emaciated arms, failing bodies along roadsides. No, hunger here in the U.S. saps people in more subtle ways: families eat only once a day or skip meals for several days, causing chronic malnutrition. There are 12 million hungry children in America whose ability to learn is being crippled. Studies show that hungry students are fatigued. They cannot concentrate. Some cannot lift their heads off their desks for long. Hungry students do worse than well-fed children on tests. Because they are ill twice as often, they miss class more frequently.

"They are dazed," explains one teacher who often dips into her own pocket to buy food for her students. "You can see it in their eyes, their hands tremble. One girl broke down in class last year describing how she had gone all weekend without eating." At another school, Christina, a soft-spoken twelve year-old with freckles, says she got dizzy on the playground and crumpled onto the blacktop. She had had no breakfast that day. Dinner the night before was a potato.

This kind of hunger is found in many U.S. schools. Most of these children suffer because their parents were laid off work or because the parents work long hours and leave their children to fend for themselves in the mornings when the refrigerators are bare. Many parents work at jobs that barely pay them enough to cover their monthly expenses.

One mother explains that the night before her three sons had to split two hot dogs for their dinner. "There are many days I don't have anything for them for breakfast," she says. "I know food is important, but I know we need a roof over our heads more." Most of her income goes to pay her $690 a month rent.

What does hunger do to children?
Why do children in a country rich with food go to school hungry?
Why are children so vulnerable to hunger?

What do hungry children's families need in order to feed themselves and become self-reliant?

MAKING A DIFFERENCE!

Many schools in the U.S. have been serving free breakfasts before school starts every morning to children whose parents do not earn enough money to pay all their bills and buy enough food. Studies show that when schools serve breakfast, these students' test-scores rise, they have more energy, and are absent less often. Hunger activists around the country are working hard to get schools without breakfast programs to sign up. Many states have passed laws that require schools to serve breakfast to hungry children, but some people on school boards in other states have voted against this law. The breakfasts are paid for with taxpayers' money. Some taxpayers, school board members, and principals say children should eat breakfast at home with their families. They insist that it is **not** the school's responsibility to feed hungry children --- it is the parents' responsibility.

What do you think? Should a law be passed in your state requiring schools to serve breakfasts to hungry children?

TEAM #2

HUNGER. USA - THE ELDERLY

(The following report was adapted from an article in *The New York Times*, November 17, 1994 called "*In Fearful Thrift, Elderly Forage in Garbage Bins.*")

A gray-haired man in a blue Yankees cap lifts the lid of a garbage bin next to a supermarket. Peering inside, he pulls out a tray of mushrooms still wrapped in plastic and slips it into a small gym bag. A few minutes later, a man in his 80's walks to another of the three green bins outside the market. He forages through the garbage, using his cane to stir the bottom, and removes a red pepper, some potatoes, an apple and wilted broccoli. While shoppers stroll in front of the bustling supermarket, elderly people go almost unnoticed as they scavenge for food in garbage bins.

They are not homeless, and they are not entirely destitute. They say they are driven to the unappealing, even humiliating, task of searching through the trash by a combination of immediate financial need and a fear of the future. Most of them are retired, and they struggle to get by on limited incomes. Sometimes what they receive each month in Social Security and small pensions simply does not meet their expenses. An unexpected medical bill may leave them short of cash. As many as **one in six elderly Americans is either hungry or has an inadequate diet** according to The Urban Institute, a research organization in Washington. The 87 year-old man said he had seen 20 to 30 different older people picking through the garbage bins there.

"I don't blame the people for doing this," he said. "They just want to have enough to get by. It's not easy for old people. I lost my pride a long time ago," he said. "What's wrong with these apples? What's wrong with this squash? The young people, they won t buy it if it has a nick or a scratch or a bump," he explained.

The man said he had begun searching in supermarket dumpsters for fruit and vegetables not long after he retired 22 years ago after nearly five decades as a shipping clerk in a warehouse along the Brooklyn waterfront. He lives with his ailing wife in a fourth floor walkup apartment they have rented for 62 years. He said he had had surgery for a hernia in August, and that even with Medicare, he had to pay about $1,000. That was a setback, he said.

"Ten dollars a day, that's what I'm trying to get by on, so I can have some money around to pay medical bills," he said. "Everyday I go look in the bins. If it's too rotten, I pass it by. But this is good stuff they put out there. My father said, 'That's God s gift to mankind --- don't throw it away!' People are starving around the world, and in this country they are throwing food away."

DISCUSSION QUESTIONS

1. Why do the elderly in this report say they have a "fear of the future"?

2. Think of your grandparents. What happens physically as people age? What are some of their special needs? Why do they live on "limited" incomes?

3. Why are the elderly among the groups most likely to be hungry?

4. Many elderly people are not able to leave their homes to buy food. What can young people do to alert people in the community to the fact that many elderly go without food? How can young people help the elderly get enough food?

MAKING A DIFFERENCE!

In 1954 some people living in Philadelphia became aware that many of the elderly people in their city were unable to shop for food and did not have enough money to buy the food they needed. All of these elderly people had worked for many years serving their community as teachers, nurses, business people, bus drivers, etc. Now they were going without food several days every month. The group of concerned citizens decided to take action. They formed an organization called MEALS ON WHEELS. The citizens pooled their own money and money collected from business people in the community to prepare and deliver meals to elderly people confined to their homes. MEALS ON WHEELS became so successful feeding the elderly that in the early 1970's the U.S. government began giving the organization money so they could expand and serve even more hungry, elderly people. By 1994 MEALS ON WHEELS had 15,000 nutrition sites and 4,000 groups working with them all across the U.S.! In most places elderly people volunteer to do much of the work.

How does Meals on Wheels help the elderly?
Is there a MEALS ON WHEELS program in your town?
Do they need young people's help?

TEAM #3

HUNGER, USA - THE WORKING POOR

Imagine that you are Mike or Karen Smith who live in a small two-bedroom house with their three children in your city. LISA (10) and TIM (8) are in public school. KATIE (1) spends the day at a child-care center. Both Karen and Mike work full-time and the two older children attend the childcare center after school.

Karen is a cashier in a supermarket a few miles away. Every morning after dropping the children off, she takes the bus to work. The restaurants in the neighborhood where she works are expensive, so Karen takes her lunch to work everyday. Mike is a construction worker and leaves before sunrise every morning to get to his job-site on time. His car is old and in constant need of repairs. In order to earn enough to pay all the monthly bills, Mike works six days a week. On Sundays he does odd jobs for people in your neighborhood to earn extra money.

Winter is coming --- the family's heating bill will be going up. Lisa needs a warm winter coat. Work out your monthly budget below and see if there is any money left for clothing, medical expenses, repairs on Mike's car, movies, etc.

SMITH FAMILY MONTHLY BUDGET

INCOME (after taxes)
Karen $ 650
Mike   1,050
Total Income: _____ $ _____

EXPENSES:
Rent $700
Utilities (heat,
electric, phone)   100
Childcare Center   300
School supplies   15
Transportation:
(bus fare, gas,
car insurance)   150
Food ($80 per **week**)   _____
TOTAL: _____ $ _____
BALANCE: _____ $ _____

EMERGENCY!!! Today Lisa fell and broke her arm. You have no health insurance. What expenses can you cut back on in order to pay this emergency hospital cost of $200? Karen has found a second-hand coat for Lisa for $20. Is there enough money?

MAKING A DIFFERENCE!

Many hardworking families like the Smiths must choose between paying medical expenses and eating enough food. Many families must choose between heating their homes and eating enough food. Fortunately, for millions of these hungry people the U.S. government has a program which provides FOOD STAMPS that can be exchanged for food in supermarkets. The money families would normally spend on food can be used to pay other necessary bills. FOOD STAMPS cannot be used to buy alcohol, cigarettes, soap or household cleaning supplies - only food. In 1994 one out of nine Americans used FOOD STAMPS.

The FOOD STAMP program has helped feed millions of hungry people but critics have found problems with the program. Some people who don't really need FOOD STAMPS are using them. Other critics of the program claim that some families who desperately need FOOD STAMPS can't get them because their incomes are higher than the "poverty line" set by the government. The Smith family earns too much money to qualify for FOOD STAMPS. The government doesn't consider them poor enough.

How do Food Stamps help hungry people? Should families like the Smiths receive FOOD STAMPS?

What does the Smith family need so that they can get out of poverty and not have to depend on FOOD STAMPS? (Karen and Mike work very hard, do they earn enough for their labor? Child-care centers are very expensive as are medical expenses when you don't have health insurance.)

TEAM #4

HUNGER, USA - ETHNIC & RACIAL MINORITIES

In the United States hunger and race are related. **Most** of the poor and hungry people in the country are white - there are more white people in the U.S. than any other race. Look at the pie below which represents the total U.S. population in 1992:

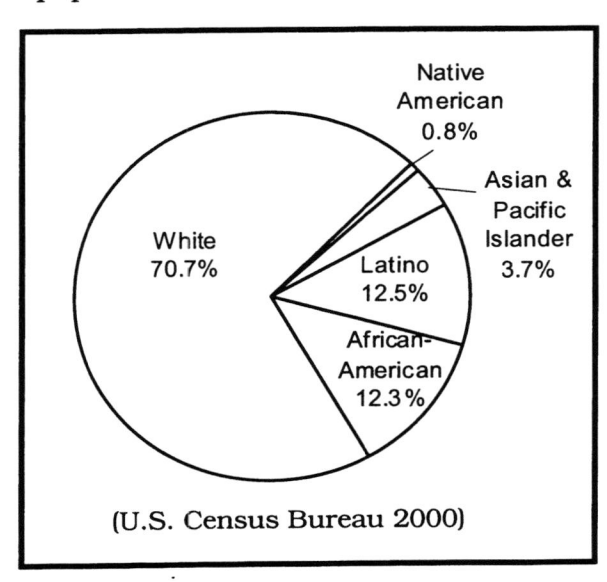

Pie chart (U.S. Census Bureau 2000):
- White 70.7%
- Latino 12.5%
- African-American 12.3%
- Asian & Pacific Islander 3.7%
- Native American 0.8%

Which group makes up most of the U.S. population?

Which group makes up the smallest percentage?

(What reasons can your group give for this difference?)

What are some of the problems people of color face in a predominantly white society?

Now look at the graph below which shows the percentage of each population group living in poverty --- and hungry --- in 2000:

Which population group has the smallest percentage of hungry people?

Which group has the highest percentage of hungry people?

Why are racial and ethnic minorities in the U.S. more vulnerable to hunger than whites?

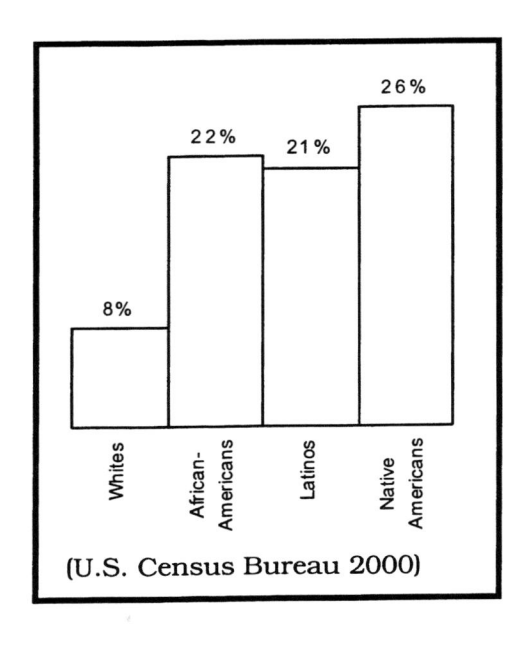

Bar graph (U.S. Census Bureau 2000):
- Whites: 8%
- African-Americans: 22%
- Latinos: 21%
- Native Americans: 26%

RACISM is the belief that one's own race is superior to others and has the right to control others.

HOW DOES RACISM KEEP PEOPLE HUNGRY?
With your group members make a list of the many ways racism keeps people hungry. The following facts will help your discussion:

In 1994 twice as many African-Americans and Latinos as whites could not find work.

Weekly earnings for Native Americans, African-Americans and Latinos were lower than they were for whites.

The Federal Reserve Bank in Boston found that banks often refuse to give loans to people of color even when they have the same income and credit history as white applicants.

Many communities, where the majority of members are people of color, do not have reasonably-priced supermarkets.

MAKING A DIFFERENCE![*]

In 1986 San Antonio, Texas was one of the poorest cities in the United States. The government officials in San Antonio were predominantly white, but most of the people living in the city were Latino. It seems Latino neighborhoods were not getting their fair share of government services and money. Things began to change, however, when some Latino men and women held a drive to register more Latinos to vote and to educate them on how they could run for government office, use the media more effectively, and insist on social justice. Before too long a Latino mayor was elected. He made sure government services flowed to **all** neighborhoods not just to white ones. New roads, sanitation services, health clinics and nutrition programs changed the poorest areas into healthier, more livable ones. Today the citizens of San Antonio are busy campaigning for better schools for Latino children, affordable health care and job opportunities.

How did San Antonio confront racism?
What is being done in your city to eliminate racism?

---

[*] The example above is from *Reinvesting in America* by Robin Garr, Addison-Wesley, N.Y. 1995.

TEAM #5

HUNGER, USA - SINGLE MOTHERS

Imagine that you are the mother of three small children: Jack (12), Annie (7) and Tommy (2). You are raising your children alone. Sometimes your parents help out but it is difficult for them because, like you, they work more than full-time and do not often have extra money or time.

You work two jobs. One is a day-position as a nurse's assistant in a hospital across town. While you are at the hospital your two oldest children are in public school. Baby Tommy must stay at a day-care center in your neighborhood; it is expensive. There are very few centers like this one in your city and it is overcrowded. Many of your friends cannot find day-care centers with space for their children. After school everyday your older children go home alone. You return home from work at around 6:30 p.m. and prepare a quick dinner. After dinner, and on weekends, you work until midnight cleaning a nearby office building. Your mother or a neighbor stays with the children. Often, however, Jack and Annie must watch Tommy alone. You would prefer to stay home in the evenings and help your children with their homework and spend time with them, but you must pay all the monthly bills alone: rent, electricity, phone, medical expenses, transportation expenses, and buy clothing and food for your children. Most of the food you buy is inexpensive food that is easy to fix such as peanut butter, macaroni, and frozen dinners.

You would like to go back to school to become a registered nurse so that you could earn more money but there simply is no time left in your day for classes. You worry that your children are not getting enough healthy foods to eat, proper medical attention, warm clothes and the love they need, but you are trying your best.

In 2000 over *half* of all families living in poverty were maintained by women alone.

What reasons can your group find for why single mothers and their children are more vulnerable to hunger than two-parent families?

What are some of the things single mothers need so that they can take care of themselves and their children?

MAKING A DIFFERENCE!*

One example of a neighborhood program that is helping single mothers get out of poverty is **Para Los Ninos** in downtown Los Angeles. This Family Center is located near the neighborhood school where children receive hot breakfasts and lunches. The Center has a food pantry where mothers can obtain extra food when their money runs out at the end of the month when bills must be paid. There is a medical clinic in the Center where families receive immunizations and a doctor's attention when they are sick. The Center provides classes in parenting and counseling for mothers and help with finding a job. There is also a first-rate day-care program in the Center for children too young to attend school. A separate area in the Center is set up for older children and teenagers who come in after school to watch movies, participate in art and dance activities as well as receive help with their homework. Many of the volunteers at the Center are mothers and fathers from the community.

What are some of the ways Para Los Ninos helps single mothers?
Is there a family center in your town helping single mothers and their children improve their lives?

---

* This example was found in *Reinvesting in America* by Robin Garr, Addison-Wesley, New York, 1995.

RAIN

When autumn rains flatten sycamore leaves,
The tiny volcanoes of dirt
Ants around their holes,
I should be out of work.

My silverware and stacks of plates will go unused
Like the old, my two good slacks
Will smother under a growth of lint
And smell of the old dust
That rises
When the closet door opens or closes.

The skin of my belly will tighten like a belt
And there will be no reason for pockets.

From *New and Selected Poems*,
by Gary Soto © 1995,
published by Chronicle Books,
San Francisco.
Reprinted with permission.

LESSON 16: WORKING & EATING

Discussions and activities in this lesson focus on the absolute necessity of work and fair wages for maintaining healthy individuals, families and communities. Students explore some of the social and political forces that deny needy people access to jobs, reasonable working conditions, and adequate pay. **POWER PLAY** is a dramatic demonstration of how employers sometimes exploit workers, why workers need to develop unions, and how their attempts to organize are subverted. **LAID OFF!** allows students to assume the identity of a worker who loses his job after seventeen years. They must plan and purchase meals on a limited budget. **UNEMPLOYMENT & DISCRIMINATION** reveals significant differences in the rates of unemployment and weekly wages for different social groups. Students explore the reasons behind these differences. Additional activities offer ideas on investigating job availability and unemployment in your community, as well as ideas on how to "create" new jobs that would benefit needy people, the entire community, and the environment.

TEACHER BACKGROUND READING*

Unemployment is the major cause of poverty in the U.S. Food, housing and health care cost money. Without a job individuals have little access to the essentials of life. Work is fundamental to the health and survival of individuals, families, communities, countries.

Matthew Fox explains in his book *The Reinvention of Work: A New Vision of Livelihood For Our Time*, (Harper, San Francisco: 1994) that every thing in nature, no matter how small, is constantly working. There is no unemployment among the planets, the trees, fishes, butterflies or ants. Their work is in harmony with the work of the universe. The only species among which unemployment exists is the human species. We see the consequences of widespread unemployment all around us: poverty, hunger, family break-ups, depression, heart attacks, child and spouse abuse, alcoholism, drug addiction, criminal activity and suicide. The cycle of poverty set in motion by chronic unemployment spirals through generations depriving future parents and their children of the right to healthy and productive lives.

The Universal Declaration of Human Rights which was adopted by the U.N. in 1948 asserts that every person has the right to work and to receive a fair wage for that work, a wage that insures "an existence worthy of human dignity." America's work ethic proudly proclaims that any of us who **can** work, **should** work --- yet millions of Americans cannot **find** work today and cannot afford the training they need to perform the jobs that are available. In 1994 surveys showed that for every vacant job there were more than five "officially" unemployed job seekers. Official statistics don't tell the whole story --- as high as they are, they don't include people who have been forced to take part-time jobs or those who have given up looking for work.

---

* Information and ideas for this introduction are from *WHY Magazine* No. 17, Winter/Spring, 1995. World Hunger Year, New York.

It is important for students to understand that most people are not out of work because they are lazy, but because there are not enough jobs to go around. Some economists claim that a certain "natural" rate of unemployment is necessary to keep inflation in check. How do those of us who are working explain this to those who need jobs desperately but can't find them? Fierce competition for too few jobs and unfair wages create hostility among social groups, and dependence on handouts. Widespread unemployment keeps wages low for the majority of workers who are afraid to speak out or strike for fear of losing their jobs. In 1994 only 11% of nongovernmental workers were unionized. Many people today work two or more jobs at or below minimum wage and still cannot rise above the poverty line.

With so much work to be done on our ailing planet, we cannot afford for even one of us to be out of work. How can we find work for everyone?

1. We can begin by saving jobs. Instead of closing sound plants and moving them to other regions or countries where labor can be had for less, we can search for creative ways to forge healthy relationships between workers and company managements, and to give workers a share of the ownership or profits of the companies they work so hard to sustain. Community-based businesses respect the rights and needs of their workers as well as the health of the surrounding environment.

2. We can redistribute some of the work that already exists. Just as hungry people exist alongside overfed people in our society, unemployed people exist side by side with over-worked people.

3. We can create much needed jobs that infuse workers' lives with meaning, care for needy people and clean up our environment. What kind of work is your community calling for? Certainly not for more automobiles, factories or chemicals. The machine driven work of the Industrial Revolution damaged our natural environment as well as the spirits of workers. The earth calls now for clean water, soil and air, for recycling and repairing, for sustainable energy, organic farming, the planting of trees and gardens. Humanity calls for compassion, understanding, trust, caring relationships, food for everyone, homes and health care for everyone, equal education and meaningful work. There is **so** much work to be done.

POWER PLAY

The classroom is transformed into an imaginary society where the resources for survival are controlled by one very powerful person. Students experience some of the pressures that lead workers to organize in order to take control of their working lives. It allows them a glimpse of the possibilities available when people work together for change.

This activity is from ***THE POWER IN OUR HANDS: A Curriculum on the History of Work and Workers in the United States***. Copyright 1988 by William Bigelow and Norm Diamond. Reprinted here by permission of Monthly Review Foundation. This is an excellent resource guide with stimulating activities and stories for a more extensive study of work. Available for $15 from Network of Educators on the Americas. See Resource Guide to order.

MATERIALS: A large machine such as a VCR or overhead projector.

PROCEDURE:

1. Close the door, pull the shades and tell students to imagine that you are all going to live in this classroom for the rest of your lives. There is no soil for growing food but you have a machine that produces artificial biscuits. Correct yourself and explain that actually **you** own the machine. Place the machine in front of the class.

2. Tell students you need workers to produce the food. They will be paid enough money to buy food to live on. Those who don't work will find it hard to survive. Ask for volunteers who want to work, eat and survive. If additional encouragement is necessary, tell students that in order to receive credit for this lesson, they must not starve. Choose only half the class as workers. The rest will be unemployed. Seat the groups at opposite ends of the room facing each other.

4. Explain the economics of your society. Put the chart below on the board. Five biscuits a day are necessary to survive in a fairly healthy manner. Anyone receiving less - the unemployed - will slowly starve. Go over the chart with your students:

DAILY BISCUIT ECONOMY

	WORKERS	**UNEMPLOYED**	**OWNER**
WAGES	$6 x no. of workers	NONE	NONE
TAXES	-$1 x no. of workers	$2 x no. of unemployed	$1 x no. of unemployed
CONSUMPTION	5 biscuits x no. of Workers	2 x no. of unemployed	6 biscuits
SURPLUS	0	0	4 x no. of workers minus 6 for daily consumption

(If there were 10 workers and 10 unemployed, a total of 110 biscuits would be produced. After taxes, the workers would consume 50. From welfare payments the unemployed would consume 20, leaving a total of 40 for the owner - 34 after consuming six. NOTE: Workers and owner need to provide $2 to each unemployed person (taxes are paid in biscuits)).

> Each worker produces 11 biscuits a day.
> All workers are paid $6.00 a day.
> A biscuit costs $1.
> $1 deducted from the pay of each worker to make welfare payments to the unemployed.
> Each worker is left with $5 a day (after taxes) just enough to survive.
>
> (No money or biscuits are actually exchanged during the game.)

4. Tell students that because you are the owner you are entitled to more biscuits --- without you and your machine everyone would starve. Everyday you receive 4 x the number of workers.

5. Show the unemployed that they will receive only $2 a day in welfare. With this they can buy 2 biscuits. They need work desperately --- they are starving.

6. Be sure everyone understands his/her position. As the owner, your goal is to increase your profits. You can do this by cutting wages.

7. Begin the game by telling students to imagine that several weeks have passed. How have they been eating? How are they feeling?

THE GAME BEGINS

Ask who among the unemployed wants to work. Offer one of them $5.50 a day (less than the other workers are making, but more than the $2 they are already receiving.) Once you have a taker, go to the workers and ask who is willing to accept $5.50. Fire the first person who refuses to accept the lower wage. Send him/her to sit with the unemployed. Hire the unemployed person willing to accept the lower wage. Continue trying to drive down wages this way.

Now and then ask workers to repeat after you "I am a happy worker." "I love my job." Fire those who refuse and hire some of the unemployed. You can refer to the unemployed as "welfare bums" and encourage the workers to do the same. Later, talk about why they were unemployed and who the real bum was.

Anyone who mentions "strike," "union" or anything disruptive is fired immediately. (Remind them that they will not be receiving enough food to remain strong.) Get all workers to sign "yellow dog" contracts promising never to join a union as long as they work for you.

Hire a foreman who will turn in subversive workers. Let workers know the foreman will be paid more than they get. Whisper something in the ear of a worker to encourage suspicion and division among workers.

If someone threatens to take over the machine hire a policeman or two to protect it. Explain that the police are there to protect "all our property", not just the owner's. (This also lets students know that taking over the machine is possible.) You want to keep workers and unemployed from uniting to strike or taking control of the machine. Offer privileges to certain workers to keep them from seeing their common interests --- higher wages, shorter work days, maybe even profit sharing.

If students are successful in stopping production, you can (1) Wait them out, indicating your surplus of biscuits and how quickly they would starve, or (2) Give in to their wage demands and a little later raise the price of biscuits. Justify your need for more income to meet your higher costs.

Announce that every 3 minutes an unemployed person will die of starvation. This adds a note of urgency and lets the class know that there will be consequences should they fail to act.

Students usually try to organize. The game ends when they have had ample **opportunity** to get together - successfully or otherwise. Participants may be totally demoralized or they may have taken over the machine and found a way to run it collectively.

Spend time discussing the experience. Have students write about how they felt.

> What did you personally do to try to stop my efforts to divide people?
>
> How effective were you?
>
> Were there actions you considered taking but didn't? Why not?
>
> If we were to repeat this activity what different actions would you take?
>
> What methods did I use to keep you from opposing me?
>
> Which ones worked? Which ones didn't?
>
> At which points were you most successful in getting together? Least successful?

What prevented you from immediately calling a meeting and demanding equal treatment or simply walking over to the machine and taking it over?

Did you think your efforts to unite would be betrayed? What in your life led you to think this?

Have you ever had an experience that convinced you that people could unite and act for an important goal?

As an owner, what kind of attitudes would I want you to have about your ability to work together? About property rights? Respect for authority?

As a follow-up to this activity have students write about a time when they were able to work together with others to achieve a common goal. Share these with classmates.

LAID OFF!

Students imagine how their lives and community would change if a major employer in their city suddenly closed down. Working with a limited budget, they visit their local supermarket and plan a week's worth of meals.

MATERIALS: Copies of *LAID OFF!*

PROCEDURE:

1. Distribute copies of *LAID OFF!* (To personalize this situation, use the name of a large company in your area that employs many people. Have students imagine that that company is closing down.) Read the handout together and discuss the questions that follow.

    How does it feel to be out of work?

    How will this lay-off change your life?

    How is the widespread lay-off affecting your community? Will other people and businesses be affected by this lay-off now that hundreds of people have less money to spend? Explain.

    How will the children of laid-off workers be affected?

    What do you think will happen to your town?

    Who has the right to make decisions that affect an entire community?

What actions could the workers have taken to prevent the closing?

What do workers bring to a company? What does the company bring to a community?

What is necessary to maintain a healthy relationship between workers and company management?

What can workers do to protect themselves from losing their jobs?

2. For homework students must visit their local market with their $25 unemployment checks and plan their meals for the coming week in their journals.

Did their money buy enough food?

Are the meals nutritious and well balanced?

Would students be healthy and content to eat these meals?

If there is not enough food, what will they do?

HAND OUT

LAID OFF!

For the past seventeen years you have worked for a company in your town which manufactures automobiles. Your father and grandfather worked for this company, as do many of your friends and their families. In fact, this one company employs thousands of people from your area. You are a loyal, hard worker. You rarely miss a day of work. One day you receive notice that the company management has decided to close the plant and move it to another country where workers are paid less and unions are illegal. You cannot believe it! The company was doing very well here.

Many other smaller companies in your town are also closing down and there are not enough jobs left to go around. Families are becoming desperate. Some have even packed up and moved to other parts of the United States in search of work. You have stayed because your family and friends are here. This is your home and you would like to see it build itself up again.

You begin receiving unemployment checks. You don't like being out of work. You know the unemployment checks will stop coming soon. You look everyday for a job. You did not make enough at the automobile plant to save enough money to get you by in case of an emergency such as this. Your resources are running low. Your car is starting to break down. Winter is coming and you need a warm coat. The heater in your home needs repairing. You are already in debt. You know you must stay healthy --- you cannot afford to get sick. Many of your friends who have lost their jobs as well are feeling depressed. Many marriages are breaking up.

You have worked out a budget that provides you with a total of $25 a week for food --- after all your other expenses have been paid. You are at the local supermarket and must plan your meals for the coming week. What kinds of food can you afford? How much food can you buy?

ADDITIONAL ACTIVITIES

1. Watch and discuss one or more of the videos listed in the Resource Guide under "WORK". **ZONED FOR SLAVERY - *The Child Behind the Label*,** for instance, is a 23 minute video about children who work in factories in Latin America making clothes for the GAP, Eddie Bauer and Walmart. For detailed lesson plans on teaching about global sweatshops send for Volume 11, No. 4 of **Rethinking Schools** Educational Journal. See Resource Guide - "Resources For Teachers".

2. Songs about work to discuss and write about:

    Hello, Brother - Louis Armstrong
    My Hometown - Bruce Springsteen
    Allentown - Billy Joel
    Livin' for the City - Stevie Wonder
    Frontline - Stevie Wonder

3. ***Workers: An Archaeology of the Industrial Age*** by Sebastiao Salgado is a remarkable book of photographs of the faces of workers from over 50 countries which tell the story of the kind of world we are building and who is doing the work.

DISCRIMINATION & EMPLOYMENT

PROCEDURE:

1. Ask students to graph the following unemployment statistics from 2008. (Have students call the Dept. of Labor in your city for current, local figures.)

CATEGORIES OF LABOR FORCE	% UNEMPLOYED
ALL WORKERS	5.8
ALL AFRICAN-AMERICANS	10.1
African-American Men	11.4
African-American Women	8.9
African-American Teens	31.2
ALL LATINOS*	7.6
Latino Men	7.6
Latino Women	7.7
Latino Teens	22.4
ALL WHITES	5.2
White Men	5.5
White Women	4.9
White Teens	16.8

    (*When examined as a subset.)

2. Explain that these figures do not include people who work part-time or who have given up on finding a job.

   What reasons can students give for the dramatic differences in unemployment among different groups?

   What are some of the consequences that occur when too many people must compete for too few jobs?

3. Graph the following statistics:

   MEDIAN WEEKLY EARNINGS IN 2008

	MEN	WOMEN
ALL	$798	$638
White	$825	$654
African-American	$620	$554
Latino	$559	$501

4. Who earns the most? Who earns the least?

   What reasons are there for these differences?

   How do these differences affect hunger, poverty and violence in our communities?

ADDITIONAL ACTIVITIES

1. Have students survey family members, business people, workers and government officials in your community for their opinions on why differences in unemployment rates and earnings exist among certain groups.

2. Encourage students to call the Department of Labor in your city to find out the "job gap" - the difference between the number of people looking for jobs and the number of jobs available. Are there enough jobs for everyone? What kinds of jobs does your community need?

3. Have students use the HELP WANTED ads of your newspaper to do research on the kinds of jobs available in your area. What skills do most of these jobs require? How do wages differ among the jobs available? Are the jobs available to both men and women? Look for ways to graph and chart jobs.

4. Research the kinds of jobs that have sustained your community (farming, fishing, mining, manufacturing, etc.). Interview workers. What kinds of jobs have been lost? Why? What kinds of jobs are needed?

5. Ask students to reflect on how the work of all other species on the planet benefits that species as well as the environment. Has anyone ever seen an unemployed tree, robin or insect? What would happen if one of the planets simply stopped working? Individually or in pairs students can create a painting, poem or story about "The Day The _____Stopped Working". (sun, trees, stars, land, birds, flowers, wind, sky, etc.) What would our world look like? How would other life on the planet be affected?

6. See Resource Guide for books and videos on homelessness.

7. See Resource Guide for books and videos on the importance of work, the history of unions and the labor movement.

8. Find out about child labor groups by writing to The Child Labor Project, 555 New Jersey Ave. N., Washington, D.C. 20001-2079.

9. For information on child labor in America and ways to fight it surf **virtually react:** http://www.react.com.

LESSON 17: THE HOMELESS

"A generation is growing up that can't remember a time when the notion of people sleeping on the streets or under bridges in this country was unthinkable. In fact, as recently as the late 1970's, homelessness was the kind of horror that Americans assumed was reserved for places like Calcutta and could never happen here. How has it come to be that homelessness became so common-place that even caring Americans simply avert their eyes?"

(Bill Ayres, World Hunger Year)

Four activities in this lesson help students confront homelessness, its causes, history, and possible solutions. Listening to homeless people tell their stories, students learn why they lost their homes, who is most likely to become homeless, what life without a home is like, and what homeless people need to become productive members of their communities.

1. **JUST ANOTHER DAY IN PARADISE** uses a popular song about a homeless woman whose pleas go ignored by a passerby. Students discuss their own reactions to homeless people, then reconstruct the scene from the song and add dialogue that builds a bridge between the woman and the passerby.

2. **IN THEIR OWN WORDS** takes students inside the personal stories of people who have lost their homes. Working in small groups, students create "dialogue" poems in which they combine their voices with those of the homeless.

3. **DISAPPEARING HOMES - A MYSTERY** turns students into private investigators. Discussing CLUES helps them figure out why so many people are showing up on the streets of Pleasantville.

4. **PLEASANTVILLE TOWN MEETING** is a role play in which students representing homeless people, local shop keepers, government officials and activists debate the mayor's decision to ban the homeless from seeking refuge in the town's historic train station.

TEACHER BACKGROUND READING[*]

No one knows exactly how many Americans are homeless. It is difficult to count them because it is difficult to find them. They have no addresses

---

[*] Statistics and other information on the homeless are from the National Law Center on Homelessness and Poverty (2003) and the National Coalition for the Homeless (2002).

except for an occasional shelter bed, cardboard box, park bench, tunnel or cave. In 2003 over 3 million men, women and children were homeless. These figures did not include the roughly 5 million people who lived doubled up in over-crowded and dangerous conditions.

WHO ARE THE HOMELESS?

Single men make up 68% of the single homeless population
40% of homeless men are veterans
39% of the homeless are children
Families amount to 40%
Nearly 1/2 are minorities
37% are substance abusers
Nearly 1/2 are high school graduates
1/4 work full or part-time
1/4 are mentally ill
Nearly 1/2 of all homeless women and children are victims of domestic violence

The stories homeless people tell about their lives are often all they own. These stories give us valuable insight into the variety of reasons why people lose their homes --- fire, chronic unemployment, mounting medical bills, divorce, mental illness, etc. Heavy drug use (particularly crack) causes homelessness. Drugs eat up money that would otherwise be used to pay rent, makes people less employable, and their friends and relatives less willing to take them in. Lack of affordable housing is another cause of homelessness. Every year hundreds of thousands of low-income housing units are torn down only to be replaced with condominiums, shopping malls, office buildings, hotels, etc. Escalating rents force many families to choose between housing and food. An increase in the break-up of marriages has led to an increase in the number of women and children who are homeless. People lose their jobs and homes as a result of AIDS or other crippling illnesses.

People who experience one or more of these serious problems become homeless when they don't have access to one of three "safety nets" that usually prevent other people who experience similar problems from ending up on the street. The three safety nets are: a personal savings account or trust fund, family help, and government benefits. Cutbacks in government benefits and services make it harder for people without jobs or adequate wages to keep a roof over their heads.

Once a person loses his job or home, he must find his way through a tangle of bureaucratic paperwork which includes standing in long lines at government offices sometimes for up to five hours at a time, or traveling hours each way to pick up a government check. Figuring out the system leaves little, time, energy or money for job and apartment searches, child care, training or education. The physical and psychological strain of living without a home is enormous.

Homeless people need **emergency** care - food, shelter, medical attention. They also need long-term help in order to return to healthy, productive lives. This kind of help includes substance-abuse programs, mental health care, job-training, a job that pays fair wages, affordable, permanent housing, child-care and political organization.

ADDITIONAL ACTIVITIES:

1. Include in your study some of the books for young people on homelessness listed in the Resource Guide. Have small groups read and discuss different books and present the stories to the rest of the class.

2. Encourage students to create lessons or role-plays on homelessness for other classes.

3. Students can organize a MAKE A DIFFERENCE club in your school that helps meet the needs of the homeless year round: collecting clothing, coats, blankets and preparing sandwiches and serving meals in soup kitchens and shelters. Students should research pantries, soup kitchens and shelters before getting started.

4. Invite a speaker from a homeless shelter, organization or soup kitchen to speak to students. Students could have a list of questions ready to ask about the history of homelessness in your area. Consider also inviting a former drug addict to talk about the connection between drugs and poverty, hunger and homelessness.

5. Students can write articles for your local newspaper comparing the homeless to refugees of war or famine. What do they have in common? What are their immediate needs? Long-term needs?

6. Watch the video FLY AWAY HOME. Host LeVar Burton talks with homeless children and their families. Viewers see the insides of shelters, hear how families became homeless, and discover how other young people are helping. To order see Resource Section - VIDEOS.

7. Read *HOME: A Collaboration of Thirty Distinguished Authors and Illustrators of Children's Books to Aid the Homeless* edited by Michael J. Rosen.

MAKING A DIFFERENCE!

Several thousand unemployed people in Cincinnati who do not have enough money to repair their furnaces, plumbing or electricity receive help from a unique community program called **People Working Cooperatively**. As of 1995 the program, organized and funded by community businesses, kept nearly 4,000 people from becoming homeless. A staff of 100 includes formerly unemployed or homeless people who have been trained by program leaders in carpentry, plumbing, electric work, painting, etc. They are paid to repair the homes of the poor. The poor pay nothing for these services but add their efforts to making the repairs. Every spring and fall the group holds a "Repair Affair" to repair and maintain the homes of needy people.

1. JUST ANOTHER DAY IN PARADISE

MATERIALS: Song by Phil Collins *"Another Day In Paradise"*
Typed lyrics for each student

PROCEDURE:

1. Play the song for students one or two times.

2. Allow time for responses.

    QUESTIONS :

    Where is "paradise"?
    Why did the songwriter choose this title?
    What is happening in the scene on the street?
    Why does the man ignore the woman?
    How would it feel to be in the woman's place?
    Has anyone ever been in the man's place?
    	Or in a similar situation? How did it feel?
    Why don't we know what to say or do in a situation such as this?

3. Ask two students to volunteer to act out the scene from the song.

4. Have students work in pairs to create dialogue and action for the scene or a similar one they create. What can the passerby say or do?

5. Invite pairs of students to perform their revised scenes for the class. Encourage the rest of the class to comment on the power of the words in the new scenes. Do they change it? How?

2. IN THEIR OWN WORDS

MATERIALS: Interviews from *Rachel and Her Children*
(A different interview for each small group of students--- enough copies for every member of the group)

PROCEDURE:

1. Ask students to close their eyes and think of a special place in their homes. Ask some students to describe the room and why it is their favorite. How important is having a home? Ask students to describe

some of the events that take place in their homes. How would their lives change if they lost their homes? How would it feel? Where would they go?

2. Read a few of the interviews with homeless people from ***Rachel and Her Children*** aloud.

QUESTIONS

Who are the homeless?

What are some of the causes of homelessness in these stories?

Other people's heaters break and yet they don't become homeless. **Why** did Kim lose her home when her heater broke? **Why** did Richard lose his home and family when he lost his job?

What is life like in a shelter or welfare hotel?

What are some of the physical, emotional and social consequences people face when they lose their homes? How does this complicate their situations?

Have there always been homeless people? (Who could students interview to find out?)

What is being done in your community to help care for the homeless? (Who can you talk to to find out?)

What do homeless people need? How can we find out?

How can students help?

What role should government play in helping end homelessness?

3. Discuss with students how often when people are oppressed for a long time and no one listens they eventually lose their "voices" in society.

DIALOGUE POEMS

4. Tell students that today they will give power to the voices of the homeless by combining their own voices with those of the homeless people in the interviews. They are going to create "dialogue poems".

5. Divide students into small groups and distribute different interview excerpts to each group. Half the small group must work separately to

create a poem about a favorite place in their homes. The other half of the small group must read their interview quietly, underlining words or phrases that strike them, then together arrange those phrases into a poem, adding their own words as well.

6. When both halves of each group are finished with their poems they come back together and find a way to combine their poems, or a way to perform them simultaneously. One way to do this is for each half to take turns reading a line at a time from each poem. Another way is to find lines that correspond or answer each other and rearrange one of the poems to be read in response to the other.

7. Encourage groups to find a creative way to perform their dialogue poems for the class or other classes. In some performances each half of the small group has stood in opposite ends of the classroom and performed the lines in a call and response technique. Other students included musical devices such as echoing certain words or repeating powerful phrases while snapping fingers, clapping hands or stamping their feet. Stress the idea that two distinctly different voices should be heard in the dialogue poems: one is someone experiencing the beauty, safety and history of a favorite room - the other is someone remembering her home or explaining how it feels to be without a home.

ADDITIONAL ACTIVITY:

Have students write in their journals about a time when their own voices were silenced. Share these with each other.

INTERVIEWS
from
RACHEL AND HER CHILDREN

(Excerpted and edited from Jonathon Kozol's book *Rachel And Her Children*, Ballantine Books, NY 1989. Printed with permission from Crown Publishers.)

#1 AN INTERVIEW WITH GWEN

Gwen is a mother of three children. She was a teacher's aide while the family lived for awhile doubled up with Gwen's relatives. When one relative died and another got married, Gwen could not pay the rent alone and she and her children ended up on the street. They have been living at the Carter Hotel for two years now and are trying to find a home they can afford.

"My rent allowance (from the government) is $270. Places I see start at $350. Even if you could pay it, landlords do not want you if you are homeless. You feel ashamed.

It's the same with public school. The teacher asks, "Where do you live?" You say the Carter. Right away they put you in a slot.

Food is short. By the eighteenth of the month I'm running out. I have to borrow. The children have got to eat. When we're low we live on macaroni and french fries. I can make a lot from two potatoes. When you're running low you learn to stretch. I don't have the money to buy meat. Even if I did, there's no refrigerator. Some mornings there's no food. The children go to school at eight. I give them a quarter if I have one. They can buy a bag of chips. After school I give them soup or bread with peanut butter. Cooking does pose certain dangers in a place like this. If you're using oil and it catches fire, it will go right up the wall."

(Many hotels for the homeless do not permit stoves or ovens in the rooms because of the frequency of fires.)

#2 AN INTERVIEW WITH RACHEL AND HER CHILDREN

Rachel is a former drug addict who lost her husband and is now living in a hotel for the homeless in New York with her three children: Angie (12), Stephen (11), and Erica (9).

RACHEL: Before we lived here we were at the shelter. People sleep together in one room. You have to dress in front of everybody. When we moved here I was forced to sign a paper. Everybody has to do it. It's a promise that you will not cook inside your room. So we lived on cold bologna. (To prevent the possibility of frequent fires, hotels for the homeless often do not permit any cooking inside the rooms.)

ANGIE: We used to live with my aunt but then it got too crowded there so we moved out. The room here is either very hot or freezin' cold. It's so cold right now you got to use the hot plate.

Christmas here is sad for everyone. They givin' you toys and that do help but I would rather that we have a place to be. There's only one thing I ask: A home to be in with my mother. That was my only wish for Christmas. But it could not be.

School is bad for me. I feel ashamed. They know we're not the same. My teacher do not treat us all the same. They know which children live in the hotel.

RACHEL: Blackness is all around me. In the night I'm scared to sleep. In the morning I'm worn out. If I eat, I eat one meal a day. I stay in this room. I hide. This room is safe to me. I am afraid to go outside. Can you get the government to know that we exist? I know my children have potential, they're intelligent. They need a chance. In this place here I am fightin' for my children. I am tired of fightin'. I want my kids to live in peace.

(One month after this interview Angie was arrested for stealing food from a supermarket.)

#3 AN INTERVIEW WITH PETER AND MEGAN

Peter worked as a carpenter doing construction work on New York City housing projects. Megan kept their home and cared for their five children. The family lived in an apartment on a pretty street near Coney Island. In this interview Peter and Megan describe a day that changed their lives.

PETER: I did carpentry. I painted. I could do wallpapering. I earned a living. We spent Sundays walking with our children at the beach.

We were at the boardwalk. We were up some. We had been at Nathan's. We were eating hot dogs. Everybody was in shorts.

(When they were told about a fire, they grabbed the children and ran home. Everything they owned had been destroyed.)

MEGAN: My grandmothers china, everything. I had that book of gourmet cooking...

(One of the children's kittens, born three days before, had died in the fire.)

PETER: I haven't had a real job since the fire. I had tools. I can't replace those tools. It took me years of work. Everything I had was in that fire. I can't see any way out. I want to go home. Where can I go?

Peter and Megan and their children moved into a hotel for the homeless in New York City. After a year all five children were adopted by different families. Peter and Megan get by asking strangers on the street for money. When the interviewer asks Peter what he had meant when he had said "We were up some," Peter laughs, then says, "It means that we were happy."

#4 AN INTERVIEW WITH RICHARD

Richard is an educated, 36 year-old Vietnam veteran who worked for seven years in data-processing until the company shut down without warning and moved out of the state. Without money to pay the bills, Richard's family lost their home and the family broke apart. Richard lives in a men's shelter in New York. The author interviewed Richard in a restaurant at 8:30 pm where, his hands trembling, Richard finished his chicken sandwich before the author put his napkin on his lap. Richard apologized but then said this was the first thing he had eaten since 8 am.

RICHARD: When the company left I could find nothing. I looked everywhere. I slept in Washington Square and Central Park. I spent most of my time just walking. I would try to bathe in public toilets. I'd wash my clothes and lay them outside in the sun to dry. I used to talk with people like yourself so that I would not begin to feel cut off. I was scared that I would fall apart.

Half the people that I know (on the street) are suffering from chest infections and sleep deprivation. The lack of sleep leaves you debilitated and shaky. If a psychiatrist came along he'd say that I was crazy. But I was an ordinary man. There was nothing wrong with me. I lost my wife. I lost my kids. I lost my home. Now would you say that I was crazy if I told you I was feeling sad?

I was a pretty stable man. Now I tremble when I meet somebody in the ordinary world. I'm trembling now. I've had a bad cold for two weeks. When you're sick there's no way to get better. You cannot sleep in at the shelter. You have to go outside and show that you are looking for a job.

If you are very hungry and you want a meal you can get it at St. Francis. You can get a sandwich at Grand Central every night at 10 o'clock. So if you want to keep from starving you are always on the move.

Listen to me! I've always worked. I need to work! I'm not a lazy man. You think to yourself: It's a dream and I will wake. Sometimes I think it's an experiment. They are watching you to find out how much you can take. Someone will come someday and say: "Okay, this guy has suffered long enough. Now we'll take him back into our world." Then you wake up and get in line.

#5 AN INTERVIEW WITH KIM

(Kim is in her twenties. She was a preschool teacher and when the heating system in her home broke down in the middle of winter, she had no wealthy friends or family to help her with her expenses. She was moved into the Martinique Hotel, a hotel for homeless families in New York City. She lives with her children in a room on the 11th floor.)

KIM: When I first came here I found I'd lost the right to vote. We're like cripples in this city. We had to fight for refrigerators. Food for children couldn't be refrigerated. You couldn't open a can of infant formula and save it overnight. If you didn't use it all you'd have to throw it out.

There's a woman on the seventh floor. She's like a broken stick. You ought to meet her. She's so timid and afraid. She gets cut off; this happens all the time because she cannot read. She's quiet. They ignore her. They don't explain things to her. Nobody says 'Wait a minute. Something here is wrong.' Why don't they teach her to read? I **know** her. This is something that she wants. If they had a decent day care set up in this building I'd go down and teach her. There's no day care, nothing you can count on. No library. No quiet place to meet and talk. Not even a pleasant place to sit and read a book.

Why don't people in the city ever look around this building? Why don't they figure out who's here, who's got some skills, who could help someone else? They look at us to see what **isn't** there, and not what **is**.

They see us like a lot of empty bottles that they don't intend to fill. LISTEN! There are gifted people in this building. Imagine, with all these children, all these people concentrated here within one building, all the useful things that you could do. You could do some good things in those empty rooms. Lectures. Movies. Every night you could have education going on. Doctors could come and talk, explain things women need to learn. Imagine all the decent things you could do with just a little common sense if you were not thinking of this situation as a punishment for failure.

3. THE MYSTERY OF THE DISAPPEARING HOMES[*]

The people of Pleasantville are baffled. Thousands of people have begun sleeping on sidewalks, living in the city's parks and the town's historic old train station. Students discuss CLUES to try to figure out what caused so many people to lose their homes.

MATERIALS: CLUES
(Cut the sentences on the following pages into strips, mix the strips up, fold them into quarters, and place them in a hat. You should have one CLUE for each student.)

PROCEDURE:

1. Sitting in one large circle, explain that the citizens of Pleasantville, where you live, have called on this select group of private investigators to solve a mystery:

    > Ten years ago in Pleasantville there was no such thing as a homeless person. Today, despite the fact that there are many new apartment buildings and neighborhoods, thousands of men, women and children are living on the sidewalks, in doorways and in the train station. No one can seem to figure out what is causing people to become homeless.

2. Tell students that each of them will be given a CLUE that will help solve this mystery. They may share the contents of their CLUES with each other by reading them and discussing them, but they may not show their CLUES to each other. (Discussion is the essence of this activity.) **Everyone** must share his or her CLUE during the investigation. Distribute CLUES.

3. Allow students to solve the mystery on their own. They must use their CLUES to reconstruct the history of what happened in Pleasantville over the past ten years. You may only intervene when students become stumped or completely frustrated. To spark discussion then, ask a student with a particularly crucial CLUE to talk about it. Encourage students to speculate on how their clue is connected to other CLUES.

4. As students begin to unravel the mystery, ask one of them to write students' ideas about what happened on the board.

5. Questions to discuss and write about after the mystery has been solved:

---

[*] This activity is modeled after mysteries found in *Learning Discussion Skills Through Games* by Barbara Dodds Stanford. Prentice Hall, Englewood Cliffs, NY: 1969.

What were some of the changes that took place in Pleasantville over the last ten years?
Would YOU call the new development progress?
How did these changes affect the people of Pleasantville?
> Developers? Well-to-do people? The poor? Women? Children? Workers?

Why do you think so many families broke up after 1985?
Why did some people who experienced problems as a result of the changes end up on the street when others didn't?
List **three** reasons for the sudden surge in homelessness.

CLUES

(To be cut into strips)

In 1980 nearly everyone in Pleasantville had a home and job.

In the early 1980's people in Pleasantville who earned very low wages or none at all lived in inexpensive, one-room apartments in a part of town called Skid Row.

The rent for one-room apartments in Skid Row was only $70 a month.

Skid Row was a run-down area of town because the city did not spend much money there. There were only a few tiny grocery stores there, no restaurants, or shops.

In the spring of 1985 citizens of Pleasantville began to complain about Skid Row. They urged the mayor and wealthy developers in town to clean up the area.

By 1986 wealthy developers had bought up all the inexpensive apartment buildings in Skid Row.

The developers tore down the inexpensive rent buildings, and built expensive high-rise apartment buildings in their places.

Once the developers bought the low-rent buildings in Skid Row, the people who lived in the buildings had to leave their homes and look for affordable apartments in other areas.

There were not many affordable apartments available in Pleasantville in 1986.

When there is a shortage of available apartments rents go UP.

Once the new apartment buildings were finished, people with high-paying jobs moved into them. These new apartments rented for $1,500 per month.

When the new residents moved into the sleek and shiny skyscraper apartments, the neighborhood around Skid Row began to change. Developers also built expensive gourmet food shops, supermarkets, and designer clothing shops.

The name of the newly developed area was changed from Skid Row to Park Place and soon even developers from outside the city were coming to Park Place to build expensive hotels, office buildings and art galleries.

In 1985 BUZZZZZZZZZZZZ, a company in Pleasantville that assembled electrical appliances, closed down and moved to another state.

Six thousand people had been employed at BUZZZZZZZZZZZ.

When a worker is laid off in Pleasantville, he receives an unemployment check for a short while, then the checks stop.

In 1985 and even today, there are not many jobs available in Pleasantville. The few jobs there are require sophisticated training in computer technology.

In the 1980's the government in Pleasantville began cutting back on services for the poor. There was less money for food programs, health services, and housing.

In 1986 doctors in Pleasantville reported an increase in the number of people being treated for depression and problems related to stress.

In 1987 the Health Commissioner in Pleasantville reported an increase in the use of alcohol and drugs.

When people become addicted to drugs all their money goes to buy more drugs. Employers don't want to hire them and their friends and families are reluctant to take them in.

In 1987 the police reported an increase in crime in Pleasantville.

The news media reported an increase in the number of divorces in Pleasantville in 1987. Families were breaking apart. Women and children searched for inexpensive apartments.

Women in Pleasantville earn less money every month than men for the same kind of work.

As a result of an increase in crime and homelessness, many small businesses closed down and left town in search of a more prosperous and safe area. More people were left jobless.

Not everyone who had to move out of Skid Row or who lost a job ended up on the street. Some people had a safety net to catch them.

For some people their safety net was the money they had been able to save while they were earning good wages.

Some people's safety nets were their families. Family members took them in, loaned them money, or gave them a job to help them get back on their feet.

Some of the workers laid off by BUZZZZZZZZZZ found other jobs in Pleasantville, but these jobs paid much less and did not provide workers with health insurance. Many people had trouble paying their monthly expenses.

By 1990 there were 10,000 homeless people in Pleasantville.

PART 4: PLEASANTVILLE TOWN-MEETING[*][†]

```
         TOWN MEETING
    TO DISCUSS HOMELESSNESS
          1:00 TODAY
          CITY HALL
       PLEASANTVILLE, USA
```

For this role-play the classroom is turned into an imaginary city. The mayor of this city has just announced that the local train station will no longer be open to the homeless people of Pleasantville who have sought refuge there. Students representing various members of the community: **homeless people, local shop keepers, activists, government officials and a charitable organization**, meet to express their opinions on the mayor's rule and to brainstorm ways to end homelessness.

MATERIALS: Enough for all students:
Copies of "The Mayor's Statement"
A role sheet for each student

PROCEDURE:

1. Write the information for the Town Meeting above on the board. Also, list the five social groups.

2. Divide the class into five groups of equal size and distribute the role sheets --- all members of one group play the homeless people, all members of another group play the government officials, etc. Ask students to read these carefully and, in their role, think about what can be done about the problem of homelessness in Pleasantville. Encourage students to underline words or phrases on their role sheets. To help them imagine these characters as real people and to get inside their minds students can write an interior monologue (five minutes) --- their thoughts about how they would like to see the problem of homelessness handled. (Remind students these are not **their** thoughts, but their **character's** thoughts.) Have them read their interior monologues to each other in their groups. **Each group should write the name of their group on a placard and place it where other groups can see who they are.**

---

[*] The structure of this activity is based on an activity described by Bill Bigelow in *Rethinking Our Classrooms: Teaching for Equity and Social Justice*. See Resource Guide for more information.

[†] The information for the role sheets and the mayor's statement are based on actual incidents found in Jonathan Kozol's book *Rachel and Her Children*, Ballantine Books, New York, 1988.

3. Hand out a copy of the mayor's statement to each student. Ask one student to introduce you as the Honorable _____, Mayor of Pleasantville. Read the statement with great conviction. Allow some students to criticize your decision, but don't respond --- you want them to reserve their energy for the town meeting which will follow their discussions. Tell them that for now you will only answer questions about your statement --- so that everyone is clear on its meaning.

4. Ask groups to discuss the town meeting questions and decide what they think. (Allow about 10 - 15 minutes for this.)

5. Explain to students that there are quite possibly other groups in the room who might agree with them. The more united people are in their opinions and goals at the town meeting the more power they will have to convince others. Have each group select two members to serve as "traveling negotiators" who will visit other groups to see if they can develop a plan together on what to do about homelessness. (Traveling negotiators may not meet with other traveling negotiators --- only with seated groups.) Tell students to look around to see which group may be an ally. Allow about 10 minutes for this. You want to end it before the energy level declines.

6. Traveling negotiators return to their original groups. Each group must prepare a brief presentation based on the town meeting questions and their discussions. A member from each group will write a one or two sentence response on the board on why they **do** or **do not** support the mayor's statement.

7. Call the town meeting to order. Groups should stay together with allies, if preferred. This is a time to debate. **Students must remain in character**. Encourage participation from everyone by asking questions, pointing out contradictions or problems.

8. After the meeting allow time to debrief. Have students step outside their character and write about the experience. What do they think about their group's ideas? Did any other group's ideas appeal to them? If this were a real town meeting what would they have said? How did it feel to be the character they played? Did this activity change the way they think about people who have lost their homes? (Be sure to tell students that in real town meetings many times the homeless are not included. How might this omission have changed the meeting?)

HANDOUT

THE MAYOR'S STATEMENT

Many citizens have complained to the city council that homeless people are turning our railroad station into a shelter. The homeless are sleeping on benches, washing up in the rest rooms and asking passersby for money or food.

I am sorry, my friends, but the railroad station was not built to accommodate overnight guests. It is not a slumming house. The hard-working people of our city who take the trains to and from work, and those people who live and work near the station have the right to a safe and clean city. They should not have to live in fear of people who are unkempt or ranting and raving, talking to themselves. Nor should they have to be exposed to people who are carriers of diseases such as TB and pneumonia which are rampant among homeless people. Our train station is a beautiful, historic landmark and the city intends to keep it that way.

The homeless people who gather in the train station are a threat to public safety. We simply will not tolerate their presence there anymore. They will have to find other places to stay. To keep them out the city will be removing the 300 benches located in the main rotunda. The few antique landmark benches will remain. Signs will be posted explaining clearly that shaving and washing clothes are prohibited in the station's rest rooms. Policemen will be posted at rest room doors to keep out all undesirables. In order to prevent the homeless from congregating outside the covered entrance to the station, the area will be mopped nightly with strong ammonia that produces a noxious smell. In addition, charitable organizations that have been distributing food to the homeless in the station each night will be denied entrance. They only attract more homeless people to the area.

Beginning today, it is the policy of this city to forbid the homeless and undesirables from using the railroad station as a shelter. Police officers will be stationed at the doors of the station to enforce the policy. It is necessary to teach the homeless, now before winter sets in, that their presence in the station will not be tolerated.

TOWN MEETING QUESTIONS

Do you support the mayor's decision? Why or why not?

Who is responsible for helping people who have lost their homes?

What measures would you like to see taken regarding homelessness?

GROUP #1 - ROLE SHEET

THE HOMELESS

It wasn't your fault that the local tire company closed down and left you without a job after you worked so hard for twelve years. You search everyday for a job but there don't seem to be any for people like you. You would like to get into a job-training program and learn to use a computer but you can't find a program that is willing to take you free of charge. Since you have been homeless no one will listen to you, look at you or come near you.

When your money ran out you were evicted from your apartment. You will not stay in a shelter because they are overcrowded, unsanitary and dangerous. You have been living on a bench in the city's old railway station. At least there you have a private corner where you can be alone and think, and a bathroom to shave and wash clothes in. You must try to make yourself presentable but your clothes are ragged and your shoes are full of holes. Some days you do not even recognize yourself in the mirror. Everyday you walk all over the city trying to find food, a job or someone who can help you.

You would like the mayor of Pleasantville to know that you and your homeless friends are not a threat to the people of the city. Have they taken a good look at you lately? You are weak and tired from hunger. You have not been able to sleep well for several months and you have a hacking cough. You are sorry that your appearance annoys people but if they had to live the way you do - **they** would look frightening too. You'd like to tell the people of Pleasantville that the homeless don't mean to expose them to any sickness - you just don't have the money to pay for a doctor and living outside all the time makes you sicker. What do they expect you to do? You are sure that the real reason many people are frightened of you is that when they look at you they see themselves. They know that if no one is helping you when you are down, then no one will help them when they are down either.

You are tired of being pushed out of every place you go. Do people think you want to live in the railway station? You are tired of people who don't even know you making policies that affect your life. Why don't the government officials ever come to the railway station and ask people like you what you need and how the people of the city can help you get it?

You would say to the mayor: "LOOK AROUND YOU! This city has enough skyscrapers and expensive hi-rise apartment buildings! What about people who don't earn lots of money? How about building some affordable apartments for us? We can even work to build them! We need jobs, decent homes and FOOD! And we're eager to work hard to get them! We used to pay taxes when we were working. Shouldn't our money be used to help us when we are down?" Today you walked all day trying to find someone who would listen. It is getting very cold and starting to rain. You are looking forward to the hot coffee and sandwich that an organization gives away free in the railway station at 10 pm. You are just too tired to think anymore.

GROUP #2 - ROLE SHEET

RESTAURANT OWNER

You are the owner of a restaurant inside Central Railroad Station in Pleasantville. You don't want the homeless to be allowed to sleep in the doorway of your restaurant or to gather in the station. Can't the city do something about these people? They are bad for business. Many people refuse to come to your area or eat at your restaurant because they fear the diseases and unpredictable behavior of the homeless there.

You are angry. You consider yourself a decent, law-abiding citizen. You pay a lot of taxes to the city out of the money you earn. You are a very hard-worker and you are not about to let anyone who doesn't want to work for a living ruin the business you have struggled so hard to build. You are a community leader. Many people agree with you and you are going to make sure the city gets your message. After all, the government officials work for YOU and the rest of the taxpayers.

You want people to know that you have a good heart. You don't like to see anybody down on her luck and having to sleep in a railroad station or on a park bench when it is cold outside. But you are sure that a lot of the homeless bring their problems on themselves. Several years ago when there were only a few homeless people in the station, you **did** try to help by offering them left-over food from your restaurant, but your charity only brought more homeless people to the area looking for your free food. There are just too many of them now. They are turning the streets and station into dormitories! You know that no one can help people who don't want to help themselves.

It just doesn't seem fair that homeless people should be allowed to sleep all day, then get free food too when you have to work so hard. You arrive at your restaurant very early in the morning and don't leave for home until dark. You have three children to support. You don't have the time to try to come up with a solution to the problems of the homeless. That's why you pay taxes. Let the city, the charities and the churches solve the problem.

It's a shame that a once beautiful station has been allowed to get so run down. You take pride in your city and your work. You want your children to be able to play in the parks without having to be exposed to homeless people sleeping on benches. You do your part to keep the area around your restaurant clean and attractive. It is not fair to allow homeless people to spoil the beauty of the area. Maybe the city could use some of the taxpayers' money to build a settlement house outside the city for all the homeless. Most of the taxes, however, should be spent on improving life in the city for the people who work and pay those taxes - on fixing up the streets, keeping the parks pretty and putting more police officers on the streets to keep them safe.

GROUP #3 - ROLE SHEET

ACTIVIST FOR HOMELESS PEOPLE

You are an activist for the homeless and you cannot believe what is happening in Pleasantville. Doesn't anyone care that men, women and children are sleeping outside in the rain and snow every night? You think the mayor should call an emergency press conference and say "This has gone on long enough! We are mobilizing our entire city immediately to find a way to help homeless people put their lives back together."

You know that once people lose everything they become weaker, and sicker from living on the street. It is impossible to get out of it alone. They need a helping hand. It is up to people who have their health and strength to help others who are down.

You have seen families sleeping in phone booths and under benches to get out of the rain. This is crazy! You feel that the people of Pleasantville have grown tired of the homeless and would just like to send them all away. But you know that the homeless aren't going away - in fact, there will probably be even more homeless people this winter because a local company that employed several hundred workers in Pleasantville is closing down and moving to another country where they pay their workers much less. There are very few jobs in this town and more and more unemployed people will have trouble paying their rents. The government has cut back on the money it spends on services such as housing and food programs for the poor.

If you could, you would like to take the mayor to the train station and introduce him to some of the people who seek shelter there. You would say to him: "Look, this is what happens when people stop caring about other people. If another country was doing this to our people we would go to war against them. Why do **we** allow it?" You have listened to the homeless and they have told you that they need food, a safe place to stay and medical attention. Many of them are sick from living outside all the time and eating unhealthy food. Then, they tell you, that when they are a little stronger, they need to be trained for new jobs. They need fair wages that will help them pay their own expenses. They need an apartment they can afford, health care and an education for their kids so they can grow up and get good jobs.

In your opinion, the city isn't paying enough to help the homeless. More of the taxpayers' money should be used to build affordable apartments, instead of expensive high-rises. You would like to explain to the mayor and the business people in Pleasantville that the best way to improve life here is to create new jobs and training for the homeless. We need to make the homeless a priority! Ending homelessness is possible. No one wants to be homeless. If we work together we can stop this from happening in our town. After all, what would the people of Pleasantville do if those people sleeping on streets and park benches on cold nights were their own fathers, mothers, brothers or sisters?

GROUP #4 - ROLE SHEET

GOVERNMENT OFFICIAL

You are a government official in Pleasantville. The salary you receive comes from the taxes paid by the working people of the city. You don't think it is fair to these working people to have to put up with the unsanitary and dangerous conditions created by the homeless. Besides, you have other problems to solve - the streets are full of pot holes, bridges and tunnels in the city need repairing, and crime is up. There is so much work to be done! You would like to see more police on the streets. All this is going to cost money - money that comes from working people's taxes. Too many people are becoming homeless and expecting the city to take care of them. This is not fair!

Of course, you care about the homeless. You hate to see them sleeping on city benches and doorways, but many of them simply don't want to work; they expect handouts from the people who **are** working. One thing is for certain: If you make homelessness acceptable, if you build a lot of shelters for them and give away food, clothes and medical care, then these people will NEVER try to get a job! That is just the way some people are. If the homeless in other cities hear about how well the homeless in Pleasantville are treated, why most of the homeless people in the country will move to your city! You surely don't want that! Some of your friends in government have said that the way to clean up the city and take care of the homeless problem is to give each of them a one-way ticket to another city. You wouldn't go that far, but you have no tolerance for freeloaders. Why can't they just clean themselves up, get a job and live like the rest of the people in Pleasantville?

You would like the city to cut back on social services for poor people - shelters, emergency food programs and health care. You don't think these programs help people get on their feet. By taking away many of these free services, you believe this will force people to get a job in order to survive. There is simply too much money being wasted on strong, young people who could be working. Too many people are cheating the system. You also want the people of Pleasantville to place a certain stigma on homelessness. People should look at a homeless person and think, "Gee, I'm going to work hard so that I don't end up like that poor person." You also think the government should make it as difficult as possible for homeless people to get free things without working for them. For instance, there should be a lot of paperwork and waiting before people get food stamps or welfare checks. Then, maybe more people would rather find a job than stand in line all day.

You want the city to cut back on programs that help the homeless stay homeless. You want more money spent on fixing up the city and putting more police on the streets. You believe this will make Pleasantville a safer, cleaner, more beautiful city.

GROUP #5 - ROLE SHEET

COMMUNITY ORGANIZER

You have joined with other concerned citizens to find creative ways to end homelessness. You have spent time talking to homeless people and finding out about the kinds of skills they have and the kinds of skills they need. You have also spoken to business people in the city who need workers or who are willing to help train workers. These business people own or run restaurants, clothing stores, printing shops, news-stands, supermarkets, etc. By introducing homeless people who want to work to business people who can hire and train them, your organization has helped many homeless people get off the street and back to work.

You have written to the mayor about the seven homeless men and women you found living in the city's parks a few years ago. Your organization found them safe, clean rooms in a small hotel, fed them at a nearby soup kitchen, and got them medical treatment. When they regained their health and confidence, you took them to meet some restaurant owners who had agreed to teach them how a restaurant works. They worked hard and were paid as waiters, waitresses, cooks, cashiers and janitors in the restaurants. Two times a week the owners and managers of the restaurant met with them and taught them how to plan a budget, order food, and maintain a restaurant. In the meantime, your organization helped the seven people find apartments they could afford. A few years and a lot of hard work later, the seven former homeless people started a restaurant of their own using loans from the owners of the restaurants where they had been trained! And who do you think they hired and trained to work in their new restaurant? Twenty homeless people from the city's parks and shelters who desperately needed work! The restaurant is doing so well that the new owners have begun paying back the loans. Every Tuesday a special dinner is held in the new restaurant to feed homeless people in the neighborhood. Business people from the community come to dinner as well and talk to people about training them for jobs in their companies. (The original restaurant owners are already training more homeless people.)

You have linked other business people with homeless people in the same way - hospitals, hotels, book stores, construction companies, typing services, etc. You would like the city government to study your successful program and spend some of the taxpayers' money to create more programs like yours. At least they know that your program works - the city's efforts so far have not helped homeless people get their lives back together the way yours has. Everyone would benefit from more programs like yours around the city. Pleasantville would be a safer, cleaner, more caring place to live.

LESSON 18: THE MEDIA

In this media workshop students explore the different ways the media complicate the hunger problem:

In PART 1: ADVERTISING students collect and study ads, identify their "target" audiences and messages and discuss who benefits from advertising. They compare a generic product with a popularly advertised one to discover that the only real difference is the price and the packaging. A discussion focuses on how advertising increases consumption and waste by getting us to buy things we don't need.

In PART 2: THE TRUTH, THE WHOLE TRUTH AND EVERYTHING BUT THE TRUTH students analyze current news reports to find out how they portray hungry people, and how much they teach about the **root causes** of hunger. They create their own honest and informative headlines and articles.

Additional activities in this lesson ask students to watch their favorite TV programs with a more critical eye. Discussions reveal how these programs often pull us away from the real world and its important problems. Several ideas for using the media more effectively can be found at the end of this lesson.

PART 1: ADVERTISING

FACTS:

The average 5 year-old will have spent 5,000 hours in front of the TV before entering kindergarten - longer than the time it takes to get a college degree. (Nielsen, Inc.)

On average children see 20,000 TV commercials a year - over 350,000 by the time they are 18. (Action of Children's Television)

DAY 1:

MATERIALS: 1 box of popular brand cereal (choose one that is heavily advertised on Saturdays mornings)

1 generic brand of cereal

Examples of ads from various magazines - if possible tape some TV ads

PROCEDURE:

1. Ask students to define "the media". What is included? Tell them they will be learning about the media over the next few days and the media's connection to the problem of hunger. (Can they imagine what that connection might be?) One area of the media includes **advertising**.

2. Ask students to list in journals their favorite brand of:
   sneakers   ice-cream   apples (!)
   computer   soft-drink   beans (!)
   cereal   chips
   soup   cookies
   candy-bar   carrots (!)

3. Once they have completed their lists chart them on the board.
   Did many choose the same brands?

   > Why are these their favorites?
   > How did they hear about them?
   > Are advertised products **better** products?

4. Present the two boxes of cereal. Which would they buy? Why? Compare the prices. Read the package labels. Compare the ingredients in each. Pass around some of each for students to taste. (Or do a blindfolded taste test.)

5. Ask how advertising and packaging influence us. Read some of the ads you've brought in or critique the taped TV commercials with students:

   > Who is the target audience?
   > What is the message of the ad?
   > What race, gender, age are the people
   >   in the ads? Why?
   > What is the **purpose** of advertising?
   > Who benefits from it?

6. Brainstorm a list of ways in which we are bombarded everyday with advertising messages (TV, radio, billboards, packaging, newspapers, magazines, even skywriting!)

WEEKEND HOMEWORK
(Assign this homework over a weekend so students can include a study of Saturday morning TV commercials)

1. Have students divide a page of their journals like this:

ITEM ADVERTISED	TV, RADIO MAGAZINE	TARGET AUDIENCE	AD'S MESSAGE

2. Tell students that as they watch TV over the weekend or page through magazines they should write down the ads they see. Explain the meaning of "target" audience - whose attention is the ad meant to attract: women, men, teenagers or young children? Explain the meaning of an ad's message - what is the ad trying to tell its audience? For example, "This cereal will make you more powerful" or "This toothpaste will make you more popular."

DAY 2:

1. Sitting in one large circle, discuss the students' ad collections.

QUESTIONS

What kinds of foods and other products were advertised most? When? To whom?

Why did the companies choose those times and those particular programs to advertise their products?

What techniques do advertisers use to get people to buy their products?

Did the ads show people wanting to have the "best" of something, or people sharing, cooperating and working together?

How are racial and ethnic minorities portrayed in the ads (if at all)? What are they advertising?

How are older people portrayed in the ads?

What are they advertising?

Why are there often attractive women in car commercials?

How does advertising affect the way we see different groups of people (women, African-Americans, Native Americans, Latinos, older people)?

How would you feel after seeing these ads over and over again?

How does advertising affect our view of cooperation and competition?

Do any of the ads exploit weaknesses or addictions such as sugar, smoking, etc.?

Are the ads honest?

Do any of the ads educate their audience about the true value of the product?

Who benefits most from these ads?

How does advertising shape consumption and life-styles? Does advertising increase waste?

What are some of the harmful effects of advertising?

Do you see any connection between advertising and the persistence of poverty and inequality?

How could advertising be used to help people make wise choices in food and other items?

ADDITIONAL ACTIVITIES:

1. Have students choose between creating an ad for a magazine or acting out a TV commercial alone or with a partner. Students choose a slip of paper from a basket. Some slips say "WHOLE FOOD", others say "A TRUTHFUL AD", others say "LUNCH".

   "WHOLE FOOD" means they must create an ad for a whole, healthy food such as apple, carrot, etc.

   "TRUTHFUL AD" means they must find an ad in a magazine or on TV and create a truthful ad for that item. For example, what does the candy bar **really** contain? What will it do to your teeth and body? Why is the company advertising it on Saturday morning? Who is going to benefit if you buy this product? (These are spoofs of real ads.)

"LUNCH" means these students must choose a food from the school lunch program and create an ad for it.

2. Look for evidence of the power of advertising in your school - slogans, labels, logos, language from ads, products used by students and teachers, teaching materials, brand-name foods, etc.

7. ***HOW ADVERTISING CONVINCED MOTHERS TO BUY SOMETHING THEY ALREADY HAD****
(and harmed many babies)

Can you imagine something that could **feed** and **immunize** every single baby on earth? Hint: It doesn't need to be heated or refrigerated. No bottles, spoons or packaging are necessary. It is highly nutritious, tastes good and is FREE!!!

ANSWER: Mother's milk

When a mother gives birth her body automatically begins to make milk to feed her baby. As the milk flows from the mother's body to the baby's, it carries with it nutrients to make the baby grow strong, and special proteins called "antibodies" to protect the baby's tiny body from infection. The mother's milk is fresh and warm. It contains proteins called "enzymes" that make the mother's milk easy to digest.

Most mothers can breastfeed. Some mothers choose to feed their babies a product called "infant-formula" from a bottle. Formula is cow's milk that has been sweetened, heated, fortified with vitamins and packaged in sterilized containers. Formula does not contain the natural enzymes or antibodies found in mother's milk. It must be heated at home and then poured into bottles that have also been sterilized. Some formulas come in a powder form and must be mixed with purified water. Any leftover formula must be refrigerated or it will spoil.

So why would a mother choose to **buy** something less healthy for her baby when her body already produces something better? Some mother's bodies can't make milk for their babies so the mothers **must** feed their babies formula. Mothers who work outside their homes must leave their babies with day-care workers or the baby's father. Some mothers who work prefer to pump their own breastmilk so that it can be fed to their babies from bottles while they are away

---

* Created from information distributed by Infant Formula Action Campaign, 30 E. 38th St. Suite 3091, Minneapolis, MN 55409

at work. Many mothers, however, prefer the convenience of having the care-giver feed their babies formula. Some mothers breastfeed for awhile, then switch to formula later.

In the 1960's mothers in industrialized countries like the U.S. began learning that their own milk was better than the formula they were buying. The message spread and more and more mothers stopped buying formula. The companies that produced the infant formula wanted to find new markets for their product so they began advertising in developing countries. Mothers in these countries had **always** breastfed their babies, so to get them to buy formula the companies created billboards, signs and magazine ads showing the bottle of formula next to the chubby, pink face of a healthy baby with bright eyes and a wide smile. This kind of advertising made mothers believe that babies who drink formula are **healthier** and **happier** than babies who drink mother's milk. Some ads even claimed that babies who drink formula are smarter than those raised on mother's milk.

Like most parents around the world, mothers and fathers in developing countries want to give their children the best they can. The messages in the ads told parents that breastfeeding was "backward" and that the "modern" mother who really cares about her babies feeds them formula. **Because of the advertising campaign, many mothers turned away from breastfeeding.**

In countries where most families cannot afford food, clean water and medicine the campaign has tragic effects. In poor households family members go without food so they can buy expensive infant formula. Mothers cannot always get clean water to mix with the formula or the fuel needed to heat the formula and sterilize the bottles. Very often dirty water and contaminated bottles are used. Mothers don't always have access to refrigeration and the formula spoils. Babies become malnourished and very sick. In some places the instructions on the formula package aren't written in the mother's language. When a mother stops breastfeeding and begins giving her baby formula her body stops making milk. The mothers and babies become dependent on formula.

Some people who learned that advertising was misleading mothers and hurting babies protested loudly. They carried signs in front of the companies that make the formula, they wrote newspaper articles and went on radio and TV to tell others what the companies were doing in developing countries. The World Health Organization developed rules against certain advertising techniques. Some companies have stopped their misleading advertising, but others continue today.

In order to teach mothers in developing countries how healthy their own free milk is, some organizations such as UNICEF and Save the Children have set up clinics and nutrition centers. It will take time to reach all the mothers and repair the damage caused by dishonest advertising.

DISCUSSION QUESTIONS

1. Why is breastfeeding healthier and more economical than bottle-feeding?

2. Why do some mothers prefer not to breastfeed their babies?

3. How did advertising hurt families and babies in developing countries?

4. Who benefits from dishonest advertising such as this?

5. How can the damage caused by misleading ads be repaired and prevented in the future?

ACTIVITIES:

1. Create a poster advertising the benefits of breastfeeding.

2. Role play an advertising campaign representative trying to sell formula to a mother.

REBELLION AGAINST THE NORTH SIDE

There will be no monograms on our skulls,
You who are training your daughters to check for the words
"Calvin Klein" before they look to see if there are pockets
are giving them no hands to put in those pockets.

You are giving them eyes that will find nothing solid in stones.
No comfort in rough land, nameless sheep trails.
No answers from things which do not speak.

Since when do children sketch dreams with price tags attached? Don't
tell me they were born this way.
We were all born like empty fields.
What we are now shows what has been planted.

Will you remind them there were people
who hemmed their days with thick-spun wool
and wore them till they fell apart?

Think of darkness hugging the houses,
caring nothing for the material of our pajamas.
Think of the delicate mesh of neckbones
when you clasp the golden chains.
These words the world rains back and forth
are temporary as clouds.
Clouds? Tell your children to look up.
The sky is the only store worth shopping in
for anything as long as a life.

                                      by Naomi Shihab Nye
                                      (Reprinted with permission of
                                      the author.)

PART 2:

THE TRUTH, THE WHOLE TRUTH AND EVERYTHING BUT THE TRUTH

MATERIALS: Several current magazines and newspapers (If possible videotape the opening segment of a television news program to critique)

One long, blank strip of paper, enough to cover one of the headlines on the newspaper

Tape

PROCEDURE:

1. Show students the magazines and newspapers. Read some of the headlines. Is there any important and urgent news missing from these reports?

2. Tape the strip of blank paper over one of the headlines. On it write in large letters: **25,000 CHILDREN DIED OF HUNGER TODAY!**

   Why don't headlines shout this crucial message?

   What sells magazines and newspapers?

   When the media **do** cover hunger do they focus on relief services or on root causes? How much do they tell us about **why** people are hungry?

   What message do the media send about hungry people? Are they portrayed as helpless and dependent - or as eager to work, skillful, talented and courageously struggling to overcome obstacles and resist oppression? How might this image affect the hunger problem?

   How does the lack of attention to hunger contribute to the problem?

   How could the media help educate the public about the root causes of hunger?

   Why is it important to read different magazines and newspapers instead of only one?

3. Have students tape paper over a newspaper or magazine headline at home and create their own hunger headlines, then write the report on the causes of hunger below the headline. They can present these to other classes or display them.

ADDITIONAL ACTIVITIES:*

1. Ask students to suggest the names of some of their favorite TV programs. Write these on the board. Tell them they are going to watch these programs with a more critical eye. Decide who will watch which program. As they watch they must pay close attention to the ways different races, genders, ages and social classes are portrayed. What roles do women (older people, racial and ethnic minorities, etc.) play and what qualities do the characters possess? Students should keep notes as they watch. How are conflicts presented and resolved? What are the goals of the main character: to get ahead, be the best, be a hero? Or to work together to make positive changes for everyone?

   At the end of the week after students have watched and critiqued their programs, have them work in small groups to compare their criticisms and to prepare a presentation for the class.

QUESTIONS:

What did you learn about TV families or people's economic situations? How does that compare to this country as a whole? Why is it different?

What did you learn about people of color? Older people? Women? Were their characters real or stereotyped?

How did characters on TV solve their problems? Was this realistic? How do you and your family solve your problems?

How do TV programs influence the way we see the world and think about ourselves? Why are people from different races, classes and ages omitted from many TV programs?

Are you letting stereotypes and omissions affect you? What can you do to change this?

How do the distortions in TV shows prevent us from understanding the reality around us?

---

* Activity #1 adapted by permission from *Open Minds to Equality* by Nancy Schniedewind and Ellen Davidson, copyright 1983 by Allyn and Bacon.

How does maintaining stereotypes perpetuate the problem of poverty and hunger?

2. Watch *Images* or *Culture Jammers*, videos listed in the Resource Guide.

MAKE A DIFFERENCE!

1. Write letters to the editor of local newspapers regarding the lack of coverage of subjects such as hunger. Write op-eds that educate readers about hunger in your community and what community members and government officials can do to end it. See Lesson 23 for letter-writing tips.

2. Encourage TV networks to create a "development desk". Send letters to local stations and major networks encouraging them to assign at least one person to be a full-time development correspondent to report on hunger and development issues. Insist that they focus on programs that help hungry people **feed themselves**.

3. Write to the producers of your favorite TV program urging them to incorporate the **real** struggles and triumphs of people who are politically disenfranchised into storylines.

LEARN HOW TO USE THE MEDIA!

4. Make your own hunger video and send it to local television stations. Brainstorm ways to get funding for this project - car-wash, bake sale, etc., or simply ask parents and community members for donations. Some students have successfully convinced local cable stations to donate time and equipment to shoot their video. In addition to alerting the public to the existence of hunger, try to educate them about the root causes in your video.

5. Create a 30-second radio commercial. Tape it and deliver it to a major radio station. Find out what the station charges to play the ad during rush hour when it will be heard by all the motorists on their way to or from work. (This charge is usually around $100.) In successful ads students often address their governor, mayor or members of the community.

6. Give a Public Service Announcement. Call your local radio station for information. (Some students have simply walked into radio stations carrying food - coffee, muffins, cookies, donuts, cheese & crackers - and requested some air-time with the disc jockeys. The food, they say, was their ticket inside. It's worth a try!

7. Create your own class newsletter about hunger and related topics. Each month have different students rotate duties - reporters investigating local news and events, layout artists, typists, editors, etc. Distribute the newsletter in the community. You might even get funding from community organizations or businesses to expand your newsletter.

8. Send for WHY's *Media Guide* for ideas on how to get the media's attention. See Resource Guide to order.

LESSON 19:
THE GRAPES OF WRATH

The Grapes of Wrath
By John Steinbeck
Penguin Books
581 Pages

John Steinbeck's novel is a landmark of American literature. Published in 1939, it is a moving and timely portrait of hardworking people and their struggle to preserve their humanity in the face of social and economic desperation.

The Joad family is forced off its beloved farm in Oklahoma by representatives of large land-owners and banks. Readers climb aboard the family's over-loaded, run-down truck and make the harrowing journey westward with them in search of the American Dream - a home, a piece of land to call their own, a job, peace and security. Each night, with little money and food, the family joins fellow migrants in recreating society on the road. Leaders are chosen, food and other necessities are rationed and shared with strangers, unspoken social codes are honored - privacy, generosity, cooperation. Rituals are maintained: loved ones are buried far from home, prayers are recited, babies are born and engagements celebrated. Relationships are either solidified or shattered. When the exhausted travelers reach California, instead of realizing their dream, they are forced to confront the same powerful forces - greed, oppression and injustice--which drove them from their homes.

This novel has been included in this program because it illuminates the root causes of hunger and poverty so clearly and poignantly. Its themes are even more relevant today than they were during The Great Depression: the emotional and social fractures that occur when people are disconnected from the land-their source of food and livelihood; the plight of the small farmer, the homeless, the unemployed and the politically disenfranchised; the disintegration of family and community; the bitter conflict between the powerful and the powerless; the crucial role of women in the family and society; the importance of a fair wage and meaningful work for all; the seeds of violence.

You may wish to begin by reading the first three brief chapters aloud in class. Have students pay close attention to Steinbeck's use of detail in describing characters and their surroundings. As they read it will be helpful if they jot down in their journals any lines or phrases that have particular meaning for them. These can kick off classroom discussions the following day. Whenever possible, encourage students to make connections among the Joad's story, current events in the news, and other lessons you have covered in your study of hunger.

THE MOVIE

When the book has been completed, or as particular sections are covered, show students the movie--or scenes from the movie. It can be found in video stores and runs 129 minutes. This film, in black and white, with beautiful and haunting images, was directed by John Ford in 1940 and stars Henry Fonda as Tom Joad.

RELATED SONGS

Listen to and discuss: "The Ghost of Tom Joad" by Bruce Springsteen and/or "The Banks Are Made of Marble" by The Weavers.

RESEARCH PROJECTS

Steinbeck's novel captures the horrors of The Great Depression. Have students research the forces behind the Depression, The Crash of 1929, the Dust Bowl, and the New Deal. Investigate local archives for photos and first person accounts. Interview local community elders for their family stories.

QUESTIONS FOR DISCUSSION

1. Imagine that you are Tom Joad. You have been away from your own home and family for four years. What changes would you expect to find upon your return? What would have remained unchanged?

2. How did the land become so poor and dusty?

3. Discuss the following passage. Find passages in the novel that contrast with this description of how the land was viewed:

    Behind the tractor rolled the shining disks, cutting the earth with blades-not plowing, but surgery, pushing the cut earth to the right where the second row of disks cut it and pushed it to the left; slicing blades shining, polished by the cut earth...And when the crop grew, and was harvested, no man had crumbled a hot clod in his fingers and let the earth sift past his fingertips, no man had touched the seeds, or lusted for the growth. Men ate what they had not raised, had no connection with the bread. The land bore under iron, and under-iron gradually died; for it was not loved or hated, it had no prayers or curses.

4. What did the land mean to Muley and the Joads?

5. Tenant farmers got to keep a very small portion of the crop they grew on the landowners land. They could use this to feed their families or to sell. How do you feel about this line by a large land-owner:

    One man on a tractor can take the place of twelve or fourteen families. Pay him a wage and take all the crop.

(Is this progress?)

6. What does the tenant farmer mean when he asks:
   How can we live without our lives? How will we know it's us without our past?

7. In small groups role play tenant farmers trying to convince large land-owners to allow you to keep your farms.

8. Why do you think the bank was called "the monster"?

9. Why did so many families have to leave their homes? Do you have any suggestions on how this could have been prevented? What will be the consequences of this uprootedness? What will be the consequences of a few wealthy land-owners holding onto the land?

10. If you were forced to leave your home and town and could carry only five items with you on the road, what would you choose? Explain.

11. How do think you would react if you and your family were forced to leave the land where your grandparents and great-grandparents have lived, worked and died?

12. What did the government camps provide that made them so attractive to migrant families? Is there anything of value here that could have been duplicated in other camps?

13. Why do you think Steinbeck chose the title *The Grapes of Wrath*?

14. Do you find any significance in the fact that the author began his story with drought and ended it with a flood?

15. Reread Chapter 3. How does the story of the turtle relate to the rest of the story?

16. Discuss or write about what may have happened to Muley, Noah, Connie or Tom.

17. What constitutes "ownership"? In Chapter five a tenant farmer says:
    ...it's our land. We measured it and broke it up. We were born on it, and we got killed on it, died on it. Even if it's no good, it's still ours. That's what makes it ours--being born on it, working it, dying on it. That makes ownership, not a paper with numbers on it.

    (See also *This We Know* by Chief Seattle in Lesson 10)

18. What are the social and environmental consequences that result when most of an area's best land is used to produce only one crop such as grapes, cotton or oranges?

19. What was the Joad family's dream? Talk about your own family's dreams. Do you think the Joad family (and your family) will achieve that dream?

20. Interview a farmer in your area about the plight of the small farmer in America today. Compare his/her story with that of the Joads. Call your local Farm Bureau or visit a local greenmarket to find a farmer who will visit your classroom or invite you to visit the farm.

21. What were Casy and the other "reds" trying to do for the workers? Do you agree or disagree with their goals and tactics? Why do you suppose Tom decided to take on Casy's work?

22. "Hoovervilles" was the word used for encampments of migrants during The Great Depression. These camps were named after Herbert Hoover who was President at the beginning of the Depression. Discuss the conditions inside these camps. How does the plight of the migrants compare with that of today's homeless? refugees of war? communities where large companies have shut down or moved? developing countries where most of the best land is used for growing cash crops? workers who are not allowed to unionize?

23. Do you see any connection between the Joad's story and the story of the Native Americans?

WRITING ACTIVITIES

1. Collect a few artifacts that remind you of your home. If they are small, bring them in to share with the class. Talk about your connection to them. If they are too large, write an essay describing them and their importance to your personal history and identity.

2. Notice Steinbeck's use of detail for making a character or place come alive for the reader. Find a favorite place inside or outside your house. Sit quietly and observe for several minutes. Close your eyes and absorb what you hear, smell and feel. Write in your journal your impressions, observations, feelings and any overheard conversations that relate to this place. Give as many details as you can in your description of the place so your audience can "see" it. Describe your relationship to this place.

3. Reread Steinbeck's description of grandpa. Observe a member of your family (or focus on a photograph of a family member) and, using words, paint a clear and colorful portrait of that person. Include the person's favorite sayings, gestures, habits, hairstyle, clothes, language, etc.--anything that makes that person unique.

4. Compare a personal experience with something experienced by one of the characters in the novel.

5. Choose a character from the book and a particular event. Write an interior monologue from that character's perspective. For example, what was Muley thinking as he watched the Joad's truck pull away for good? What was Rose of Sharon feeling when she realized Connie had left her?

6. Write a poem about exile--being forced to leave the land or home you love. If you wish, choose three characters from the novel and write each stanza of your poem in a different character's voice. Find other poems of exile and bring in to read.

7. Why is it so important to put down roots? Choose a family photograph (or story) that you feel encapsulates a lot of your family history. Bring your photo or story to class and talk about it in your small group. Write an essay describing it and how it explains your roots.

8. Write an ending to this story. What happens to the Joads? What happens to Tom? Muley? Rose of Sharon?

9. After a discussion of Casy and his mission to help the workers, write about a time in your own life when you tried to make a difference.

10. Reread Tom's discussion with his mother about Casy in Chapter 28. Tom decides to take up Casy's cause:

> *I'll be aroun' in the dark.*
> *I'll be ever'where - wherever you look.*
> *Wherever they's a fight so hungry*
> *people can eat, I'll be there.*
> *Wherever they's a cop beatin' up a*
> *guy, I'll be there. If Casy knowed,*
> *why, I'll be in the way guys yell when*
> *they're mad an' - I'll be in the way*
> *kids laugh when they're hungry an they*
> *know supper's ready. An' when our folks*
> *eat the stuff they raise an' live in the*
> *houses they build - why, I'll be there.*

Some teachers have asked students to engage in simple "subversive" acts as a way of connecting with Tom and Casy. This can be a very exciting and inspiring activity, HOWEVER, be sure students know exactly what is expected and just how far they can go with this assignment. If you decide to do this with students, inform parents about what is being asked of students and how this connects to your hunger-study. Students may choose whether or not to participate. You may decide collectively to perform a local boycott or protest. Discuss the meaning of subversive--"to undermine the principles of corruption." Obviously, there are various degrees to which subversion can be carried. For this assignment students should be aware of simple, everyday opportunities for subversion. These acts may be small, but they often carry dramatic consequences and sharpen our awareness of injustices around us. Some examples of simple subversive acts performed by students are: standing up for someone who is oppressed, discriminated against or mistreated; choosing to do what you believe is right instead of what may be popular; getting to know someone who has been ostracized by your group of friends. Ask students to be aware of simple opportunities for undermining corruption or injustice that present themselves regularly. You may wish to share a subversive act you have engaged in and how you felt afterward. After students have performed their simple subversive acts have them write about them, then share their experiences with the class. How did the act make them feel? What were the immediate consequences? Would they do it again? Some classes have collected these in an album and placed it in the school library for others to read.

11. Create a comic strip, visual or poem based on one of the themes from the novel (the uncontrollable forces of Nature, the "American Dream", the tyranny of machines, the security of home, life on the road, etc.)

12. Write an essay in which you compare and contrast this story with "Maria's Dream" in Lesson 5.

The Ghost of Tom Joad
Bruce Springsteen
(Reprinted by permission)

Men walkin' 'long the railroad tracks
Goin' someplace there's no going back
Highway patrol choppers comin' up over the ridge

Hot soup on a campfire under the bridge
Shelter line stretchin' around the corner
Welcome to the new world order
Families sleepin' in their cars in the Southwest
No home no job no peace no rest

The highway is alive tonight
But nobody's kiddin' nobody about where it goes
I'm sittin' down here in the campfire light
Searchin' for the ghost of Tom Joad

He pulls a prayer book out of his sleeping bag
Preacher lights up a butt and takes a-drag
Waitin' for when the last shall be the first and the first shall be the last
In a cardboard box 'neath the underpass
Got a one way ticket to the promised land
You got a hole in your belly and a gun in your hand
Sleeping on a pillow of solid rock
Bathin' in the city aqueduct

The highway is alive tonight
Where it's headed everybody knows
I'm sittin' down here in the campfire light
Waitin' on the ghost of Tom Joad

Now Tom said "Mom, wherever there's a cop beatin' a guy
Wherever a hungry newborn baby cries
Where there's a fight 'gainst the blood and hatred in the air
Look for me Mom I'll be there
Whenever there's somebody fightin' for a place to stand
Or a decent job or a helpin' hand
Wherever somebody's strugglin' to be free
Look in their eyes Mom you'll see me"

Well the highway is alive tonight
But nobody's kiddin' nobody about where it goes
I'm sittin' down here in the campfire light
With the ghost of Tom Joad

LESSON 20:
ANCIENT FUTURES: LEARNING FROM LADAKH

Students watch a video of a remarkable and prosperous culture located high in the Himalayas where despite few resources, a harsh climate and rocky ground, human beings and Nature have flourished for over a thousand years. A class discussion focuses on the social and psychological forces that hold Ladakhi society together: frugality, cooperation and an intimate understanding of the environment. During the second half of the video students witness the breakdown of this society and environment as western-style development --- tourism, industrialization and consumerism --- rapidly dismantle centuries of social and ecological harmony. Activities and discussion help students connect the forces destroying Ladakh to the forces at work in U.S. communities.

The **Ancient Futures** video was produced by The International Society for Ecology and Culture, P.O. Box 9475, Berkeley, CA 94709. An edited version suitable for classroom use can be obtained by contacting:

KIDS CAN MAKE A DIFFERENCE®
140 East 72nd Street, #14B   Running time: 40 Minutes
New York, NY 10021
(212) 861-0911; www.kidscanmakeadifference.org

TEACHER BACKGROUND READING

What does the study of an ancient society on the Tibetan Plateau have to do with the study of hunger in American classrooms?

1. ***ANCIENT FUTURES*** offers students the opportunity to step outside what we in the West have come to think of as the **only** way of seeing the world. It provides a model of a successful society whose values and vision were shaped --- **not** by a western industrial perspective that emphasizes independence, competition, and the technological domination of Nature --- but by a deep-rooted respect for one another's needs and an acceptance of the limitations of the environment. Ladakh's economic and social philosophies embrace **inter**dependence and cooperation. As a result, poverty, hunger, even crime are non-existent. The culture generates a sense of security, fulfillment and contentment. It teaches us about the social wonders human beings can achieve.

2. Witnessing the "wealth" of traditional Ladakh can help dispel the notion that ignorance, disease and constant drudgery are the lot of pre-industrial societies.

3. Ladakh's serene and healthy civilization is bombarded by "development". The video shines a spotlight on the effects of this

invasion --- dislocation from the land and each other, greed, hunger, intolerance, aggression, dissatisfaction fueled by false promises of leisure and luxury, inflation, unemployment, ethnic and religious rivalries, pollution and waste. We are urged to turn the spotlight inward and re-examine our own values and visions and ask, What kind of society do we want to be? What is "progress"? What is "wealth"? Has all our technology made us happier, healthier, more civilized?

4. Around the world, with break-neck speed, western development is creating a monoculture erasing centuries of valuable knowledge, languages and customs. ***ANCIENT FUTURES*** asks the question: Is a more humane and sustainable life possible in today's rapidly changing, technological world? Ladakhis offer a hopeful answer. Refusing to let go of traditions that infused their lives with meaning, they are finding creative ways of integrating the best of their traditional culture with modern-age technology. Ladakhis are re-defining "development" --- small scale renewable energy sources such as solar heated walls, small-scale organic farming, increased literacy and better communication --- in ways that are more democratic and environmentally sound than conventional methods.

The story of Ladakh has been documented by Helena Norberg-Hodge, a western linguist who has lived closely with the Ladakhis for several years, learning their language, observing their ancient and modern ways of living, and developing The Ladakh Project to protect their culture and environment.

A TEACHER'S GUIDE
TO ANCIENT FUTURES[*]

I. THE PAST

Ladakh, or "Little Tibet" as it is also known, belongs to the Indian state of Jammu and Kashmir, is 40,000 square miles (about the size of England) with a population of around 130,000. The name "Ladakh" means "the land of mountain passes". It describes a high altitude desert region hidden among white-capped mountain ranges. For eight months of the year the ground is frozen solid and temperatures fall as low as 40 degrees below zero. During the brief planting season rain is rare and tornadoes whip furiously around Ladakh's stony edges. Humans and domesticated animals (sheep, horses, cows, goats, donkeys and yak) share this rough terrain with snow leopards, wolves and wild blue sheep. Animals play a crucial role in Ladakh's economy providing dung --- the main fuel --- transport, labor, wool and milk. Most Ladakhis are

---

[*] Adapted from the book *Ancient Futures*, by Helena Norberg-Hodge, Sierra Club Books, San Francisco, 1991.

self-supporting farmers. The principle crop grown is barley, although several acres of fast-growing wheat are also cultivated, as well as small gardens of peas and turnips. In the lower valleys can be found giant walnut trees and apricot orchards.

Culturally, Ladakh is Tibetan. Its language, art, architecture, medicine and music reflect this. Tibetan Mahayana Buddhism is the predominant religion and permeates all aspects of traditional life in Ladakh.

Interdependence
From birth a traditionally-reared Ladakhi child learns that everything is connected --- elements, plants, animals, human beings. Every living thing depends on every other living thing. Ladakhis have a deep and lasting relationship with the earth from which every resource is gathered, used, then returned: mud and stones for homes, wool from animals for clothing, food from the soil and animals, water from glaciers (one stream for drinking, another for washing). Skills, finely tuned to the environment, and honed by the centuries are handed down to everyone in Ladakh. Each person knows, for instance, how to build a house, make shoes and grind grain. This special kinship with the land extends even to the naming of children. There are no last names in Ladakh, only first names taken from the name of one's house or landholding. Land here is not owned but cared for. Each working member of a household is considered the "guardian" of one acre of land.

No money is spent in this society. People help for free - for the security of knowing they can depend on each other. "Ladakhis have inherited a society in which the good of the individual is not in conflict with that of the whole community," explains Norberg-Hodge.

The Role of Women
The focus of Ladakh's economy is the household. Women make the important decisions here and their knowledge and work is highly valued. They excel in maintaining good relations among families, in their understanding of the processes of Nature, of growing and preparing food and caring for children. In an agrarian society their knowledge is the "lifeblood" of the entire community. As a result of their highly respected position in the society, Ladakhi women exhibit great self-confidence, strength of character and dignity. A balance between male and female (the essence of Buddhism) resonates throughout the society: the female is symbolic of wisdom, the male of compassion.

II. THE PRESENT

Ladakh's traditional culture survived unthreatened by colonialism and development for so long because of its inaccessibility, its harsh climate and its scarcity of resources. Located on one of Asia's major trade routes, Ladakh was exposed to the influences of other civilizations but changes were integrated gradually into Ladakhi culture.

Then in 1974 the Indian government opened the area to tourism. Western-style development quickly followed and was concentrated mainly in Leh, the capital. By the 1990's 70% of Ladakh's population continued traditional lifestyles, but the psychological, social and environmental impact of modernization reverberates throughout the region.

Development now takes place (not at the communal level) but faraway in Kashmir or Delhi where programs are administered by officials who are not Ladakhi and do not speak the language. Development includes building roads, huge energy plants, over a hundred hotels, a large police force, a court, radio, western television, movies, medicine and western education. Trucks of foreign grown wheat and rice, firewood and water converge in Leh with busloads of tourists causing congestion, pollution and the clash of cultures.

As Norberg-Hodge explains, "To the Ladakhis these tourists seem to have lives of leisure and inexhaustible wealth," spending as much as $100 a day --- what a Ladakhi might spend in an entire year. The tourists, for their part, see only the material side of Ladakh --- worn-out handmade robes, an animal pulling a plow and barren land. To them the Ladakhis are backward and severely poor. The visitors do not stay long enough to uncover the social and spiritual wealth of Ladahis, their peace of mind and the ties that bind them to one another and their land.

Tourists, TV and films send out overwhelming images of luxury, glamour and power that are especially irresistible to the young who see their own lives, in contrast, as empty and dull. Feelings of self-consciousness, insecurity and pressures to conform to the images rob people of their individuality. People become anonymous, identified only by what they **have**, instead of what they **are**. Relationships are brief and superficial. The young reject their traditional culture and covet the symbols of the West they see in the shops in Leh - sunglasses, walkmans and tight jeans. They become aggressive and reckless. "To be modern means smoking cigarettes, driving fast and shooting at people." In their idolatry of the West they don't see the negative consequences of modernization - stress, loneliness, depression, inflation, unemployment, hunger and environmental damage.

Money and Technology
Values are changing ruled by Leh's new master, money. Labor, once shared, is now paid for. Land, once free, is now expensive as individual living spaces become smaller and smaller. Free handmade wool clothes have been replaced by expensive synthetic fibers or imported wool. The new economy operates on the mercy of forces very distant. As wages decrease and food prices increase, relationships change. Money pushes people further and further apart. One needs money today to be a farmer --- for labor, tools, animals, etc. Many Ladakhis are abandoning their farms and moving to the cities for paying jobs. People are cut off from their land, each other and themselves.

Machines, far from improving conditions in Leh, are complicating them and poisoning the air and water. For example, diesel-powered mills in the city grind grain many times faster than the traditional communal water wheels. But loads of wheat and barley must be transported at some expense to the distant mill where, for a price, the grain is ground. The high speed of the machine heats the grain reducing its nutritional value as the mill spews dark fumes into the thin mountain air. "You can't have a relationship with a machine. You become like them," says Norberg-Hodge.

In traditional Ladakh life was lived and work performed at a **human** pace. Technology turns time into a commodity --- something to buy and sell. As people acquire more and more "time-saving technological wonders" the pace of their lives actually speeds up. They must constantly keep up with ever more efficient technology. Ladakhis now have less time for themselves, their land and each other.

Education

In traditional Ladakh there were no schools. Children learned all that was required from tradition, from others and from observing Nature --- how to grow barley at 12,000 feet, how to shape and sundry mud bricks. Modern schools in Ladakh teach none of this. Instead children are trained to become specialists in a technological (not an ecological) society. Most of their newly acquired skills will be of no real use to them --- how to construct a building of concrete and steel or to farm using chemical fertilizers and machinery they will probably never be able to afford. Young Ladakhis are left unable to use their own resources. They are squeezed between the past and the present --- unprepared psychologically and practically to live the way their parents did, and incapable of applying their "education" to their present, everyday lives. Western style education in Ladakh leaves people poorer, less knowledgeable about themselves and their culture, dependent, and ashamed of their own traditions. Competition for space, food and jobs fuels rivalries. A dependence on abstract faraway forces makes people feel powerless and apathetic. Gaps form between old and young, male and female, rich and poor. "The biggest division of all in Ladakh is between the 'modern, educated expert' and the illiterate 'backward' farmer," according to Norberg-Hodge.

Men vs. Women

Male and female roles, once intertwined, are becoming more differentiated. Men are leaving their families to become part of the money-driven and technologically-based life outside the home. They are seen as the only productive members of the society, while women become shadows. In government statistics 10% of Ladakhis who work are listed according to their occupations - the other 90% (housewives and traditional farmers) are lumped together as "non-workers". Women and farmers see themselves as inferior. Men are deprived of prolonged contact with their children. They assume new macho identities based on characters and behavior in western films, while the women become more passive and overly concerned with appearance.

Health Hazards

All the elements of modern living in Ladakh (as in other places) work like a whirlpool pulling people to the center of modernization. The population of Leh has doubled while the rural population decreases steadily. Diseases of civilization --- cancer, stroke and diabetes --- unknown in traditional Ladakh --- are common now, the consequences of stress, western style diets and environment pollutants. Information about nutrition or the dangers of chemical fertilizers and pesticides rarely reaches "underdeveloped" areas. In Leh, Norberg-Hodge reports bread is often baked on scraps of asbestos and pesticide tins are used as salt shakers. 70% of the pesticides used in India have been outlawed or restricted in the West. Against the pristine, ancient backdrop of the Himalayas, modern, western artifacts pile up --- plastics, styrofoam, metal packing materials, etc.

III. THE FUTURE

The positive changes development has brought to Ladakh should not be discounted: heating, electricity, communication with the outside world, literacy (a necessity in today's world) and medicine that has reduced the child mortality rate and increased life expectancy. Ladakhis can travel more easily today, a sense of freedom and mobility releases them from bonds to place or people.

These positive changes deal mostly with comforts at the expense of relationships and the health of people and the environment. In Ladakh, as well as other places, the benefits of development are not available to everyone, only those who can pay for them. In "raising the standard of living" in Ladakh, development has sacrificed the social and ecological balance.

Norberg-Hodge urges us to learn from Ladakh's successful attempts to regain their humane and sustainable way of life. Recent projects in Ladakh are proof that a higher standard of living need not mean abandoning economic independence or traditional values. A necessary component of these projects is a return to life on a smaller, more human scale.

Ladakhis are finding ways to incorporate technology with their traditional principles and to educate others. A far-reaching information campaign based in Leh advocates lobbying for subsidies for decentralized, renewable energy sources (wind, sun and water), supporting small scale organic farming, raising the status of farming as an occupation, strengthening the position of women, and demystifying-glamorous images from the West.

ANCIENT FUTURES

PRESENTING THE VIDEO:

1. Explain to students that they have been invited inside a culture that is very different from ours --- a healthy culture that has survived for over two thousand years. Ask students why it might be helpful to study an ancient civilization still thriving. As they watch, have students make notes of any reasons that explain how this culture survived for so many years.

2. Play the first half of the video. Stop it before images of western development begin to dominate the screen. Ask for students reactions to life in traditional Ladakh. Would they want to live there? Why or why not?

3. Divide the board into two separate sections: **LADAKH** and **OUR CULTURES** (You may have different cultures in your classroom). Brainstorm some of the differences between OUR CULTURES and LADAKH'S. List these under the appropriate heading on the board. Encourage students to think of some things in OUR CULTURES that aren't working well (people are out of work, racism, pollution, hunger, crime, etc.) Discuss how these problems might be handled and resolved in LADAKH.

   What are some of the supports that held Ladakh together so strongly for so many centuries? Would you say that Ladakh is "wealthy"?

4. Before presenting the second half of the video tell students that in the 1970's something happened that began to threaten the health and harmony of life in Ladakh. Can students imagine what it was? As they watch the rest of the video ask them to make note of any changes they see taking place.

5. After the video, while images are still fresh in their minds, ask students to choose a scene that reminds them of something in their own communities or families. Ask them to write about it for two or three minutes then share it with the class.

QUESTIONS:

Would you call the development taking place in Ladakh "progress"? Why or why not?

Compare the following in both traditional and modern Ladakh:

physical comforts role of women
relationships role of elders
connection to nature food production/distribution
education

Has development in Ladakh made people happier? healthier? Explain.

What caused the break-up of families and communities in Ladakh? Why did people leave the land? What were some of the consequences?

Can or should Ladakh go back to its traditional way of life? What positive aspects of their traditional culture would you suggest they keep? Can they integrate some of these into their new way of life? How?

What can Ladakh's traditional culture teach us about the root causes of hunger in our own country? What can Native **American** cultures teach?

Western movies, products, advertising, clothes, etc. are changing cultures around the world. Do you see this change as positive or negative?

ADDITIONAL ACTIVITIES:

1. Have small groups of students create a poster or TV commercial advertising travel to traditional Ladakh. Have other groups prepare posters advertising travel to your city (to traditional Ladakhis).

2. Students imagine they are traditional Ladakhi teenagers visiting your American town and seeing western culture for the first time (automobiles, restaurants, hotels, television, computers - as well as pollution, hunger, homelessness and crime). From this perspective have them write letters to their families and friends back in Ladakh describing this "strange" American culture.

3. Ask each student to choose a partner and together rehearse then perform one of the following scenes (or they can create scenes of their own):

    1. A Ladakhi teenager has just accompanied you to the latest popular American movie. The teen thinks the movie portrays life the way it really is in the U.S.

    2. A Ladakhi teenager from a traditional household accompanies you to a popular fast-food restaurant in your town. You both compare a traditional Ladakhi food and an American fast-food --- where the foods come from, how they are grown and prepared, their nutritional value, etc.

    3. A Ladakhi teenager from a traditional village, where education means learning to plant barley, how to build a house or turn wool into a shirt, visits your school to discuss American education.

4. What occupations were valued in traditional Ladakh? In small groups have students create a list of occupations that are valued in our society. Then have them organize these occupations according to the contributions each makes to the well-being of society. Which occupations are at the top of their lists? Which are at the bottom? In reality, which ones are seen as most valuable (highest paid)? Ask groups

to compare their lists with each other. (Don't forget actors, rock stars, models, athletes, CEO's advertising execs.)

5. Have students choose one of the themes from the Ladakh video and interview grandparents or other community elders on how that particular subject has changed in the U.S. since the grandparents were teenagers. Students can share these with the class. Subjects include:

Education
The way land is used
Food production and preparation
The role of women in the family and community
The role of elders in the family and community
Rituals (births, marriage, deaths, holidays, etc.)
Time - leisure, work time, time for oneself, for family, etc.
The role of the family in the community

Before interviewing, ask students to brainstorm questions they will ask. Are there any positive aspects of the traditional ways that have been lost? How can they be integrated into modern life?

6. Have students research an ancient culture that existed at one time in what is now your community. What Native American cultures lived on the land you now live on? Use the questions from **LESSON 10: THE LEGACY OF COLONIALISM - Additional Activity #8** as a guide. Compare these Native American cultures with the traditional culture of Ladakh. What can we learn from our own ancient cultures? How can we integrate their wisdom and practices into our modern lives to insure a healthy, humane future? (Discuss the video's title: *Ancient Futures*.)

7. The International Society For Ecology & Culture also puts out a comic book called *Journey to New York* which helps counter the overly glamorous image of modern urban life. It is the story of a young Ladakhi's journey from his village through New York City and home again.

To order contact KIDS CAN MAKE A DIFFERENCE - See Resource Guide.

UNIT III:

WHAT CAN WE DO TO HELP END HUNGER?

Hunger will be eliminated when people come together to help each other. People need to take an active role in changing politics and society, but first, they need to change themselves and their own hearts.

Rep. Tony Hall
Democratic Task Force on Hunger

...two people fighting
back to back can cut through
a mob, a snake-dancing file
can break a cordon, an army
can meet an army.
Two people can keep each other
sane, can give support, conviction,
love, massage, hope, sex.
Three people are a delegation,
a committee, a wedge. With four
you can play bridge and start
an organization. With six
you can rent a whole house,
eat pie for dinner with no
seconds, and hold a fundraising party.
A dozen make a demonstration.
A hundred fill a hall.
A thousand, have solidarity and your own newsletter;
ten thousand, power and your own paper;
a hundred thousand, your own media;
ten million, your own country.

It goes on one at a time,
it starts when you care
to act, it starts when you do
it again after they said no,
it starts when you say We
and know who you mean, and each
day you mean one more.

The Low Road from **The Moon is Always Female** by Marge Piercy. Copyright 1980 by Marge Piercy. Reprinted by permission of Alfred A. Knopf, Inc.

LESSON 21:
FIND OUT WHAT PEOPLE THINK

Before launching a neighborhood awareness campaign to teach others about hunger, students can get an idea of how well (or un-) informed people in their communities are about hunger --- its root causes and solutions. An interesting way to do this is to have students create a survey. (A sample survey can be found on the following page.) Students can brainstorm questions about hunger for their own surveys. Type up the survey and have students distribute copies to a family member and two other people in their communities. (Students should survey family members with whom they have **not** had on-going conversations about hunger during the study.)

Once the surveys have been collected, students can work in small groups to analyze and summarize the results. It can be especially empowering when young people discover that they are better informed about a crucial subject than many of the adults around them! Together look for ways to graph and chart the survey responses, then plan your awareness campaign. Some students have kicked off their campaigns with a hunger banquet to which they invited the press, local officials and community members. (See Lesson #2.) Others have held workshops in the town hall, library, or traveled to other schools. Students have created and distributed hunger newsletters, given public service announcements, and created and shown hunger videos in their communities. (See Lesson #18, Part 2 for suggestions on how to use the media effectively to spread your message about hunger in your community and gather community support.)

DISCUSSION:

According to the survey results, what are people's attitudes toward hunger?

What percentage of those surveyed were aware of how widespread hunger is?

Are people aware that hunger exists in the U.S.?

Do people believe the myths about hunger - that it is caused by a shortage of food, by people who don't know how to produce food, or by too little U.S. foreign aid?

How many people surveyed believe hunger can be eliminated? Are their suggestions for ending hunger realistic?

What can students do to inform their community about hunger?

(Answers to survey questions: 1-D, 2-B, 3-B, 4-B, 5-B, 6-B)

A SAMPLE SURVEY

AGE_____   OCCUPATION_____

1. How many children does the United Nations estimate die every **day** from causes related to hunger and poverty?

    A. 25
    B. 250
    C. 2,500
    D. 25,000

2. People are hungry because there is not enough food for everybody on our planet.

    A. TRUE   B. FALSE

3. People in places such as Africa and India are hungry because they don't know how to grow their own food.

    A. TRUE   B. FALSE

4. If the United States sent more food to hungry countries hunger could be eliminated.

    A. TRUE   B. FALSE

5. Hunger is not a problem in a powerful, wealthy country such as the United States.

    A. TRUE   B. FALSE

6. There is not much one person can do to help end hunger in the world.

    A. TRUE   B. FALSE

7. Do you think ending hunger is possible?

    A. YES   B. NO

8. If you answered YES to question #7 list two ways to end hunger:
   _____
   _____

9. What questions or comments do you have about hunger?
   _____
   _____
   _____
   _____

LESSON 22: SHINE A LIGHT ON HUNGER

This is an on-going art project that allows students to express their feelings about hunger in a creative way. They draw or collect images that **symbolize** hunger (its causes and solutions) on a class visual modeled after Picasso's *Guernica*. Get the art teacher to help with this one.

MATERIALS:

Large roll of white paper to cover one or more walls
Markers, paint, brushes, pens, colored pencils, charcoal
Magazines
Scissors
Glue
Handouts: *Guernica* - one for each student
The Great Tablecloth - one for each student

PROCEDURE:

1. Hand out copies of Picasso's *Guernica* and discuss its history and meaning. Ask students to suggest possible meanings for some of the images in the mural. These images will have different meanings for different students. The following are some suggestions that have been made by art critics:

    1. The broken sword symbolizes heroic resistance.
    2. The light above the horse resembles an eye. This represents reason - the need to see the truth clearly in order to bring an end to war.
    3. The hand holding the lamp looks like the Statue of Liberty. It could represent a beacon in the dark guiding those who have lost their way.
    4. The open window in the upper right corner symbolizes freedom or openness to other's differences.
    5. The mother holding the dying child has often been compared to the Pieta.
    6. The human-headed bull stands for intolerance, or the refusal to change.

2. Discuss the meaning and power of symbolic images. They are the artist's tool for sending powerful messages. Much is said with one simple image. Symbols evoke strong emotions. (Remind students of how the dying plant helped symbolize hunger's effects on human bodies.) Ask them to write down an image that might symbolize each of the following: courage, timidity, greed, freedom, hope. What **colors** might each of these be?

3. Tell students they will be creating their own mural with images that symbolize hunger and how to end it. Together choose a place where the mural's message will reach the most students - hallways, lobby, library, lunchroom, etc.

   Your mural will take shape over the next several weeks as students hear more about the root causes of hunger. Have them decide whether they will work alone, in pairs or in small groups. Some murals use multi-media and combine drawings, magazine cutouts, newspaper headlines, statistics, photographs, poetry, etc. The mural should depict some of the **causes** of hunger as well as **what is needed to end it.**

4. Ask students to brainstorm images that come to mind when they hear the word "hunger." Write these down. Ask them to write down an image in response to the following:

   > What color is famine?
   > What color is chronic hunger?
   > What kind of animal represents hunger?
   > What sound best represents hunger?
   > Write down a root cause of hunger -
   >   next to it write down an image
   >   that symbolizes that cause.

   Have them share these with each other.

5. Picasso combined images of war with images of what was needed to end the war. Brainstorm anything necessary to **end** hunger. (Some of these may include: awareness, compassion, generosity, work, equality, sharing of resources, education, etc.) Next to each item ask students to suggest an image that represents it.

6. Words can inspire. As you slowly read the following passages to students they can write down any images that come to mind to be used later in their designs. (You can repeat this exercise in following classes.)

   > *...Hunger is a curious thing: At first it is with you all the time, waking and sleeping and in your dreams, and your belly cries out insistently, and there is a gnawing and a pain as if your vitals were being devoured, and you must stop it at any cost...then the pain is no longer sharp but dull, and this too is with you always, so that you think of food many times a day and each time a terrible sickness assails you...then that too is gone, all pain, all desire, only a great emptiness is left, like the sky, like a well in drought.*
   >   from ***Nectar in a Sieve***
   >   by Kamala Markandaya

The peasant in the field
ate his poor quota of bread,
he was alone, it was late,
he was surrounded by wheat,
but he had no more bread;
he ate it with grim teeth,
looking at it with hard eyes...

Eating alone is a disappointment,
but not eating matters more,
is hollow and green, has thorns
like a chain of fish hooks
trailing from the heart,
clawing at your insides.

Hunger feels like pincers,
like the bite of crabs,
it burns, burns, and has no fire.
Hunger is a cold fire.
Let us sit down soon to eat
with all those who haven't eaten;
let us spread great tablecloths,
put salt in the lakes of the world,
set up planetary bakeries,
tables with strawberries in snow,
and a plate like the moon itself
from which we can all eat.

For now I ask no more
than the justice of eating.

The Great Tablecloth
From **Selected Poems** by Pablo Neruda, translated
by Nathaniel Tarn. Reprinted with permission from
Jonathan Cape, Ltd., London.

7. Take time to examine the images in the poem. Why does the speaker see hunger as green? Describe "hard eyes." How is hunger a cold fire? How do students interpret the message of Neruda's poem? What are some **positive** images?

8. If students wish they may share their images with a partner or keep them on a separate page to be developed later for their design.

9. Begin covering the wall for your mural and determine times during which students may work on it. **Everyone** must contribute something to the mural!

© 1997 Estate of Pablo Picasso / Artists Rights Society (ARS), New York.
Giraudon / Art Resource, NY.
Museo Nacional Centro de Arte Reina Sofia, Madrid.

GUERNICA

The original mural is 11' x 25'. It was created by Pablo Picasso, a Spanish 20th century painter. One of the most famous of all modern artists, Picasso was stirred to action by the Spanish Civil War in the late 1930's. During the war the beautiful, ancient city of Guernica in northern Spain was bombed. Picasso created this mural to protest the savagery of the war. Just as a writer might be moved or angered toward using words to provoke people into action, an artist uses images that make people feel, think and act. Picasso's visual is called *Guernica* and has become one of his most famous works. He did not paint the actual bombing; instead, he used powerful images to make the viewer feel what war does and what is needed to eliminate the forces that cause war. Each person who views *Guernica* will interpret the images in his or her own way.

LESSON 23: COMBINE OUR TALENTS

This activity connects students with people in their community who are working in a variety of ways to help hungry people become healthy and self-reliant. These include working in soup kitchens, food pantries and shelters, caring for the elderly, growing community gardens, creating jobs, training unemployed people for new jobs, ending racism and discrimination, teaching, writing or singing about hunger and poverty, reporting on the causes of hunger, lobbying government officials and designing legislation, etc.

Students interview these people who are making a difference in the community. They work alongside them if possible, and introduce them to their classmates during a Local Heroes Day. The names, addresses and phone numbers of the organizations for which these and other community members work are compiled in student journals to serve as a resource guide for continued student involvement in the community.

Remind students that in addition to spreading the message about hunger, they must also find creative ways to help hungry people get food as well as to help remove obstacles that prevent people from becoming self-reliant. Everyone's skills, ideas, talents and labor are necessary. Students can begin thinking about what they might bring to the movement by considering what they are good at and what they like - writing, drawing, speaking, singing, working one-on-one with the elderly, children, the sick, working the land, making videos, etc.

Students can work in groups, pairs or alone to seek out people already working in their communities, hear their stories, observe them at work and write about them. Some students may know of individuals, organizations, or church groups helping hungry or poor people. They can share these with the class. Together brainstorm ways to go about finding out who is helping the homeless, getting laws passed that end racism, discrimination, secure affordable housing, etc., educating people, etc. Have a telephone directory or two available. Students are always surprised at how easy it is to find these organizations and people! Most organizations are very open to young people who are interested in what they do.

Set a due date for presentations. If possible, invite the entire school, the media and local politicians to a Local Heroes Day. Students can introduce their guests, explain briefly their experience working with them, and how this work contributes to ending poverty and hunger. Compile written presentations in an album with names of organizations, addresses and phone numbers and place in the library so that other students have access to it.

LESSON 24: WRITE LETTERS

This lesson provides an outline and suggestions for organizing a successful letter-writing campaign to alert government officials, newspaper editors, local business leaders, producers of television news programs, etc. of the knowledge students have gained about the root causes of hunger and what can be done locally or nationally to eliminate it. This activity demonstrates that when people with a common purpose combine their skills and energies the results are magnified.

MATERIALS: paper
pens
envelopes
stamps
students' journals (for first drafts of letters)

PROCEDURE :

1. Explain to students that even while they are educating others about hunger and working with local organizations to end hunger's causes, it is also important to write letters to elected officials, newspaper editors or television news producers, and company presidents because this can often lead to getting **policies** changed. If they can get government officials and members of the media talking about their ideas then they will have a better chance at winning support for their cause and possibly getting laws changed or instituted to improve people's lives.

2. Decide on a **topic** for your letter campaign. This should grow out of research or discussions students have engaged in because their knowledge will validate their letters and enable them to suggest possible solutions. The recipients of their letters will take them very seriously.

    Some topics include: homelessness, hunger and the elderly, children, unemployment, unequal education, environmental protection, discrimination, the media's role in educating about hunger, etc. Choose an example related to your community's needs or one currently being discussed in your newspapers.

3. Decide who should receive your letter. If writing to editors of newspapers bring in some "LETTERS TO THE EDITOR" from your local newspaper to read to students as examples of what they will be writing.

    (Students may choose to write on a separate topic all their own; however, it is usually more effective if a flood of letters arrives for the same individual urging action on the same topic.)

4. Review the letter-writing format with students. How will they organize the content of their letters?

5. Students should write rough drafts in their journals, revise these, then copy their final copies on special paper.

6. Each student should keep a copy of his/her letter.

SOME SUGGESTIONS FOR WRITING EFFECTIVE LETTERS:

1. Handwritten letters and envelopes stand out more than the usual typewritten correspondence.

2. Address letters to a specific individual.

3. Keep letters brief and to the point.

4. Students should mention how old they are and let the recipient of their letter know that young people are the caretakers of the future and the recipient should be aware of what concerns them.

5. Students should give specific examples of the causes of and solutions to the problems they are addressing based on their research.

6. If students are writing to government officials they might ask what that official is personally doing about the problem. (This is more likely to get a response.)

7. Include the student's name, address and phone number in his/her letter just in case the recipient needs to write or speak to the student.

8. If possible, as a group, hand-deliver your letters. This will draw more attention.

9. Encourage family members and friends to write letters as well.

ADDRESSING ENVELOPES

THE PRESIDENT (THE VICE-PRESIDENT)
The White House
Washington, D.C. 20500

THE HONORABLE *name of senator*
Senate Office Building
Washington, D.C. 20510

THE HONORABLE *name of representative*
House Office Building
Washington, D.C. 20510

THE HONORABLE *name of governor*
Your state capitol

The names and addresses of your local officials can be obtained by calling The League of Women Voters, your public library, or by consulting the telephone directory. Addresses of companies can usually be found on the labels of their products.

CORRECT SALUTATIONS AND CLOSINGS:

Dear Mr./Mrs. President
Very respectfully yours,

Dear Mr./Mrs. Vice President
Sincerely yours,

Dear Senator   *name*
Sincerely yours,
Very truly yours,

Dear Mr./Mrs.   *name of rep*.
Very truly yours,

Dear Governor   *name*
Respectfully yours,
Very truly yours,

Dear Assemblyman/woman   *name*
Sincerely yours,

MAKE A DIFFERENCE!

RESULTS is the name of an organization whose volunteers write to elected officials asking them to vote for laws that will help end hunger. RESULTS has volunteer groups all across the United States who lobby officials, call them and work with the media. To become part of their letter-writing campaigns contact them at:

RESULTS / RESULTS Educational Fund
750 First Street NE, Suite 1040
Washington, DC 20002
(202) 783-7100; www.results.org

LESSON 25: GIVE TESTIMONY

Twelve year-olds in Sandwich, Massachusetts testified at their state capitol to help pass a law that would ban smoking on public school grounds. The law was passed and several other states adopted similar laws.

In Chelmsford, Massachusetts a twelve-year old started a petition and testified with friends at a town meeting to protect a wooded area from being destroyed by a condominium development project. The woods are still there.

A Chicago community health clinic that provides services for poor, pregnant women and infants was about to be shut down for lack of funds. Fifty children organized a protest in front of the clinic drawing the attention of the media and lawmakers. The clinic remained open.*

Young people have two distinct advantages over adults when it comes to testifying before legislative bodies --- they stand out in the usual crowd of adults, and committee members know that children have no vested interest in getting a particular law passed other than their own passionate belief that the law will protect people or their natural surroundings. Helping shape legislation this way is an extremely empowering and exciting experience for young people. It can set the foundation for a lifetime of activism and community involvement.

Here are two suggestions on how to begin:

1. Students may already have a **specific** idea on what can be done in your community, such as turning a vacant city lot into a community garden or urging the local Department of Education to insure students who need them get free breakfasts and lunches or school supplies.

2. Another way to approach this is to support a cause already underway in your community. Pay close attention to related hunger issues being debated by the media. When issues have received media attention there is often an outspoken, visible leader pushing for legislation. If this leader's ideas connect with those of the students, they can call the legislator **after they have researched the topic** and tell her they want to testify.

---

* Information for this lesson was adapted with permission from *NO KIDDING AROUND! America's Young Activists Are Changing Our World & You Can Too* by Wendy Schaetzel Lesko. This very resourceful guide for organizing and petitioning contains success stories and the names and addresses of congressional committees and state legislators.

It is essential that students research their issue thoroughly before approaching City Hall or the local school board. (For instance, who owns the vacant lot? Does the surrounding community want it turned into a garden? Are they willing to help tend it? How will it help the community? How will the food be distributed?)

Students might consider getting a petition together and asking community members to sign it. Knowing their stuff is important. Some people will have questions or may need some persuading before signing. Students will also have to convince others to join their cause. Research the opposition's opinions and proposed actions as well. When they testify, students can present members of the city council with copies of their petitions.

TIPS ON TESTIFYING:

1. Prepare students for what they will be doing. If possible visit a council meeting or call the council office to find out how the room is arranged and how many people are expected to attend.

2. Time students' testimony. Find out what the limit is for the legislative committee they will be appearing before. Witnesses are usually given two to three minutes. The more students the better. Have students coordinate their speeches so they don't repeat each other but cover the important ideas - speeches should be concise and to the point.

3. Testimony should be in students' own words and grounded by their own experience or feelings. **Storytelling is a powerful technique.** Include facts and statistics as well.

4. Have students practice their speeches with friends, parents or other teachers and ask for suggestions on how to improve them.

5. Students should be prepared to answer questions by committee members as well as the media. Try to anticipate what questions will be asked and encourage students to come up with informed, quick answers. A legislator on your side of the issue can help provide possible questions.

6. On the day of the hearing call to confirm time and location of hearings.

7. Students should type up their speeches, make several copies and pass them out to lawmakers on the committee and members of the press.

8. After testifying give students a chance to talk about the experience. How did they feel? Did they agree or disagree with anything that was said? Would they testify again? Follow the progress of your issue in the media and by writing to lawmakers.

RESOURCE GUIDE

FUND-RAISING IDEAS

JUSTICE-QUILT RAFFLE - Organize reading groups in your classroom. Have each group read and report on three or four books related to social justice. Choose books from this resource guide. Each group must illustrate a fabric panel for each book and include the title of the book and the author. The panel can depict a central theme of the book or a favorite scene. Use fabric paint. When all the panels are finished, have students and parents sew them together in quilt form. Hang the quilt in the school lobby and raffle it off. Donate the money to a local hunger organization or use it to fund a hunger commercial for radio.

ART SHOW - Hold an art contest where local artists and students enter up to three pieces of their art at $5 per entry. Try to get a local gallery owner to donate space for the event and recruit local celebrities as judges. You could also sell this artwork and donate a portion of the proceeds to your favorite organization.

POETRY READING - Hold a poetry reading in your favorite café. Get students or family members to volunteer to read their own or other's poems related to hunger, homelessness, discrimination, etc. Pass the hat and ask diners to contribute. Explain where the money will go. Try to get local news coverage for your event --- this will also appeal to the restaurant owner whose establishment gets free advertising!

BAKE SALE - Everyone's favorite! Include baked foods from around the world.

NEIGHBORHOOD FLEA-MARKET - Students and their families can get their books, used clothes, tapes or hand-made crafts together to sell. Ask them to donate part or all of their profits to a particular cause.

COSTUME BALL - Hold this event around Halloween. Give it an international theme. Charge admission.

READ, DANCE OR WALK-A-THON - Collect pledges from family, friends and community members for each hour or mile students walk or dance, or for each book read.

STUDENT-FACULTY PLAY-OFF - Compete for the benefit of others. Choose a sport - volleyball, basketball, etc., and invite the rest of the school as well as parents to watch and cheer. Sell tickets or charge admission at the door.

TALENT SHOW - Hold a student-faculty talent show. Sell tickets. Advertise the event. Donate the proceeds.

COMMUNITY AUCTION - Ask families, friends and community businesses to donate their specialties - including skills - to be auctioned off. Be creative! Some teachers and students have had themselves auctioned for a day of baby-sitting, or a day of museum-gazing with a small child, etc. Teachers have made videos of their classroom over the course of the year and auctioned them off to parents. Restaurant and theater owners can donate dinners and seats to shows. This takes some organizing but can raise lots of money for your cause and will alert the community and get everyone involved as well. Students can create posters, canvas the neighborhood for donations, etc.

FAST - Give up one meal a week or give up junk food for one week and donate the money to a cause. Get the school involved by going around to other classes and explaining where their money will go. Place large containers in each classroom in which students can place their change.

SEASONAL CELEBRATION - Hold a seasonal pot-luck dinner. For instance, in autumn ask participants to bring a seasonal dish. Eat outside under colorful trees. Organize simple games and activities to attract children to the event - leaf rubbings, scavenger hunt, story-telling, autumn poetry readings, etc. Charge admission.

WORLD MAP-A-THON - *Save the Children*'s project helps raise money while teaching students about geography. Students learn the location of as many countries as possible in two weeks and collect pledges from family and friends based on the number of countries correctly identified during the Map-a-thon. Send for the kit which contains maps, information and certificates of achievement. See Organization Guide.

CAR-WASH - Students can hold a weekend car-wash to raise money or they can make themselves available to run errands, do yard work or walk dogs, etc. Have them make up fliers to advertise their services and explain where the money will go that is earned.

BIRTHDAY DONATIONS - On birthdays students can ask parents, friends and grand-parents to make a donation to a special organization instead of buying a gift. Students can do the same for other people's birthdays. Make up a card for the birthday person explaining that a donation was made in honor of his/her birthday to a local organization. Explain how the organization works.

ORGANIZATIONS

AFRICARE
440 R. Street N.W.
Washington, DC 20001
(202) 462-3614; www.africare.org
Africare's programs help improve living conditions in 25 countries. Students can participate by collecting donations that will be used by Africare to buy seeds, fertilizer, plant trees, etc.

BREAD FOR THE WORLD INSTITUTE
50 F Street N.W.
Suite 500
Washington, DC 20001
(202) 639-9400; www.bread.org/BFW-Institute
Bread for the World Institute provides policy analysis on hunger and strategies to end it. The Institute educates its advocacy network, opinion leaders, policy makers and the public about hunger in the United States and abroad. Educators can visit their website to access educational activities and resources about domestic and world hunger. Their annual report called *Hunger* contains facts, statistics and ideas for affecting government policy and using the media to end world hunger. Bread for the World Institute is the research and educational partner of Bread for the World, a 54,000-member Christian citizens' movement against hunger.

CARE
151 Ellis Street N.E.
Atlanta, GA 30303
(800) 422-7385; www.careusa.org
CARE is the world's largest relief and development organization not affiliated with a government or religion. They send teachers, health and agriculture experts to impoverished areas to help people improve their lives. Send for a CARE package of information on their hunger videos, teaching materials, programs and case studies.

CONGRESSIONAL HUNGER CENTER
Hall of the States Building
400 North Capitol Street, NW
Suite G100
Washington, DC 20001
(202) 547-7022; www.hungercenter.org
The Congressional Hunger Center trains and inspires leaders who work to end hunger, and advocates public policies that create a food secure world.

ENDING HUNGER NETWORK
P.O. Box 3032
Santa Monica, CA 90408
(310) 454-3716; www.endhunger.com
This organization works with the entertainment industry to spread the word about hunger.

FEEDING AMERICA (FORMERLY NAMED AMERICA'S SECOND HARVEST)
35 East Wacker Drive
Suite 2000
Chicago, IL 60601
(800) 771-2303; http://feedingamerica.org
The country's largest hunger-relief organization. Students can contact them for information on volunteering to work with their local affiliates in food banks, soup kitchens and food pantries.

HEIFER PROJECT INTERNATIONAL
P.O. Box 8058
Little Rock, AR 72203
(800) 422-0474; www.heifer.org
Heifer Project International sends farm animals such as cows, pigs, goats and chickens as well as llamas, honeybees and seeds to hungry villagers in developing areas so that they have access to food and a livelihood. $10 buys a share of rabbits, $20 a flock of chicks or share of a llama.

THE HUNGER PROJECT
5 Union Square West
New York, NY 10003
(212) 251-9100; www.thp.org
This organization seeks to identify "what's missing" in the global effort to end hunger and finds ways to provide it. The *Youth Ending Hunger* project is one of its many programs. Send for a description of educational resources and programs.

THE HUNGER SITE
One Union Square
600 University Street
Suite 1000
Seattle, WA 98101-4107
www.thehungersite.org
An on-line activism site that provides hunger statistics, classroom activities and resource links.

INSTITUTE FOR FOOD AND DEVELOPMENT POLICY
398 60th Street
Oakland, CA 94618
(510) 654-4400
www.foodfirst.org; Email: info@foodfirst.org
This is a hunger research and educational center. Contact them for their catalogue of books on hunger, development and nutrition.

INTERNATIONAL EYE FOUNDATION
10801 Connecticut Avenue
Kensington, MD 20895
(240) 290-0263; www.iefusa.org
The International Eye Foundation is focused on reducing vitamin A deficiency and improving pediatric eye care services worldwide. The ***Vitamin A+ Kids*** campaign integrates vitamin A capsule distribution, nutrition education, vitamin A vegetable gardens, food fortification programs and control of childhood diseases to save children's sight and lives. See Unit 1, Lesson 4 for ways students can participate in Vitamin A+ Kids.

KIDS CAN MAKE A DIFFERENCE®
140 East 72nd Street, #14B
New York, NY 10021
(212) 861-0911; www.kidscanmakeadifference.org
KIDS Can Make A Difference, a program of WHY, is an innovative educational program for middle- and high-school students. KIDS offers informational resources, speakers, a website and newsletter to educate young people about issues related to hunger. Students and teachers can write articles for the KIDS newsletter and website and learn about what other schools are doing to eliminate hunger. Send your name and address to be placed on their mailing list.

NATIONAL STUDENT CAMPAIGN AGAINST HUNGER AND HOMELESSNESS
407 S. Dearborn
Suite 701
Chicago, IL 60605
(800) NO-HUNGR; www.studentsagainsthunger.org
A coalition of student-community activists who, understanding the causes of poverty, initiate positive change through service and action. They also provide a clearinghouse of information and contacts pertaining to hunger.

OXFAM AMERICA
226 Causeway Street, 5th Floor
Boston, MA 02114
(800) 77-OXFAM; www.oxfamamerica.org
Oxfam America creates lasting solutions to hunger and poverty by working in partnership with grassroots groups in Africa, Asia, the Caribbean and the Americas, including the United States. To foster an environment supportive of long-term development, Oxfam also advocates for policy change and produces educational materials for the U.S. public on poverty and hunger issues.

RESULTS / RESULTS Educational Fund
750 First Street NE, Suite 1040
Washington, DC 20002
(202) 783-7100; www.results.org
RESULTS organizes massive letter-writing campaigns to encourage elected officials to vote for laws that will end hunger. Their network of volunteers across the country also lobbies lawmakers and works with the media on issues related to poverty and hunger.

ROOTS & SHOOTS-USA
The Jane Goodall Institute
4245 North Fairfax Drive
Suite 600
Arlington, VA 22203
(800) 592-JANE; www.rootsandshoots.org
Founded by Dr. Jane Goodall, this global program emphasizes the principle that knowledge leads to compassion, which inspires action. Roots & Shoots engages and inspires youth through community service and service learning. With tens of thousands of young people in almost 100 countries, the Roots & Shoots network connects youth of all ages through service projects, youth-led campaigns and an interactive website. See Unit 1, Lesson 5 for a description of the ***ReBirth the Earth: Trees for Tomorrow*** campaign.

SAVE THE CHILDREN
54 Wilton Road
Westport, CT 06880
(203) 221-4030; www.savethechildren.org
Save the Children's development programs make a lasting difference in the lives of children in more than 50 countries including the U.S. Your school can sponsor a child or an entire school through this organization.

SHARE OUR STRENGTH (SOS)
1730 M Street N.W.
Suite 700
Washington, DC 20036
(800) 969-4767; www.strength.org
The nation's leading anti-hunger organization, SOS works toward ending hunger and poverty in the U.S. and abroad by supporting food assistance programs, treating malnutrition and other consequences of hunger and promoting economic independence among people in need. Contact SOS for ideas on how to end hunger in your community.

UNITED FOR A FAIR ECONOMY
29 Winter Street
Boston, MA 02108
(617) 423-2148; www.faireconomy.org
This organization raises awareness and demonstrates how concentrated wealth and power can undermine economic justice, corrupt democracy, deepen the racial divide and tear communities apart. Teachers will find statistics, stories, research, information and graphs for classroom use.

U.S. FUND FOR UNICEF
125 Maiden Lane
New York, NY 10038
(800) 4-UNICEF; www.unicefusa.org
UNICEF saves the lives of children in more than 100 countries by helping villagers create nutrition and education programs, gain access to safe water and emergency medical care. UNICEF puts out valuable information and source books include *The*

State of the World's Children, an annual report on nutrition, health and education issues and programs affecting the lives of children everywhere.

WHY (WORLD HUNGER YEAR)
505 Eighth Avenue, 21st Floor
New York, NY 10018
(212) 629-8850; www.whyhunger.org
WHY is a leading advocate for innovative community-based solutions to hunger and poverty. WHY challenges society to confront these problems by advancing models that create self-reliance, economic justice and equal access to nutritious affordable food. The ***WHY Media Guide*** offers advice on how to get the media's attention in order to get your students' message out to others.

WORLD SAVVY
999 Sutter Street, 4th Floor
San Francisco, CA 94109
(415) 292-7421; www.worldsavvy.org
World Savvy is a global education nonprofit whose mission is to educate and engage youth in community and world affairs, to prepare them to learn, work and live as responsible global citizens in the 21st century. World Savvy runs three programs (World Affairs Challenge, Global Youth Media and Arts Program and Global Educators Program) in San Francisco, New York and Minneapolis that encourage youth awareness and understanding of current international affairs, either during or after school hours. The *World Savvy Monitor* is an online, bi-monthly, subscription-based "one-stop shop" for the 21st Century K-12 educator who wants to address complex global issues.

RESOURCES FOR TEACHERS

ADBUSTERS
1243 West 7th Avenue
Vancouver, BC
V6H 1B7 Canada
(604) 736-9401
www.adbusters.org
Distributes a terrific "anti ads" video called ***Culture Jammers*** (12 Mins.). Their quarterly critique of advertising is also an effective and fun classroom tool.

THE COMPLETE GUIDE TO LEARNING THROUGH COMMUNITY SERVICE
By Lillian S. Stephens. Allyn & Bacon, Needham Heights, MA, 1995. For K-9 this guide includes over 400 activities organized by subjects or interdisciplinary themes and drawn from actual teaching experience. Contains unusual and exciting examples of how to build school/community partnerships and an excellent section on poverty, hunger and homelessness.

THE GUIDE TO SOCIAL CHANGE LED BY AND WITH YOUNG PEOPLE by the Freechild Project. The mission of the Freechild Project is to advocate, inform and celebrate social change led by and with young people around the world, especially those who have been historically denied the right to participate. This publication, which centers on the "Cycle of Youth Engagement" strategy, is a summary of the social change issues and actions addressed by and with young people around the world. www.commonaction.org/SocialChangeGuide.pdf; www.freechild.org

DO SOMETHING
A journal and website for educators who want to improve students' academic and leadership skills through meaningful community involvement. There is also a website for young people who want to get informed, get connected and take action. www.dosomething.org

EDUCATORS FOR SOCIAL RESPONSIBILITY
23 Garden Street
Cambridge, MA 02138
(617) 492-1764; www.esrnational.org
ESR's mission is "to help young people develop the convictions and skills to shape a safe, sustainable, and just world." This organization supports educators and parents with professional development networks and teaching materials that focus on conflict resolution, violence prevention, inter-group relations and character education. Send for their catalogue: ***Resources for Empowering Children***, or browse their online store for educational materials.

GROWING TOGETHER: A Guide to Building Inspired, Diverse and Productive Youth Communities (Ages 12 and up) also ***FRENCH FRIES AND THE FOOD SYSTEM: A Year Round Curriculum Connecting Youth with Farming and Food***. Both resources are available from The Food Project, P.O. Box 705, Lincoln, MA 01773 (781) 259-8621. Website: www.thefoodproject.org. Their quarterly newsletter reports on activities that involve youth in community service, organic gardening and leadership training.

CAMPUS ORGANIZING GUIDE FOR SOCIAL JUSTICE GROUPS by Rich Cowan, Nicole Newton, Jeremy Smith, Alex Brozan, Niels Burger and Maia Homstad. (Mildly revised in 2002 by Aaron Kreider.) This online publication was created by the Center for Campus Organizing in 1994 to help student activists learn the basics of campus organizing. Since 2002, when the Center for Campus Organizing closed, the guide has been updated and hosted by CampusActivism.org, an interactive website. www.campusactivism.org/uploads/orgguide.pdf

TEACHING FOR CHANGE
P.O. Box 73038
Washington, DC 20056-3038
(800) 763-9131; www.teachingforchange.org
This organization works with school communities to promote teaching methods and resources for social and economic justice.

NO KIDDING AROUND! America's Young Activists Are Changing Our World & You Can Too, by Wendy Schaetzel Lesko of Activism 2000 Project. This is an excellent handbook on activism, which explains strategies for launching projects, and over 1,000 resources to help develop proposals for social, legal and political change. P.O. Box E. Kensington, MD 20895 (800) KID-POWER. www.youthactivism.com.

OPEN MINDS TO EQUALITY: A SOURCEBOOK OF LEARNING ACTIVITIES TO PROMOTE RACE, SEX, CLASS AND AGE EQUALITY by Nancy Schniedewind and Ellen Davidson. Allyn & Bacon, Publishers. 160 Gould Street, Needham Heights, MA 02194, 1998. For grades 3-12, lessons address communication and cooperation, stereotypes, the impact of discrimination, and creating change. Available through ***Rethinking Schools***, 1001 E. Keefe Avenue, Milwaukee, WI 53212. (800) 669-4192. www.rethinkingschools.org. This organization also publishes a quarterly journal ($17.95 annual subscription rate) with articles emphasizing school reform and social justice.

A PEOPLE'S HISTORY OF THE UNITED STATES By Howard Zinn. Harper & Row. An essential classroom resource, it contains all the people, facts and stories missing from the usual textbooks. Available through the Zinn Education Project, a collaborative effort by Rethinking Schools and Teaching for Change. www.zinnedproject.org.

RETHINKING OUR CLASSROOMS: TEACHING FOR EQUITY AND JUSTICE Edited by Bill Bigelow et. al. 1994. (New Edition, revised and expanded 2007) Contains inspiring teaching narratives, creative examples of how teachers can promote values of community, justice and equity, as well as an extensive resource guide. Available for $16.95 from ***Rethinking Schools*** above.

SING THE SUN UP: CREATIVE WRITING IDEAS FROM AFRICAN-AMERICAN LITERATURE. Edited by Lorenzo Thomas. Teachers and Writers Collaborative, NY, 1998. This resource uses poetry, fiction, essays and drama to inspire students to reflect on and write about important social issues. Available for $16.95 through the **Teachers and Writers Collaborative**, 520 Eighth Avenue, Suite 2020, New York, NY 10018. (212) 691-6590. www.twc.org

TEACHING TOLERANCE
c/o The Southern Poverty Law Center
400 Washington Avenue
Montgomery, AL 36104
(334) 956-8200; www.teachingtolerance.org
A nationally acclaimed classroom kit for grades K-12 that is sent out free to teachers to promote interracial and intercultural understanding. Contact them for their video, teachers' guide and magazine.

THE STATE OF AMERICA'S CHILDREN Available through The Children's Defense Fund, 25 E Street NW, Washington, DC 20001. This is a thorough sourcebook with graphs, research and statistics on all issues facing America's children. (800) CDF-1200. www.childrensdefense.org.

THE STATE OF THE WORLD'S CHILDREN Published by UNICEF. A comprehensive sourcebook with annual research, statistics, facts and case studies regarding progress in health, nutrition and education around the world. Available from UNICEF Publications, 2 United Nations Plaza, Room DC2-853, New York, NY 10017. (212) 963-8302. www.unicef.org.

THE ULTIMATE FIELD GUIDE TO THE U.S. ECONOMY by James Heintz, et al.
A compact and irreverent guide to economic life in America. Contains graphs, charts, comic strips and current statistics on wealth, poverty, workers, women, people of color, government spending, education, welfare, health, environment, macroeconomics and the global economy.

WHY MEDIA GUIDE Available from WHY (See Organizations), this slim volume offers valuable tips from the pros on how to use the media to teach others about hunger and build community support.

COLONIALISM, SLAVERY, RACISM & RESISTANCE

COLONIALISM IN THE AMERICAS: A CRITICAL LOOK by Susan Gage. Produced in 1991 by Victoria International Development Education Association (VIDEA), 407A - 620 View Street, Victoria, BC V8W 1J6, Canada. (250) 385-2333. www.videa.ca. An absolutely must-have resource in a comic-book format, with lively dialogue and illustrations. This forceful guide traces the history of the first peoples of South, Central and North America – how they lived, the impact of colonialism on their lives and its continuing effects today. Contains case studies, class activities and a colonial simulation game. The series includes separate guides on: **COLONIALISM IN AFRICA** and **COLONIALISM IN ASIA**.

DANGEROUS MEMORIES - INVASION & RESISTANCE SINCE 1492
by Renny Golden, et al. Chicago Religious Task Force, 1991. Documents the untold stories of African-African and indigenous resistance.

EVERYBODY SAYS FREEDOM: A HISTORY OF THE CIVIL RIGHTS MOVEMENT IN SONGS AND PICTURES By Pete Seeger and B. Reiser. W.W. Norton & Co., New York, 1989.

KEEPERS OF THE EARTH by Michael J. Caduto and Joseph Bruchac. Fulcrum, Inc., Golden Colorado: 1988. A teaching guide with a collection of Native American stories and environmental activities.

LETTERS TO MARCIA - A Teacher's Guide to Anti-Racist Education by Enid Lee. Cross Cultural Community Center, Toronto, Canada, 1985.

THE PEOPLE SHALL CONTINUE by Simon Ortiz, Children's Book Press. San Francisco, CA, 1988. A "teaching story" of Native Americans from the time of creation to the present and how they fought back against destruction.

RETHINKING COLUMBUS Edited by Bill Bigelow, et al. Engaging collection of essays, stories, interviews, poems and lessons that present the discovery of America as an invasion from the perspective of indigenous peoples. www.rethinkingschools.org

WOMEN OF HOPE: African-Americans Who Made a Difference.
Posters of African-American women who have had a profound impact on American life: Maya Angelou, Ella J. Baker, Alexa Conady, Septima P. Clark, Ruby Dee, the Delaney Sisters, Marian Wright Edelman, Fannie Lou Hamer, Mae C. Jemison, Toni Morrison, Alice Walker and Ida B. Wells. (Study guide included.) Available from Bread and Roses, 322 West 48th Street, 6th Floor, New York, NY 10036. www.bread-and-roses.com

FOR YOUNG PEOPLE

Carter, Forrest. **The Education of Little Tree**, University of New Mexico Press. This touching Native American boy's story reveals how a dominant white culture negates the social and ecological traditions of his heritage.

Cooper, Michael L., **Bound For The Promised Land**. Dutton, 1995.
A history of the great black migration from 1915 to 1930 when a million black southerners left their homes for the promise of a better life in the industrial cities of the Northeast and Midwest. With photographs and first person observations.

Everett, Gwen. John Brown, **One Man Against Slavery**. Rizzoli Children's Library, 1994. (26 pages) A powerful read-aloud book for all ages with stunning illustrations by Jacob Laurence. Through this story, told from a fictional daughter's point of view, readers confront the dilemma John Brown faced: Was it right for one man to seek an end to slavery through bloodshed?

Feelings, Tom. **The Middle Passage.** Through haunting images, this book tells the story of how Africans were taken out of their homeland to work as slaves in the Americas. See also his book **Soul Looks Back in Wonder**, a collection of poems by African-American poets.

Hamilton, Virginia. **Anthony Burns: The Defeat and Triumph of a Fugitive Slave.** Knopf, 1988. Anthony Burns was raised a slave in Virginia. In 1854 when he was 20, he ran away to Massachusetts, was captured and tried under the Fugitive Slave Act. His incarceration was hotly debated and marked a turning point in the northern anti-slavery movement. Also **Many Thousands Gone** by Hamilton.

Kelso, Richard. **Days of Courage: The Little Rock Story.** Steck-Vaughn Co., Austin, 1993. One of a series edited by Alex Haley, this book describes how high school students struggled to integrate Little Rock Central High School.

Meyer. Carolyn. **Voices of South Africa.** Harcourt Brace, 1986. The author's moving account of a visit to South Africa where she interviewed young people, black and white, to find out what growing up is like in a country torn apart by racial strife.

Morrison, Toni. **The Bluest Eye.** Washington Square Press, NY, 1970. (260 pages) "In a land that loves its blond, blue-eyed children, who weeps for the dreams of a black girl?"

Naidoo, Beverly; illustrated by Eric Velasquez. **Chain of Fire.** HarperCollins, 1993. (245 pages) Fifteen year-old Naledi and her friends are forced by the South African government to leave their village and live in a barren land. They refuse and the consequences are "a chain of fire." See also her book **Journey to Jo'burg**.

O'Dell, Scott. **My Name Is Not Angelica.** Dell Publishers, New York, 1989. (130 pages) Taken from her home in Africa, sixteen year-old Raisha begins a new life on a sugarcane plantation on the island of St. John. A sheltered house servant, she cannot ignore the suffering of the slaves who work in the fields and risks her life to help a group of runaways.

Pinkney, Andrea Davis. **Hold Fast to Dreams.** Morrow Junior Books, 1995. Twelve year-old Camera Dee's family must move from home in an African-American community to the uncertainty of a predominantly white community.

Paulsen, Gary. **NightJohn.** Delacorte Press, 1993. Set in the 1850's. Having escaped to freedom in the North, NightJohn returns to a life of slavery in the South to secretly teach slaves to read even though the punishment for reading is dismemberment. One of his students is twelve year-old Sarney.

Smucker, Barbara. ***Runaway To Freedom.*** The story of the underground railroad based on first-hand experiences found in the narratives of fugitive slaves and the accounts of two abolitionists.

Taylor, Mildred. ***Roll of Thunder, Hear My Cry.*** Puffin Press, NY, 1976. Four African-American children growing up on a farm in rural Mississippi during the Depression, the story is told through the eyes of nine year-old Cassie. Honesty, integrity and perseverance overcome hatred, resentment and revenge. A strong focus on the family's land as a source of courage and pride. See also her books ***Let The Circle Be Unbroken*** and ***The Road to Memphis*** which continue the family's story.

Webb, Sheyann and Rachel Best Nelson. ***Selma, Lord Selma: Girlhood Memories of the Civil Rights Days.*** University of Alabama Press, Tuscaloosa, 1980. Two women who, as children, participated in the civil rights movement tell their stories.

Eyes On The Prize - A compelling six-part series on the history of the civil rights movement (See Videos).

HOMELESSNESS

Fox, Paula. ***Monkey Island.*** Dell Publishers, NY, 1991. (151 pages)
Eleven year-old Clay's father has lost his job and left the family. When his mother does not return to their welfare hotel, Clay must survive on the streets of New York City. A homeless man tries to help.

Crew, Linda. ***Children of the River.*** Bantam, 1989. (213 pages)
A captivating story inspired by the Cambodian refugees who had come to work the land near Crew's home. The author describes the move to America and the conflict between Cambodian and American culture as seen through the eyes of a teenage girl.

Gates, Doris. ***Blue Willow.*** Puffin Books, NY. (172 pages)
Janey cherishes a blue willow plate, the symbol of a home she can only dimly remember. Her father is an itinerant worker and the family must follow the crops from farm to farm. Janey longs for the kind of home pictured on the plate where she and her family can put down roots.

Hamilton, Virginia. ***Plain City.*** Scholastic, Inc., 1993. (194 pages)
Bulhair Sims is a twelve year-old of mixed race in search of her identity and a place to live where she will be accepted by those around her.

Hamilton, Virginia. ***The Planet of Junior Brown.*** MacMillan Publishing Co., 1971. (217 pages) Already a leader in New York's underground world of homeless children, Buddy Clark takes on the responsibility of protecting his overweight, emotionally disturbed friend, Junior, with whom he has been cutting eighth grade classes all semester.

Harris, Mark Jonathan. **Come the Morning**. Bradbury Press, New York, 1989. (169 pages) Presents a believable portrait of the way homeless children live in the U.S. Ben, his mother and two siblings become homeless when they go to Los Angeles in search of his father.

Ho, Mingfong. **The Clay Marble.** Houghton, 1991. (163 pages)
A compelling drama of life in the refugee camps of the Cambodian border, told through the character of preadolescent Dara. Hope and dreams must override the hardships the refugees face as they struggle to return to their homeland. Ho created the story from her experience doing volunteer work at the camps.

Holman, Felice. **Secret City USA**. Simon & Schuster / Atheneum, 1990. (199 pages)
Two thirteen year-old homeless friends get the idea of developing a broken-down area of their city into a safe place for homeless families. Their determination and imagination outwit the opposition.

Holman, Felice. **Slake's Limbo.** Simon & Schuster / Atheneum, 1974. (126 pages)
Pushed around by everyone, Aremis Slake finds refuge in the subways of New York City and sets up housekeeping. Using his wits, he satisfies most of his needs, including human contact and compassion, with those who become regulars in his newspaper business. (See Video section for **Runaway**, adapted from this novel.)

Holman, Felice. **The Wild Children**. Puffin Press, 1983. (152 pages)
The story of Alex, set in the 1920's in Moscow, he becomes homeless and survives through his bravery and friendships.

Hubbard, Jim. **Lives Turned Upside Down: Homeless Children in Their Own Words and Photographs**. Simon & Schuster, 1996.

Hubbard, Jim. **Shooting Back: A Photographic View of Life by Homeless Children**. Chronicle Books, 1991.

Hurwitz, Eugene and Sue Hurwitz. **Working Together Against Homelessness**. Rosen Publishing, 1994. (64 pages) Presented in a dialogue format, this book describes the various ways people are helping the homeless. Their examples could be replicated in other schools and communities.

Hyde, Margaret O. **The Homeless: Profiling the Problem**. Enslow, 1989. (96 pages)
The author uses an ethnographic approach to explain why people become homeless, their location, the challenges facing them and the services available in communities. She also offers ideas on how to get involved.

Kosof, Anna. **Homeless in America.** Watts, 1988. (110 pages)
This book describes the homeless in America, a day in the life of the homeless, and the constant search for food and shelter. The Heights in Manhattan is used as an example of a successful program in which homeless people are helped to get back on their feet.

Mathis, Sharon Bell. ***Sidewalk Story***. Puffin Publishers, NY, 1986. Lilly Etta comes to her best friend's aid when she and her family are evicted from their home.

Nichelason, Margery G. ***Homeless or Hopeless?*** Lerner, 1994. (112 pages)
This book raises several questions for discussion: Do we as a society have a moral obligation to help the homeless? If so, is it the responsibility of the government or private charities? Or is it time for the homeless to take responsibility for themselves?

Orlev, Uri. ***Lady with the Hat***. Houghton, 1995. (192 pages)
Yulek, a teenage survivor of the Holocaust, returns to his home in Poland to find it occupied by a Communist Party leader. He and other refugees are forced to seek refuge in Palestine. (Fiction)

Rosen, Michael J., Editor. ***Home: A Collaboration of Thirty Distinguished Authors and Illustrators of Children's Books to Aid the Homeless.*** HarperCollins, 1992.

Rozakis, Laurie. ***Homelessness: Can We Solve the Problem?*** Holt, 1995. (64 pages)
A handy resource, this book analyzes the causes of homelessness, the people most likely to become homeless, the myths associated with homeless people, their daily struggles and some of the successful ways to overcome homelessness.

Seymour-Jones, Carole. ***Past and Present: Homelessness***. Simon & Schuster/New Discovery, 1993. (48 pages) Presents a historical look at homelessness and its causes: war, natural disasters, accidents, limited natural resources and politics.

Voigt, Cynthia. ***Homecoming***. Atheneum, NY, 1981.
Four children who have been abandoned by their mother must look out for each other while they try to find relatives to take them in.

Zamenova, Tatyana. ***Teenage Refugees from Russia Speak Out.*** Rosen, 1995. (64 pages) Teenage refugees from Russia tell their own stories about their experiences in Russia as well as the U.S.

HUNGER

D'Aluisio, Faith and Peter Menzel. ***Hungry Planet—What the World Eats.*** Random House, 2005. A stunning photographic study of families from twenty-four countries revealing, what people eat during the course of one week. Each family's profile includes a detailed description of their weekly food purchases and a photo of the entire family surrounded by a week's worth of groceries.

Hamilton, Virginia. ***Drylongso***. Harcourt Brace Jovanovich, San Diego, 1992. A family struggles to overcome drought and dust storms on their farm. A young man named Drylongso comes to their aid.

Ho, Minfong. ***Rice Without Rain***. HarperCollins, 1990. A novel about Jinda Boonreung's participation in student demonstrations at Thamasart University in

Thailand in 1976. Jinda's family, while living in a farming village, is slowly starving. Jinda joins revolutionary students to bring change.

Hosteler Marian. **African Adventure**. Herald Press, Scottsdale, PA, 1976. A Christian-based novel about a family who becomes part of an emergency food-relief program in Chad.

Howard, Tracy Apple and Sage Alexandra Howard. **Kids Ending Hunger: What Can We Do?** Universal Press Syndicate Co., Kansas City, 1992. This is an inspirational and informative book containing stories, hunger facts and 50 practical activities that help end hunger.

Lutzeier, Elizabeth. **The Coldest Winter**. Oxford University Press, 1991. An Irish boy and his family must survive the bitter winter of 1846 when a potato blight ruins the crop and English soldiers turn people out of their homes.

Markandaya, Kamala. **Nectar in a Sieve**. J. Day Co., New York, 1954.
The riveting story of an Indian family's struggle to survive famine and severe poverty in India. (Ages 13-adult)

McBrier, Page, illustrated by Lori Lohstoeter. **Beatrice's Goat**. Simon & Schuster / Atheneum, 2001.The inspiring true story of Beatrice, a young Ugandan girl, whose life in a small, impoverished village is changed forever by a wonderful gift.

McKissack, Patricia C. and Frederick L. McKissack. **Rebels Against Slavery.** Stories about the unsung heroes who fought against slavery from colonial times to the Emancipation Proclamation.

McKenna, Marita Conlon. **Under The Hawthorne Tree.** Puffin Press, NY, 1992. (124 pages) A moving story of how three children survive the famine in 19th century Ireland. Abandoned by their parents they are forced into a workhouse from which they escape to search for a great-aunt.

Rocha, Ruth and Octavio Roth. **The Universal Declaration of Human Rights, An Adaptation for Children**. United Nations Publications, 1989. This is a short, read-aloud book for all ages that explains clearly and beautifully the rights shared by every human being and why they must be respected.

Voigt, Cynthia. **Jackaroo.** Fawcett, 1985. A 16 year-old woman with a forceful nature helps the poor and hungry who are preyed upon by thieves and soldiers. (Ages 12-16)

WAR

Burton, Hester. **In Spite Of All Terror**. World Publishing Co., 1968. (203 pages) The story of a teenage orphan whose courage helps save English soldiers during World War II. (Fiction)

Filipovic, Zlata. **Zlata's Diary.** Viking Penguin Press, NY, 1994. This is the personal diary kept by a thirteen year-old girl during the war in Sarajevo. Her account helps students see that children experiencing war and hunger have the same needs and dreams as children in the U.S. (Non-fiction)

Frank, Anne. **The Diary of a Young Girl**. 1952. This famous diary kept by a thirteen year-old Jewish Dutch girl, describes how her family was forced into hiding by the Nazis during World War II. (Nonfiction)

Hayslip Phung Thi Le Ly. **When Heaven and Earth Change Places**. Doubleday, 1989. The author's account of life in Vietnam during the war.

Kosinski, Jerzy. **The Painted Bird**. Houghton Mifflin, 1965. Based on the author's childhood in Europe during World War II.

Seredy, Kate. **The Singing Tree**. Puffin, NY, 1990. (247 pages) The inspiring story of a Hungarian family's determination to remain true to its farming and cultural heritage despite the onset of World War I. The story balances the horrors of war with hope for the future. (Fiction)

Temple, Frances. **Taste of Salt: A Story of Modern Haiti**. Harper Trophy, NY, 1992. (179 pages) Two seventeen year-old Haitians caught up in their country's struggle for democracy. The story takes place after Aristede's election to the presidency.

"War" a song by Bob Marley and the Wailers from the **Rastaman Vibration** album. From Island Records.

Wiesel, Elie. **Night**. 1960. On the horrors of the Holocaust.

See also: **If The Mango Tree Could Speak** about children and war in Central America, **The Four Seasons: Winter, Winter, Winter** about children and the war in Sarajevo. Listed under Videos.

WORK

BREAD & ROSES: The Struggle of American Labor 1865-1915
Vintage Press, NY, 1973. Dramatic short stories for grades 6 and up on early U.S. labor struggles.

CHILD LABOR IS NOT CHEAP. Sanders, Amy and Meredith Sommers. 1997.
This curriculum for grades 8-12 as well as adults focuses on the millions of children who spend their days making products for the U.S. market. It contains handouts, posters, maps and web sites. (Use with video ***Zoned for Slavery***.) Order from the ***Resource Center of the Americas***. (612) 276-0788, www.americas.org.

CHILD LABOR COALITION, c/o National Consumers League, 1701 K St. NW, Suite 1200, Washington, DC 20006. Contact this organization for a teen organizer's kit and information.

THE COST OF YOUR SHIRT. A role-play for Grades 8-12 and adults based on the real life drama of a Guatemala City maquiladora. Students play plant managers, workers, government representatives and concerned U.S. citizens. Order from ***Resource Center of the Americas*** above.

LOST FUTURES: THE PROBLEM OF CHILD LABOR. Child Labor Project, American Federation of Teachers. 555 New Jersey Ave., NW, Washington, DC 20001-2079. ($10) An educational resource designed for classroom use, including a 16-minute video and teacher's guide. www.aft.org

MICKEY MOUSE GOES TO HAITI. A 20-minute video from the ***National Labor Committee***, 5 Gateway Center, 6th Floor, Pittsburgh, PA 15222. (412) 562-2406, www.nlcnet.org. Exposes working conditions for Haitians who manufacture products for Disney.

A NIKE PRODUCTION PRIMER by "Justice. Do it Nike!"
P.O. Box 219231, Portland, OR 97225. (503) 292-8168. e-mail: maxw@rain.com.
Helpful teaching tools include articles on Nike: "Six Cents An Hour" by Sydney Schanberg, "The Globetrotting Sneaker" by Cynthia Enloe, and Nike's Code of Conduct. This packet also includes names and addresses for student letter-writing campaigns. The organization requests a $10 donation for the primer.

THE POWER IN OUR HANDS: A Curriculum on the History of Work and Workers in the United States. Bigelow, Bill and Norm Diamond. Monthly Review Press, 1988. Role-plays and writing activities take students inside real-life situations throughout history. ($18) Highly recommended.

SOMETHING TO HIDE. A 25-minute video that exposes how corporations hide production behind locked gates. Order from the ***National Labor Committee*** above.

TOMORROW WE WILL FINISH. A UNICEF video distributed by Maryknoll World Productions. (800) 227-8523. This 26-minute video focuses on one young girl, Suri, to describe the lives of girls who weave rugs in factories in Nepal.

UNITED FOR A FAIR ECONOMY.
Call or visit their web site for information on ***High Pay, Low Pay, Fair Pay!*** This is a workshop for youth on wages and the American Dream. It contains information and classroom exercises that explain income differences and suggest ways to work toward fairness. (See Organizations)

ZONED FOR SLAVERY: The Child Behind the Label. This is a 23-minute video from the National Labor Committee that exposes the exploitation of children who work in factories in Mexico and Central America making clothes that are sold in major U.S. stores. ($20) Order from the ***National Labor Committee*** above.

FOR YOUNG PEOPLE

Beatty, Patricia. ***Lupita Manana***. Morrow, NY, 1981. When thirteen year-old Lupita enters the U.S. she must work hard to feed her family.

Buck, Pearl. ***The Good Earth***. 1931. Set in China before the revolution, this compelling story explains a poor farmer's rise to wealthy landowner and his wife's special love of the land.

Conroy, Pat. ***The Water Is Wide***. 1972. Bantam, NY. (260 pages) A handful of families live on Yamacraw Island. For years they have lived proudly from the sea – now its waters are not safe – waste from industry threatens their existence unless they can learn a new way of life. Focus is on work, education and ecology.

Kincaid, Jamaica. ***Lucy***. 1990. A teenage girl from the Caribbean comes to New England to work as an au pair. (See also ***Annie John***).

Kraft, Betsy Harvey. ***Mother Jones - One Woman's Fight for Labor***. Clarion Books, 1995. "When she died in 1930, more than 10,000 people gathered to mourn the "miner's angel" - the prim-looking labor leader who wore flowered hats and whose rhetorical style and organizing skills are still remembered today." (NY Times) Ages 9 and up.
Paterson, Katherine. ***Lyddie***. Trumpet Club, Brandon, FL, 1991. Set in Massachusetts in the 1800's. A teenage farm girl becomes a mill worker and dramatically influences working conditions.

Steinbeck, John. ***The Grapes of Wrath***. 1939. An account of the efforts of an emigrant farm family from the dust bowl of the West to reach the "promised" land of California.

Steinbeck, John. ***Of Mice and Men***. 1937. The story of two itinerant farm laborers - one of huge strength and weak mind exploited and protected by the other. See also ***The Pearl*** by Steinbeck.

BOOKS ABOUT PEOPLE WHO HAVE MADE A DIFFERENCE

Ashby, Ruth and Deborah Gore-Ohrn, Editors. **Herstory: Women Who Changed The World**. Viking Press, 1995. 120 biographical sketches of women from around the world – from ancient times to the present.

Barry, David. **THE RAJAH'S RICE, A Mathematical Folktale from India.** Scientific American, W.H. Freeman & Co., New York, 1994. A picture book for all ages. A powerful rajah, twenty elephants and a clever girl who feeds the hungry people of the village. Great for reading aloud. Also contains mathematical explanation of how powerful "doubling" numbers can be.

Coerr, Eleanor. **Sakado And The Thousand Cranes**. Dell Publishers, New York, 1979. The true story of an 11 year-old Japanese girl who suffered radiation poisoning from the bombing of Hiroshima. Believing that they would keep her alive, she tried to create 1,000 paper cranes before she died. She finished only 700 but her spirit and courage inspired the world. The children of Japan finished the remaining 300 and today 1,000 cranes symbolize peace across the world. Sakado's statue stands in the Hiroshima Peace Garden.

Garr, Robin. **Reinvesting In America**. Addison-Wesley: New York, 1995. Stories about people and the creative programs that are feeding the hungry, housing the homeless and putting Americans back to work. These successful programs are being replicated around the country.

Hoose, Phillip. **IT'S OUR WORLD TOO: Stories of Young People Who Are Making A Difference**. Little Brown & Co., New York, 1993. Gives an account of young activists throughout history and tells stories of how teenagers have worked to eliminate social injustices such as racism and sexism in their schools.

Karnes, Frances A. **GIRLS AND YOUNG WOMEN LEADING THE WAY: Twenty True Stories About Leadership.** Free Spirit Press, 1993. Stories of girls and women who have confronted hunger, homelessness, environmental problems and illiteracy. (Ages 10-14)

Larned, Marianne, Ed. **STONE SOUP FOR THE WORLD: Life Changing Stories of Kindness and Courageous Acts of Service.** Conari Press, Berkeley, CA, 1998. An extensive collection of inspirational true stories that profile historical, popular and everyday "heroes."

Moore, Yvette. **Freedom Songs.** Puffin Press, 1991. A fourteen year-old girl learns about prejudice and racism on a visit to the South in 1963. She and her friends band together to support the Freedom Riders. (Ages 12-14) (Fiction)

Schami, Rafih. **A Handful Of Stars**. Puffin Publishers, New York, 1990. This is the fictional journal of a teenage boy who publishes an underground newspaper after his father is arrested by the Syrian government.

See also books listed under other headings in this section especially COLONIALISM, SLAVERY, RACISM & RESISTANCE.

See also VIDEOS: *Children of Soong Ching Ling*, and *Raising Voices*.

VIDEOS

ANCIENT FUTURES
Order from KIDS CAN MAKE A DIFFERENCE®
140 East 72nd Street, #14B
New York, NY 10021
(212) 861-0911; www.kidscanmakeadifference.org
See Lesson 19: **ANCIENT FUTURES: Learning From Ladakh** for a detailed description of this video and a lesson plan with several activities. (40 mins.)

BULLFROG FILMS
(610) 779-8226; www.bullfrogfilms.com
This company specializes in videos on agriculture, energy, economics and globalization. Of interest is Risky Business: Biotechnology & Agriculture, a 24-minute video in which scientists, industry proponents, environmentalists and activists discuss the effects of bio-technology on the world's food supply, health and environment.

CHILDREN OF SOONG CHING LING (1984). Tracks the history of the children's movement in China, emphasizing the life and work of Soong Ching Ling, who was a pioneer in the fight for children's rights. (30 mins.) Available from Pyramid Media. www.pyramidmedia.com.

CHURCH WORLD SERVICE
28606 Phillips Street
P.O. Box 968
Elkhart, IN 46515
(800) 297-1576; www.churchworldservice.org
This organization has an extensive video library and sends out free videos to teachers. Contact them for a video listing. Select videos can also be streamed online at www.youtube.com/churchworldservice. Some titles are listed below:

> *The Business of Hunger* (28 mins.)
> Demonstrates how multinational corporations exploit resources and labor in developing nations.

Don't Eat Today or Tomorrow (43 mins.)
Explores the root causes of hunger and debt in developing countries and the role governments, banks, corporations and the International Monetary Fund play.

Hunger No More: Faces Behind the Facts (58 mins.)
Introduces students to some of the hungry families in the U.S. who do not earn enough money to live healthy lives.

With These Hands (33 mins.)
Focus is on the lack of support for Africa's women farmers. Three women from Burkina Faso, Kenya and Zimbabwe tell how discrimination against women is a root cause of hunger and explain what can be done to end it.

THE COLA CONQUEST (Excellent for use with Lesson 10 and ***The Curse of Sugar***) Documents how a soft drink which is more than 99% sweetened water, came to wield enormous power over the world's people and become the most recognized brand name on Earth. 1999. (50 mins.) Available from DLI Productions. (514) 272-2220. www.dliproductions.ca

DANCES WITH WOLVES documents dramatically the effects of white encroachment on the Sioux culture.

EYES ON THE PRIZE. A compelling six-part series (one hour each) on the history of the civil rights movement in the U.S. from 1960 to 1965. Originally broadcast on PBS. Available in video stores and from Blackside, Inc. (617) 482-2195

FACETS VIDEO CATALOGUE
(800) 331-6197; www.facets.org
This comprehensive video collection includes independent African-American films, feature films about Africa and African-American history, apartheid and civil rights. Of particular interest: **AND THE CHILDREN SHALL LEAD** about a young black girl who is profoundly moved by the coming of the civil rights movement to her Mississippi town.

FAMINE AND CHRONIC PERSISTENT HUNGER: *A Life and Death Distinction*
(11 mins.) Available from **The Hunger Project.** (See Organizations) This video is also available from the **African Studies Center Lending Library** at Boston University. This Outreach Resource Library houses a substantial collection on several African countries and is open to the public. The collection focuses on material of use to classroom teachers. Audio-visual materials may be borrowed through the mail, print materials are generally lent only to visitors. 270 Bay State Road Boston, MA 02215. www.bu.edu/africa/outreach/library

THE FLAME Demonstrates how a development program assists women by providing them with food and income-producing animals and training in environmentally-sound farming, leadership and community development. Available from **Heifer Project International.** (See Organizations)

FLY AWAY HOME (30 mins.) Hosted by LeVar Burton this is the story of a homeless boy and his father interwoven with talks with homeless children and their families and ways young people are working to make a difference in the fight against homelessness. To order contact: GPN Educational Media, 1407 Fleet Street, Baltimore, MD 21231. (800) 228-4630. www.shopgpn.com

THE GRAPES OF WRATH (129 mins.) John Ford's 1940 film of Steinbeck's novel about the Oklahoma farmers' migration from the dustbowl to the California Eden during the Depression. The migrants were unwelcome in California because they threatened the jobs of the locals. Their attempts to form unions sparked violence and left the farmers with few possessions and little hope.

HARVEST OF HUNGER (20 mins.) OXFAM America, 1987. Creative graphics to Jackson Browne music combine with stunning photos of overseas projects in this exploration of the underlying causes of world hunger. Includes teacher's guide with quizzes, exercises and maps. Available from the **African Studies Center Lending Library** (see above.)

THE HOUSE OF DIES DREAR based on the book by Virginia Hamilton involving slavery and the Underground Railroad. 1984.

NEW DAY FILMS
(888) 367-9154; www.newday.com
This cooperative of independent producers and filmmakers creates and distributes videos "that foster social justice and respect diversity." Some examples include:

HUNGRY FOR PROFIT by Robert Richter. (86 mins.)
Is Third World famine the price we're paying for our food? A penetrating look behind the famine headlines of today. This is a provocative investigation of the link between world hunger and the global agribusiness system.

IF THE MANGO TREE COULD SPEAK by Pat Goudvis. (58 mins.)
An award-winning documentary about children and war in Central America.

THE GLOBAL ASSEMBLY LINE by Lorraine Gray. (58 mins.)
From Tennessee to Mexico's northern border, from Silicon Valley to the Philippines, this video offers a vivid portrayal of the lives of working men and women in "free trade zones" of developing countries and North America as U.S. industries close their factories in search of lower-wage workers.

THE LONG ROAD HOME by Andrea E. Leland. (30 mins.)
(Excellent for use with Lesson 5 and **Maria's Dream**) This visually compelling documentary follows a 19 year-old Mayan refugee from his home in Chicago to a Guatemala refugee camp in Mexico. It illuminates current refugee situations and their causes.

RUNAWAY adapted from Felice Holman's book **Slake's Limbo** about a boy hiding among the homeless in New York subways.

SOMETHING TO HIDE A 25-minute video that exposes how corporations hide production behind locked gates. Order from the **National Labor Committee** (see above).

SWEATING FOR A T-SHIRT College student Arlen Benjamin documents her journey to Honduras to investigate the living and working conditions of workers who make T-shirts and sweatshirts sold to U.S. students. From Global Exchange, (800) 505-4410. www.globalexchangestore.org

TROUBLED HARVEST (30 mins.) This award-winning documentary examines the lives of Latin American women migrants as they work in grape, strawberry and cherry fields in California. Interviews reveal the dangerous effects of poverty, environmental degradation, and pesticides on the women and their children. From Women Make Movies, (212) 925-0606. www.wmm.com

UNICEF VIDEOS - To order the following videos or a complete UNICEF catalogue of videos – contact UNICEF Distribution Unit, Division of Communication, 3 UN Plaza, New York, NY 10017. (Videos $100-$500)

> **FISTFUL OF RICE** - Follows a mother in Nepal as she struggles to feed her malnourished family and exposes how hunger creates a cycle of poverty through the generations. (27 mins.)
>
> **FOR A FEW PENNIES MORE** (23 mins.) Dwi Asnawan is three years old but cannot yet walk or talk because of the lack of iodine in his diet.
>
> **LIKE ME** (1995). Through the eyes of children, this film depicts the challenges that face children in developing countries who do not have access to basic necessities. Viewers learn how UNICEF works to improve the survival, development and protection of children. (10 mins.)
>
> **MEENA** (1992). A cartoon depicting the life of a young Indian girl and how she is discouraged from pursuing education. The story explores traditional cultural values, which often emphasize the educational advancement of boys and suppress the educational development of females. (Elementary ages - 6 mins.)
>
> **MISSING OUT** (27 mins.) Niger is one of the world's poorest countries. Students learn how malnutrition affects pregnant mothers and infants.

WHERE ARE THE BEANS? (13 mins.) Linda Shelly returns to Honduras to discover that beans are no longer a staple of the Honduran diet thanks to policies that the International Monetary Fund pressed the government to adopt. Order from American Friends Service Committee's Lending Library, (617) 497-5273.

WORDS BY HEART based on the novel by Ounida Sebestyen about a black family living in an all-white Missouri town.

ZONED FOR SLAVERY: The Child Behind the Label (23 mins.) Exposes the exploitation of children who work in factories in Mexico and Central America to make clothes that are sold in major U.S. stores. Some children earn as little as 12¢ for a shirt that sells for $20 or more. Available from the **National Labor Committee** (see above).